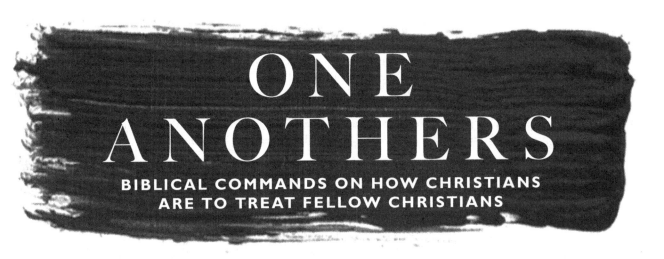

ONE ANOTHERS

BIBLICAL COMMANDS ON HOW CHRISTIANS ARE TO TREAT FELLOW CHRISTIANS

CHRISTIAN HOUSE RULES

DAVID A. EDMISTON

WESTBOW
PRESS®
A DIVISION OF THOMAS NELSON
& ZONDERVAN

WestBow Press books may be ordered through booksellers or by contacting:

WestBow Press
A Division of Thomas Nelson & Zondervan
1663 Liberty Drive
Bloomington, IN 47403
www.westbowpress.com
844-714-3454

All Scripture quotations are taken from The Holy Bible, New International Version®, NIV® Copyright © 1973, 1978, 1984, 2011 by Biblica, Inc.® Used by permission. All rights reserved worldwide.

ISBN: 978-1-6642-4465-8 (sc)
ISBN: 978-1-6642-4464-1 (e)

Library of Congress Control Number: 2021918483

Print information available on the last page.

WestBow Press rev. date: 10/08/2021

CONTENTS

INTRODUCTION TO THE ONE ANOTHERS

We find in the New Testament directions/commands to over fifty different "one anothers" or "each others." These directions/commands are found in the books of John, Romans, 1 and 2 Corinthians, Galatians, Ephesians, Colossians, 1 Thessalonians, Hebrews, James, 1 Peter and 1 and 2 John.

Who or what are the "one anothers"? Why would so many Bible writers feel the need to give guidance to the "one anothers"?

Actually it is simple. The "one anothers" are any Christians, fellow believers in Christ, then and now. These commands and instructions are directed to us. They are directions on how to relate to and treat our brothers and sisters in Christ. When we accept Christ as our Lord, we have joined the family of God. We become adopted sons and daughters of God, thus brothers and sisters. We become part of the body of Christ, the church. My Ohio pastor, Dr. Jim Smith, calls these directions/commands "house rules." Most every family has certain house rules: how all in the household are to treat each other. No lying, don't hold a grudge, do your part and then some, show respect, be kind, share, and show consideration are just a few that come to mind. This study is how we are to treat our family, our Christian family. That is what the "one anothers" are all about.

JOHN 1:12–13, *YET TO ALL WHO RECEIVED HIM, TO THOSE WHO BELIEVED IN HIS NAME, HE GAVE THE RIGHT TO BECOME CHILDREN OF GOD— CHILDREN BORN NOT OF NATURAL DESCENT, NOR OF HUMAN DECISION OR A HUSBAND'S WILL, BUT BORN OF GOD.* We become His children, not because of someone else's will, nor our heredity but because of a decision we personally make to be a follower of Christ. **1 JOHN 5:1–3** tells us this, *EVERYONE WHO BELIEVES THAT JESUS IS THE CHRIST IS BORN OF GOD, AND EVERYONE WHO LOVES THE*

FATHER LOVES HIS CHILD AS WELL. THIS IS HOW WE KNOW THAT WE LOVE THE CHILDREN OF GOD: BY LOVING GOD AND CARRYING OUT HIS COMMANDS. THIS IS LOVE FOR GOD: TO OBEY HIS COMMANDS. AND HIS COMMANDS ARE NOT BURDENSOME. We are expected to obey His commands since we are His children. As parents, don't we expect our children to obey what we say? The reason, as parents, we give commands to our children is because we know what is best and we want the best for our children. The same holds true for our heavenly Father. We will carry out His commands because we love Him and want to please Him. To be like Him. We have become part of the church family.

By joining together into one family, the Lord expects us to act in certain ways to one another. That is what this study is all about. All of these commands are ways we are directed to act and feel toward our brothers.

By following the commands of the Father, we become more like Him. We imitate Him. Haven't you ever heard, "he is just like his father"? Why does this happen? Since we have been with our father, and tried to be like him, we have picked up his traits, his way of doing things. His likes and his dislikes. I have tried to emulate my father, the way he lived his life. By doing this I hear comments "you are more like him every day." This is what is expected of us as we emulate our heavenly Father. **EPHESIANS 5:1–2,** *BE IMITATORS OF GOD, THEREFORE, AS DEARLY LOVED CHILDREN AND LIVE A LIFE OF LOVE, JUST AS CHRIST LOVED US AND GAVE HIMSELF UP FOR US AS A FRAGRANT OFFERING AND SACRIFICE TO GOD.*

When we become Christians, we have a new family, new brothers and sisters. Jesus says in **MATTHEW 12:50,** *"FOR WHOEVER DOES THE WILL OF MY FATHER IN HEAVEN IS MY BROTHER AND SISTER AND MOTHER."*

Recognizing and accepting that we become brothers and sisters in Christ is key to the study of the "one anothers." **1 TIMOTHY 5:1–2** gives us these directions: *DO NOT REBUKE AN OLDER MAN HARSHLY, BUT EXHORT HIM AS IF HE WERE YOUR FATHER. TREAT YOUNGER MEN AS BROTHERS, OLDER WOMEN AS MOTHERS, AND YOUNGER WOMEN AS SISTERS, WITH ABSOLUTE PURITY.* As we go through this study, we should ask ourselves, "If I am the older brother, how would I treat my younger sister or brother? How can I help them grow?" The answer is we must follow the directions that have been left for us on how we are to treat one another.

This is key for a couple of reasons.

1.   We are directed to help our brothers in so many ways.

2.   We need to set an example of how Christians are to live with and love one another.

There must be a real and visible difference between Christian relationships and worldly relationships that is clearly observable. If not, there is a problem with my relationship with Jesus, not with the other people. There is nothing more upsetting to see than two or more Christians not getting along, much less not loving one another.

From a personal standpoint, when I started putting these chapters together, I would ask my wife to proofread and give me honest feedback on the chapters. After the fourth chapter, about kindness, she said, "You don't live like this." The problem is, she is right. I can write about the "one anothers," but I cannot live them all. When I wrote the chapter on "be kind to one another," I decided to act it out starting in the secular world. I do the grocery shopping, and I made up my mind that every time I went to the grocery store I would do a kind deed. It consisted of some of the following:

Helping a short person get something off the top shelf.
Helping a handicapped person empty his electric cart at the cash register.
Not only putting my cart away in the parking lot but one to five more as well.
Telling an 80-90, year old woman, all dressed in red on Valentine's day, that she looked
      marvelous. (She giggled!)
Smiling and addressing all the workers.
Picking up items that had fallen on the floor.
Putting items in placc if thcy wcrc mixed up on thc shclf.

Notice, that these were all very simple things to do. What it did for me, was make me look forward to grocery day and wondering how I could help someone in some way. From speaking to the crew, many now greet me as if they know me.

Try doing acts of kindness in church. Greeting and smiling to everyone, complimenting people, looking to lend a helping hand. These acts will change both parties.

Start with one chapter and try my example. Once it becomes part of you, move on to the next *One Another* and work on that one. These 50 chapters will take work. Some for me are very difficult, but I need to work on them to follow what I have been commanded.

There are lots of scriptures. I have taught a Sunday School class for over fifty years. When I teach, I use lots of scriptures. Why? Without scripture the words would just be man's opinion. With scripture I have the backing of the Lord.

Questions are included throughout each chapter to encourage each of us to get more in depth in the study. We need to figure out how to apply each lesson to our own lives. These are not tests, just ways to help as a study guide.

We can grow more Christ-like as we commit ourselves to following the "one anothers" and make them a part of our everyday lives.

May I urge all of us to start living our lives with the love that is talked about in the chapter on "love." Without having the love of the Lord in our lives, it would be impossible to act out any of the "one anothers" on a consistent basis.

A personal thanks goes to my former pastor and friend Tom Swank for his insight and additions to this Introduction.

Enjoy the study, and I hope it changes lives.

ACKNOWLEDGMENTS

I want to thank my two great pastors: Dr. James Smith, my Ohio pastor and Gregg Heinsch, my Florida pastor. This book would not have come to fruition without Pastor Jim. When I got stuck on a verse or a subject that was beyond my Christian understanding, he would patiently explain it to me so that my mind was open to the meaning of the subject. His vast knowledge of the original Greek enlightened me on the different directions to take on various "one another" chapters. He was always there in a time of frustration. And Pastor Gregg gave me continual support and encouragement. On more than one occasion when he was speaking on a set of verses, he would come across a one another and again, and as he would expound on the verse he would even, without knowing it, give me more determination to finish what I had started. He said to me that a book was needed on the "One Anothers" so Christians would know how they were to treat fellow Christians.

I would like to thank my great friend Ruth Hossler. Her guidance on composition, subject matter, layout and verb tense was indispensable. She continually challenged me with "What are you trying to say here?" or "I want to hear your voice." As a retired teacher of English composition, she was a tough grader, thank goodness!

My wife and I have a special relationship with my cousin Dean Aldridge and his wife LouSena (Lucy). Lucy had no idea what she was letting herself in for when she agreed to edit this book. Her experience as a copy editor was a remarkable help. Her patience with me was over and above the call of duty as she corrected formatting, verb tense, spelling, punctuation and wording. She was always dead on. Thank you so much.

I also want to thank Luke Heinsch for designing the cover. Thanks for sticking with it Luke.

A huge thank you goes to my wife of 55+ years, Naomi. Her encouragement and her continual "You can do this!" always seemed to come at the right time. Her editing and particularly her spelling skills were much appreciated. Thank you for allowing me all the time it took away from our time. "Love you hon."

Also, thanks to my multiple friends who read a chapter and gave input and continual encouragement. I would also like to give praise to the Holy Spirit who guided my fingers on the keyboard and my thoughts in the direction that gives praises to our Lord.

The Bible references are from the NIV study Bible by the Zondervan Corporation copyright 1985, unless noted otherwise.

CHAPTER ONE

LOVE

JOHN 13:34, *"A NEW COMMAND I GIVE YOU: LOVE ONE ANOTHER. AS I HAVE LOVED YOU, SO YOU MUST LOVE ONE ANOTHER."*

JOHN 15:12, *"MY COMMAND IS THIS: LOVE EACH OTHER AS I HAVE LOVED YOU."*

JOHN 15:17, *"THIS IS MY COMMAND: LOVE EACH OTHER."*   [1]

There are multiple commands in the Bible to love one another, Christian to Christian. Why would I pick these three? These were the commands the Lord gave His disciples in the upper room just prior to His crucifixion. He had been with these men for about three years and these were part of His last instructions. This command was so important to Him that He repeated it three times. If it was important then, it is just as important now.

We must first look at what love is. In the New Testament Greek there are four words to define love. They are:

Eros. Sensual love. Where we get the word erotica.
Philia. The type of love we have for our friends. Philadelphia, the city, using part of this word, calls itself the city of brotherly love.

Storge. The love a family shares.
Agape. Unconditional love.

Agape love is what Jesus is saying to us when He commands us to love one another and when He says to love your neighbor and to love your enemies. He expects us to show love, unconditional, to our brothers, to others and even to our enemies.

I sent out over forty emails to my friends asking them to give me their definition of love. I received all kinds of answers, none of which totally defined what I thought love meant. I even Googled the question, "What is love?" I found many, many, many responses, but none exactly the way I felt about love. My wife and I have been married over fifty years and this is how I personally see love for my spouse. We were both freshmen at Bethel College in Mishawaka, Indiana. The first time I saw my future wife, it was not a feeling of love at first sight, it was a desire to meet and get to know her. Of course there was a physical attraction, since my wife, to me, is a very beautiful, petite lady. But seeing how she was reacting with others, I was also drawn to her personality. She had a twinkle in her eyes and seemed to laugh easily. As we made a connection, we found out we were both "going steady" with someone else. We both decided to break off those relationships so we could get to know each other without being encumbered. We talked over what was important to a real sincere relationship. As Christians, we knew the main thing that was important to us was to do what the Lord directed in our lives. With the Lord directing us, we knew we were in the right hands. As we began to date and spend time together throughout our freshman year, other feelings started to come into play. We developed a strong, intense affection for each other. From this we both devoted ourselves to the other's well-being. This included helping each other as we studied, listening to the other person's goals and fears as we looked ahead to the future. We both knew that the future would be with each other. We had a commitment to our relationship and an unconditional understanding of our feelings for each other.

This commitment developed a trust, a feeling of respect and of being honest with one another. This allowed us to openly share our growing, self-sacrificing love for each other. This brought about actions that showed we cared about the other person over self. This love was demonstrated in our acts of kindness, compassion and devotion to one another. We could not demonstrate it in money or things, since we had none of these. As this love continued to grow, we took the step of marriage.

Is our love still the same? No, it has grown over the years in many ways, even with the bumps in the road all relationships have. I have a deeper respect for my wife as I have seen her using her gift she has with kids. Not just our own but also as she taught two- to five-year-old kids in Sunday School class. I respect her for the way she is a mother and now a grandmother. This love is more intense today because we both love the Lord and seek to do His bidding as both of us put the Lord first in our lives. We both continue to do random acts of love and kindness within our marriage as we gain more and more respect for each other.

This, to me, is love; self-sacrificing, putting the other person first, totally without conditions in actions and words. Love must have actions of some sort. I truly believe we love one another more intensely today than when we first dated and got married.

Can I explain love? Not really, but I am experiencing it. Not only with my wife, but also my Christian brothers. My love for them has grown stronger over the years. It makes me want to do all the "one anothers" that are listed in the Bible. **[2]**

Where does love come from? Love comes from God. **1 JOHN 4:7–8, *DEAR FRIENDS, LET US LOVE ONE ANOTHER, FOR LOVE COMES FROM GOD. EVERYONE WHO LOVES HAS BEEN BORN OF GOD AND KNOWS GOD. WHOEVER DOES NOT LOVE DOES NOT KNOW GOD, BECAUSE GOD IS LOVE.***

The Wycliffe Bible Commentary says: the absence of the article (***GOD IS <u>the</u> LOVE***) indicates that love is not simply a quality which God possesses, but love is that which He is by His very nature. Furthermore, because God is love, love which He shows is occasioned by Himself only and not by any outside cause. By doing a good deed today, or being kind to someone, it does not make God love me, because He already loves me.

God shows us His love. We respond by showing love, but our love is not the basis for God's love. God showed us His love, and the key way He showed His love was by the giving of His Son for our redemption. The key verse is **JOHN 3:16, *"FOR GOD SO LOVED THE WORLD THAT HE GAVE HIS ONE AND ONLY SON, THAT WHOEVER BELIEVES IN HIM SHALL NOT PERISH BUT HAVE ETERNAL LIFE."*** This showing of God's love for us is almost impossible for us to understand. So unconditional. So truly self-sacrificing. So loving.

John restates God's action of love in **1 JOHN 4:9–12. *THIS IS HOW GOD SHOWED HIS LOVE AMONG US: HE SENT HIS ONE AND ONLY SON INTO THE WORLD***

THAT WE MIGHT LIVE THROUGH HIM. THIS IS LOVE: NOT THAT WE LOVED GOD, BUT THAT HE LOVED US AND SENT HIS SON AS AN ATONING SACRIFICE FOR OUR SINS. DEAR FRIENDS, SINCE GOD SO LOVED US, WE ALSO OUGHT TO LOVE ONE ANOTHER. NO ONE HAS EVER SEEN GOD; BUT IF WE LOVE ONE ANOTHER, GOD LIVES IN US AND HIS LOVE IS MADE COMPLETE IN US.

God showed His love to us by giving His Son as a sacrifice. This has brought about in us a need to respond. John is saying this need to respond brings about a need to show love to others, particularly to our brothers in Christ. This is shown in our actions. These actions make up all the "one anothers." For example, without the love of God in us, we cannot be kind and/or serve one another. This love comes from God, but it comes to us because of the indwelling of the Holy Spirit. **COLOSSIANS 1:8,** *AND WHO ALSO TOLD US OF YOUR LOVE IN THE SPIRIT.* The NIV footnote says: *The Holy Spirit is the source of all Christian love.* The Holy Spirit is the Lord living in us, thus without the Holy Spirit in us, it would be impossible to show the love of God flowing through us to others. By loving others, our love makes God's love complete. [3]

For us to truly understand the love we are to have for one another, we need to look at a couple of areas of love we learn about in the Bible. Let us look at the love of God. **1 JOHN 4:16** tells us *GOD IS LOVE.*

How big is God's love for us? David says in **PSALM 108:4A,** *FOR GREAT IS YOUR LOVE, HIGHER THAN THE HEAVENS.*

PSALM 103:11, *FOR AS HIGH AS THE HEAVENS ARE ABOVE THE EARTH, SO GREAT IS HIS LOVE FOR THOSE WHO FEAR HIM.* Who can measure the heights of heaven? Not man. Even with the world's largest telescopes, we cannot see the end of the heavens. God's love just goes on and on.

God expresses His love by action. He speaks of His love for His Son. **MATTHEW 17:1–13** tells of the transfiguration. God speaks of His Son in **VERSE 5,** *WHILE HE WAS STILL SPEAKING* (Peter), *A BRIGHT CLOUD ENVELOPED THEM, AND A VOICE FROM THE CLOUD SAID, "THIS IS MY SON, WHOM I LOVE; WITH HIM I AM WELL PLEASED. LISTEN TO HIM!"*

Another occasion when God speaks of His love for His Son is told in **MARK 1:9–11,** *AT THAT TIME JESUS CAME FROM NAZARETH IN GALILEE AND WAS BAPTIZED BY JOHN IN THE JORDAN. AS JESUS WAS COMING UP OUT OF THE WATER, HE SAW HEAVEN BEING TORN OPEN AND THE SPIRIT DESCENDING ON HIM LIKE A DOVE. AND A VOICE CAME FROM HEAVEN: "YOU ARE MY SON, WHOM I LOVE; WITH YOU I AM WELL PLEASED."*

Everyone wants to be loved by his earthly father. Jesus was loved by His Father because He followed the will of the Father, even unto death. As He prays in the garden in **LUKE 22:42,** *"FATHER, IF YOU ARE WILLING, TAKE THIS CUP FROM ME; YET NOT MY WILL, BUT YOURS BE DONE."* If we desire the love of our heavenly Father then we, as well, must follow the will of the Father and the Son and obey their commands.

There are benefits and rewards for loving God and loving Jesus.

1. God works for our good. **ROMANS 8:28,** *AND WE KNOW THAT IN ALL THINGS GOD WORKS FOR THE GOOD OF THOSE WHO LOVE HIM, WHO HAVE BEEN CALLED ACCORDING TO HIS PURPOSE.*

2. As Christians, we cannot be separated from the love of God that is in Jesus. **ROMANS 8:35A,** *WHO SHALL SEPARATE US FROM THE LOVE OF CHRIST?* **VERSES 38–39,** *FOR I AM CONVINCED THAT NEITHER DEATH NOR LIFE, NEITHER ANGELS NOR DEMONS, NEITHER THE PRESENT NOR THE FUTURE, NOR ANY POWERS, NEITHER HEIGHT NOR DEPTH, NOR ANYTHING ELSE IN ALL CREATION, WILL BE ABLE TO SEPARATE US FROM THE LOVE OF GOD THAT IS IN CHRIST JESUS OUR LORD.*

3. God demonstrates His love for us by sending His Son, Jesus. **ROMANS 5:8,** *BUT GOD DEMONSTRATES HIS OWN LOVE FOR US IN THIS: WHILE WE WERE STILL SINNERS, CHRIST DIED FOR US.* He also demonstrates His love to us by sending the Holy Spirit. **ROMANS 5:5,** *AND HOPE DOES NOT DISAPPOINT US, BECAUSE GOD HAS POURED OUT HIS LOVE INTO OUR HEARTS BY THE HOLY SPIRIT, WHOM HE HAS GIVEN US.*

4. He makes us alive with Christ and through His kindness raises us up to heaven with Him at His appointed time. **EPHESIANS 2:4–7,** *BUT BECAUSE OF HIS GREAT LOVE FOR US, GOD, WHO IS RICH IN MERCY, MADE US ALIVE*

WITH CHRIST EVEN WHEN WE WERE DEAD IN TRANSGRESSIONS—IT IS BY GRACE YOU HAVE BEEN SAVED. AND GOD RAISED US UP WITH CHRIST AND SEATED US WITH HIM IN THE HEAVENLY REALMS IN CHRIST JESUS, IN ORDER THAT IN THE COMING AGES HE MIGHT SHOW THE INCOMPARABLE RICHES OF HIS GRACE, EXPRESSED IN HIS KINDNESS TO US IN CHRIST JESUS.

5. Because of His great love for us, we are called children of God. **1 JOHN 3:1,** *HOW GREAT IS THE LOVE THE FATHER HAS LAVISHED ON US, THAT WE SHOULD BE CALLED CHILDREN OF GOD! AND THAT IS WHAT WE ARE! THE REASON THE WORLD DOES NOT KNOW US IS THAT IT DID NOT KNOW HIM.*

6. When we love others He lives in us, and His love is seen in us by others. **1 JOHN 4:12,** *NO ONE HAS EVER SEEN GOD; BUT IF WE LOVE ONE ANOTHER, GOD LIVES IN US AND HIS LOVE IS MADE COMPLETE IN US.*

7. By loving God, He, in His love, prepares us a place. **1 CORINTHIANS 2:9–10,** *HOWEVER, AS IT IS WRITTEN: "NO EYE HAS SEEN, NO EAR HAS HEARD, NO MIND HAS CONCEIVED WHAT GOD HAS PREPARED FOR THOSE WHO LOVE HIM"—BUT GOD HAS REVEALED IT TO US BY HIS SPIRIT. THE SPIRIT SEARCHES ALL THINGS, EVEN THE DEEP THINGS OF GOD.*

8. We are known by God. **1 CORINTHIANS 8:3,** *BUT THE MAN WHO LOVES GOD IS KNOWN BY GOD.*

9. We are disciplined. **REVELATION 3:19,** *"THOSE WHOM I LOVE I REBUKE AND DISCIPLINE. SO BE EARNEST, AND REPENT."* What is the benefit of being disciplined? **1 CORINTHIANS 11:32,** *WHEN WE ARE JUDGED BY THE LORD, WE ARE BEING DISCIPLINED SO THAT WE WILL NOT BE CONDEMNED WITH THE WORLD.*

The advantage is we are disciplined because we are loved just like a parent with their child. We are disciplined so we will be able to receive the reward God has planned for us.   [4]

All these verses point to the key point, God loves us. In **JOHN 16:27,** Jesus points out, *"NO, THE FATHER HIMSELF LOVES YOU BECAUSE YOU HAVE LOVED ME*

AND HAVE BELIEVED THAT I CAME FROM GOD." Our belief in Jesus brings us love from God.

Jesus loves us as well. Yes, just like the song we sang as children. A song with a powerful message and truth. It is such a simple song, but with an awesome message. *Jesus loves me this I know, for the Bible tells me so.* Many people take this to mean, since Jesus loves all the people in the world, at end times they will be saved. This is a false belief. Jesus does love all the people of the world, but He will only bring with Him to heaven people that have claimed Him as their Savior and have asked forgiveness from their sins. We are now Children of God. Do not think we have to be good enough to be saved or that we are not lovable because of whom we are personally. No matter the sins in our lives or our lifestyles, if we freely confess our sins to the Lord, and take Him as our Savior, we are now His children. Period.   [5], [6]

We have insight into Jesus' love for individuals in the New Testament. **JOHN 11:3,** speaking of Lazarus, *SO THE SISTERS SENT WORD TO JESUS, "LORD, THE ONE YOU LOVE IS SICK."* Later after hearing of the death of Lazarus and standing in front of the tomb, the crowd saw Jesus weeping. **VERSES 35–36,** *JESUS WEPT. THEN THE JEWS SAID, "SEE HOW HE LOVED HIM!"* He demonstrated His love by bringing Lazarus back from the dead. When we think about it, this is exactly what He will do for us. Defeating death so we can spend eternity with Him in heaven.

Jesus even shows love while hanging on the cross. **JOHN 19:26–27,** *WHEN JESUS SAW HIS MOTHER THERE, AND THE DISCIPLE WHOM HE LOVED STANDING NEARBY, HE SAID TO HIS MOTHER, "DEAR WOMAN, HERE IS YOUR SON," AND TO THE DISCIPLE, "HERE IS YOUR MOTHER." FROM THAT TIME ON, THIS DISCIPLE TOOK HER INTO HIS HOME.* Jesus is speaking to John, and there are other times in the book of John that John speaks about himself as "the disciple whom He loved." Jesus loved John so much He entrusted His mother's care to him, and John recognized this love, just as we should.

Paul speaks about Jesus loving him. **GALATIANS 2:20,** *I HAVE BEEN CRUCIFIED WITH CHRIST AND I NO LONGER LIVE, BUT CHRIST LIVES IN ME. THE LIFE I LIVE IN THE BODY, I LIVE BY FAITH IN THE SON OF GOD, WHO LOVED ME AND GAVE HIMSELF FOR ME.*

Jesus loves us, as His fellow brothers. **EPHESIANS 5:1–2,** *BE IMITATORS OF GOD, THEREFORE, AS DEARLY LOVED CHILDREN AND LIVE A LIFE OF LOVE, JUST AS CHRIST LOVED US AND GAVE HIMSELF UP FOR US AS A FRAGRANT OFFERING AND SACRIFICE TO GOD.*

Jesus loves the church. **EPHESIANS 5:25,** *HUSBANDS, LOVE YOUR WIVES, JUST AS CHRIST LOVED THE CHURCH AND GAVE HIMSELF UP FOR HER.*

Jesus loved his apostles. **JOHN 13:1,** *IT WAS JUST BEFORE THE PASSOVER FEAST. JESUS KNEW THAT THE TIME HAD COME FOR HIM TO LEAVE THIS WORLD AND GO TO THE FATHER. HAVING LOVED HIS OWN WHO WERE IN THE WORLD, HE NOW SHOWED THEM THE FULL EXTENT OF HIS LOVE.* Jesus was prepared to lay down His life for His followers because He loved them.

Jesus loves each of us as individuals. He has demonstrated this love by laying down His life for us. He speaks of this in **JOHN 15:13,** *"GREATER LOVE HAS NO ONE THAN THIS, THAT HE LAY DOWN HIS LIFE FOR HIS FRIENDS."* He not only spoke about laying down His life for His friends, He fulfilled what He was talking about.

John recognized how important this was by also talking about it in **1 JOHN 3:16A,** *THIS IS HOW WE KNOW WHAT LOVE IS: JESUS CHRIST LAID DOWN HIS LIFE FOR US.* Jesus' love for us had an action. The action was freely laying down His life for us per His Father's will. When love is involved there are actions that take place. We love God, and He reacts for our good. But with our love we must have an action as well. It is all well and good to tell someone we love them, but if we never show any affection or action toward them, do we really love them? If I tell my wife I love her and never show any type of actions of love, will she believe me? There must be some kind of action in my love, so she can see what I am saying is true. The same holds true when we tell the Lord we love Him and we love Him only. There are actions of love we must show to the Lord.

When we say we love the Lord, the Lord expects us to obey Him. In **JOHN 14,** Jesus is explaining He must leave them (His disciples). But at the same time He tries to bring them comfort. **VERSES 15–17A,** *"IF YOU LOVE ME, YOU WILL OBEY WHAT I COMMAND. AND I WILL ASK THE FATHER, AND HE WILL GIVE YOU ANOTHER COUNSELOR TO BE WITH YOU FOREVER—THE SPIRIT OF TRUTH."* He is asking them to obey His commands and they will receive the Holy Spirit.

The same holds true for us. If we put our trust in the Lord, He sends us the Holy Spirit. The Holy Spirit, in us, is our confirmation of our salvation. **ROMANS 8:9,** *YOU, HOWEVER, ARE CONTROLLED NOT BY THE SINFUL NATURE BUT BY THE SPIRIT, IF THE SPIRIT OF GOD LIVES IN YOU. AND IF ANYONE DOES NOT HAVE THE SPIRIT OF CHRIST, HE DOES NOT BELONG TO CHRIST.*

JOHN 14:21, *"WHOEVER HAS MY COMMANDS AND OBEYS THEM, HE IS THE ONE WHO LOVES ME. HE WHO LOVES ME WILL BE LOVED BY MY FATHER, AND I TOO WILL LOVE HIM AND SHOW MYSELF TO HIM."* Another promise to us. If we love and obey the Lord, we receive the Love of the Father. We are loved by God. We also will be shown Jesus. What does this mean? He will manifest Himself to us. We will see Him clearly, in all His glory. We will understand and recognize the sovereignty of who Jesus really is. We will know His commands in our hearts and listen to them and obey what He commands. The Holy Spirit will guide us. We will do this out of love for Him. As we study the Bible, the Spirit will open our eyes and hearts to the scripture that will enable us to see the Lord in all His glory. [7]

JOHN 14:23, *JESUS REPLIED, "IF ANYONE LOVES ME, HE WILL OBEY MY TEACHING. MY FATHER WILL LOVE HIM, AND WE WILL COME TO HIM AND MAKE OUR HOME WITH HIM."* Again, by us obeying the commands of the Lord, He and the Father will love us and make their home in us. We will never be alone.

When we obey the Lord's commands it is not to be done as, "I guess I have to do this." No, it should be our desire to want to please our Father. As a child, did we want to please our parents out of love or because we had to? We wanted them to be proud of us.

Obeying must come from love or there is resentment. Obeying is how we show our heavenly Father we love Him. [8]

If we are to show our love to the Lord through obeying His commands, what are His commands? Where is the list? Can we just check them off as we do them? No, it is not like that. We can look at some of the commands of the Lord, but the commands are inside our hearts. The Holy Spirit has come to lead us into the path of the Lord. But we must listen to the Holy Spirit and obey.

Here are some commands about love we should know. Jesus tells us to love the following:

1. **MATTHEW 5:44,** *"BUT I TELL YOU: LOVE YOUR ENEMIES AND PRAY FOR THOSE WHO PERSECUTE YOU."*

Love my enemies. But they are mean to me. I don't like them. They treat me badly. Even so we are called to love them. Jesus did not say it was easy, just that we are to love them. Jesus showed this love when He died for all, friends and enemies alike. **[9]**

2. **MATTHEW 5:43A,** *"YOU HAVE HEARD THAT IT WAS SAID, LOVE YOUR NEIGHBOR."*

Love my neighbors. For me that might be possible. I hardly ever see them. They are not a part of my life. Oh, wait, who is my neighbor? Actually, it is anyone and everyone. We are to show love to everyone. Why do this? So, others will see the love of Jesus coming from us. They should see a difference in our lives since we are doing our best to be Christ-like as we go through our lives. If we ever have any doubt of who our neighbor is, reread the parable of the good Samaritan. **[10]**

3. **MATTHEW 22:39B,** *"LOVE YOUR NEIGHBOR AS YOURSELF."*

We are to love ourselves. This can be very difficult for some of us. It can be a major problem for some who have an unhealthy self-image of themselves. Just remember, we are loved, and we are to pass that love to others starting with ourselves. We have been made in the image of God. **1 CORINTHIANS 6:19–20,** *DO YOU NOT KNOW THAT YOUR BODY IS A TEMPLE OF THE HOLY SPIRIT, WHO IS IN YOU, WHOM YOU HAVE RECEIVED FROM GOD? YOU ARE NOT YOUR OWN; YOU WERE BOUGHT AT A PRICE. THEREFORE HONOR GOD WITH YOUR BODY.* God does not make mistakes. We were each made for a reason and given gifts to be used by each of us for the betterment of the church. We are neither to puff ourselves up or knock ourselves down, but to realize God has a purpose for all of us. **[11]**

4. **MARK 12:30,** *"LOVE THE LORD YOUR GOD WITH ALL YOUR HEART AND WITH ALL YOUR SOUL AND WITH ALL YOUR MIND AND WITH ALL YOUR STRENGTH."*

Jesus said in **VERSE 29** this is the most important commandment. We are to love our God with all of our heart, soul, mind and strength. This is everything we are. All our being. We are to totally love Him with everything that is in us.

5.   **MATTHEW 10:37, *"ANYONE WHO LOVES HIS FATHER OR MOTHER MORE THAN ME IS NOT WORTHY OF ME; ANYONE WHO LOVES HIS SON OR DAUGHTER MORE THAN ME IS NOT WORTHY OF ME."***

We are also called to love the Lord above our families. We must put family second to our Lord. We cannot fully love our families if we don't put the Lord first. He expects and demands this of us.   [12]

After looking at how both God and Jesus have lavished their love on us, we must now use those examples to love one another. Why love one another? Going back to the beginning verses, Jesus said in **JOHN 13:34–35, *"A NEW COMMAND I GIVE YOU: LOVE ONE ANOTHER. AS I HAVE LOVED YOU, SO YOU MUST LOVE ONE ANOTHER. BY THIS ALL MEN WILL KNOW THAT YOU ARE MY DISCIPLES, IF YOU LOVE ONE ANOTHER."*** Do others see the love of the Lord as we live our lives with other Christians? They should.

To love one another, it must be a sincere love. **ROMANS 12:9A, *LOVE MUST BE SINCERE.*** Have we ever been around someone whose love was insincere? It is a very bad feeling. When we first notice it, we are not sure what is going on. But as we spend time around the person, we figure out that their love is nothing but words. It is not real. It is fake. It is not coming from the Lord.   [13]

When we are around our fellow Christians we must be involved, through our love for them, in serving others in love, building them up. We are to be kind, patient, and united with them in showing others love. We need to encourage others and we are to labor together in love. We should want our love to increase. **1 THESSALONIANS 3:12, *MAY THE LORD MAKE YOUR LOVE INCREASE AND OVERFLOW FOR EACH OTHER AND FOR EVERYONE ELSE, JUST AS OURS DOES FOR YOU.*** Do we love our Christian brothers more today than yesterday? If our answer is no, look for the reasons it is not growing. **EPHESIANS 4:16, *FROM HIM THE WHOLE BODY, JOINED AND HELD TOGETHER BY EVERY SUPPORTING LIGAMENT, GROWS AND BUILDS ITSELF UP IN LOVE, AS EACH PART DOES ITS WORK.*** The church will not grow without the love for each other being prevalent. But as love grows and we learn to work together using our supporting parts, the church will grow. Without love, it cannot.

In **2 CORINTHIANS 5:14A,** Paul talks about how *CHRIST'S LOVE COMPELS* him and his companions to bring the gospel message of the Lord to others. This is how the Lord's love works in our hearts. He does not demand we do things for our Christian brothers; His love in us compels our actions. His love, directed by the Holy Spirit.

We are to live a life of love. **EPHESIANS 5:2,** *AND LIVE A LIFE OF LOVE, JUST AS CHRIST LOVED US AND GAVE HIMSELF UP FOR US AS A FRAGRANT OFFERING AND SACRIFICE TO GOD.* Personally, I am not sure I am living this type of life consistently, but I must try to grow and obtain what the Lord wants and expects from me.

How important is love in our Christian service from one to another? It is the key to our service. **COLOSSIANS 3:12–14,** *THEREFORE, AS GOD'S CHOSEN PEOPLE, HOLY AND DEARLY LOVED, CLOTHE YOURSELVES WITH COMPASSION, KINDNESS, HUMILITY, GENTLENESS AND PATIENCE. BEAR WITH EACH OTHER AND FORGIVE WHATEVER GRIEVANCES YOU MAY HAVE AGAINST ONE ANOTHER. FORGIVE AS THE LORD FORGAVE YOU. AND OVER ALL THESE VIRTUES PUT ON LOVE, WHICH BINDS THEM ALL TOGETHER IN PERFECT UNITY.* Here is the key on how we are to live in love on a day by day basis. Each day as we leave the house, we are to clothe ourselves. We are to put on all the virtues mentioned in the above verses. But over top of all these virtues we clothe ourselves with, we are to put on love. Right on top. It is the key on how we are to possess and use the virtues as we love one another. All our actions need to come about with love. **1 JOHN 3:18** says it best. *DEAR CHILDREN, LET US NOT LOVE WITH WORDS OR TONGUE BUT WITH ACTIONS AND IN TRUTH.* [14]

We have been reviewing the positive aspects of love, what we are to do and what are the reasons and rewards. Within the Bible are many verses telling us about the wrong things to love. These are given so they will have no part of our Christian lives.

MATTHEW 23:6A, *"THEY LOVE THE PLACE OF HONOR."*

JOHN 3:19B, *"MEN LOVED DARKNESS INSTEAD OF LIGHT BECAUSE THEIR DEEDS WERE EVIL."*

JOHN 12:25A, *"THE MAN WHO LOVES HIS LIFE WILL LOSE IT."*

2 THESSALONIANS 2:10B, *THEY REFUSED TO LOVE THE TRUTH AND SO BE SAVED.*

2 TIMOTHY 3:2A, *PEOPLE WILL BE LOVERS OF THEMSELVES, LOVERS OF MONEY.*

2 PETER 2:15B, *WHO LOVED THE WAGES OF WICKEDNESS.*

1 JOHN 2:15A, *DO NOT LOVE THE WORLD OR ANYTHING IN THE WORLD.*

3 JOHN 9, *LOVES TO BE FIRST.*

REVELATION 22:15B, *"EVERYONE WHO LOVES AND PRACTICES FALSEHOOD."*

If we review these areas, most all of them have the same base, self or self-indulgence. Love is not about us; it is about others.   [15]

1 JOHN 4:19–21, *WE LOVE BECAUSE HE FIRST LOVED US. IF ANYONE SAYS, "I LOVE GOD," YET HATES HIS BROTHER, HE IS A LIAR. FOR ANYONE WHO DOES NOT LOVE HIS BROTHER, WHOM HE HAS SEEN, CANNOT LOVE GOD, WHOM HE HAS NOT SEEN. AND HE HAS GIVEN US THIS COMMAND: WHOEVER LOVES GOD MUST ALSO LOVE HIS BROTHER.*

Over twenty times in the New Testament we are told to love one another. There are also fifty-one "one another" or "each other" commands, but without love it would be impossible to do even one of them on a consistent basis. We, as Christians, must have love in our hearts so we will be capable to follow through on doing what has been commanded of us as we serve together with our fellow Christian brothers. This is the key chapter to the whole study. If we cannot get past this chapter, reread it and pray for love to grow in our hearts for our fellow Christian brothers.

Love is summed up in **1 CORINTHIANS 13:3–8A,** *IF I GIVE ALL I POSSESS TO THE POOR AND SURRENDER MY BODY TO THE FLAMES, BUT HAVE NOT LOVE, I GAIN NOTHING. LOVE IS PATIENT, LOVE IS KIND. IT DOES NOT*

ENVY, IT DOES NOT BOAST, IT IS NOT PROUD. IT IS NOT RUDE, IT IS NOT SELF-SEEKING, IT IS NOT EASILY ANGERED, IT KEEPS NO RECORD OF WRONGS. LOVE DOES NOT DELIGHT IN EVIL BUT REJOICES WITH THE TRUTH. IT ALWAYS PROTECTS, ALWAYS TRUSTS, ALWAYS HOPES, ALWAYS PERSEVERES. LOVE NEVER FAILS.

QUESTIONS ON LOVE

1. What does it mean to love one another?

2. What is your definition of love?

3. Explain how our acts of love make God's love complete.

4. Review the nine benefits and rewards for loving God.

5. Do you believe that the Lord loves you personally?

6. Do you remember the song? What does it say to you?

7. Do you agree with the paragraph on **JOHN 14:21?** What are your thoughts?

8. Do you agree we should obey out of love, not duty?

9. Who is your enemy?

10. Who do you think is your neighbor?

11. Do you have a problem loving yourself?

12. Why would Jesus say we need to put Him first over our families?

13. Have you ever been around someone that had insincere love? How could you tell?

14. Explain **1 JOHN 3:18.**

15. Do you agree with this statement?

CHAPTER TWO

HOSPITALITY

1 PETER 4:9, *OFFER HOSPITALITY TO ONE ANOTHER WITHOUT GRUMBLING.*

The dictionary defines hospitality as: *friendly, generous, reception, and entertainment of guests.* [1]

Peter could be talking about everyday Christian friends or he could be talking about the different people that come into our churches at different times. For instance, a special speaker, a traveling choir, a visitor, or a missionary.

Hospitality in Peter's day was crucial. They did not have a motel in every town. Christian travelers had to rely upon others to house and feed them. Peter was saying for them to open their homes to fellow Christians. It was a cultural necessity. Yes, it cost food and time, but this was to be done in the name of the Lord. What Peter was saying applies to us today. [2]

Why would Peter need to tell Christians to provide for the needs of fellow Christians, and then say not to grumble about it? Because he knew they would complain about having to make room for someone to come into their homes—the inconvenience of it all. [3]

It is probably for the same reasons we do not entertain Christians today.

Our house is such a mess.
It costs money.
We don't know them that well.
We are too busy, let someone else do it.
Our house is not as nice as theirs.
They always come to our house and never invite us to theirs.
We just don't have the time.
We always invite the special speaker to our house. It is someone else's turn. [4]

What is the advantage of inviting fellow Christians into our homes? It is not about the way our house looks or even what food we prepare. [5]

It is about the time we spend together.
It is about the breaking of bread together.
It is about getting to know fellow Christians and finding out what is going on in their lives.
It allows us to understand better how to pray for one another.
It is an example by us that hopefully others will follow.
It is an example to our children.
It is what the Lord commands.
It gives us a special bonding with our house guests.

Some of my fondest memories as a child and later as a teenager were all the fellow Christians that came into our home. It was just being together. It was enjoying each other and getting to know them. My father was a nurse at the local Veterans Hospital, and he frequently brought Christian paraplegic patients home, particularly during the holidays. This taught me that life can be a struggle as I watched how these Christian guys handled their struggles. It also taught me how to be around handicapped people and how to interact. [6]

The lessons my parents' hospitality taught me were plenty:

How to behave in front of others.
How to get along with other children (some of whom I did not like).
How a simple evening can bring amazement to all.
How I learned to interact with adults.

How it brought about the natural caring for them in the future.

How I learned about their ministries if they were missionaries, pastors, or evangelists.

How it opened my vision of the Lord at work in the world when missionaries visited.

How I could see the love that my parents bestowed on others and received in return.

How I learned that hospitality is about others, not about me. It's about giving not receiving.

How the house does not have to be a mansion to show love for others.

How I could see the pleasure it brought visitors.

How they never kept track of whose turn it was to invite friends over.

How, even if busy, I should take time for friends.

How to be a host, and the joy I receive when guests come into my home.

Many times when visitors came to our church, my dad would invite them home for Sunday dinner. Knowing my dad, he might not even have checked with my mom. I don't remember her complaining, maybe she just expected it (or maybe she complained in private). Because of this my parents had friends all over the world. Friends that kept in touch over the years. Even to this day people talk about coming to our house and the good times we all had. This is the fellowship of believers.

Recently I ran into a young woman who, as a child, came into our home for a Sunday dinner because of an invitation from my father to her family when they visited our church for the first time. Our parents remained friends until their passing. She is now married to a minister and talks about the influence of my parents on her parents, and on her and her sister. It all started with hospitality.   [7]

These are the lessons I have tried to apply in my life, sometimes to the rightful frustration of my wife, just like my dad brought to my mom. She tells me it has something to do with moderation.

Sometimes people just need a time away and to be with someone else. We give this when we open our homes to the hospitality of others. It can give them a lift in life that we may never know about.

The Bible explains that church leaders and members are to show hospitality. (See **1 TIMOTHY 3:2** and **TITUS 1:7–8**.) As a leader, this is to be a part of our makeup.

This is to be who we are. If it does not come easy to us, we must work on it. The rewards are plenty.

Think of what it was like for Jesus. He received hospitality from Zacchaeus, a tax collector. **LUKE 19:1–9** tells the story with Zacchaeus and Jesus meeting. **VERSE 6, *SO HE CAME DOWN AT ONCE AND WELCOMED HIM GLADLY.*** By Jesus going into his home, Zacchaeus' life was changed forever. Plus, the people he cheated had their lives changed as well.   [8]

In **LUKE 5:27–32** Jesus called Matthew (Levi, a tax collector) to follow Him. He immediately left everything to follow Jesus. **VERSE 29, *THEN LEVI HELD A GREAT BANQUET FOR JESUS AT HIS HOUSE, AND A LARGE CROWD OF TAX COLLECTORS AND OTHERS WERE EATING WITH THEM.*** These people were hated by the Jews. The influence of this visit must have been great on Matthew, Jesus' disciples, the tax collectors and the teachers of the law.

LUKE 10:38–42 tells of one visit of Jesus who was often in the home of Mary and Martha. He was able to get away from the crowds and do more personal teaching to His followers and friends.

MATTHEW 26:6–13 talks about the time He was in the home of Simon the Leper when the woman came and anointed Him with precious oil. By Simon opening his home it allowed another teaching time for the followers of Jesus.

LUKE 24:13–35 tells us another time of hospitality and the effect it had for many. After Jesus' resurrection He walked with two disciples on the way to Emmaus. They did not recognize Him. They urged Him to stay with them to eat. During the breaking of bread, they realized who was with them. Without showing hospitality, they would never know that the man they were traveling with was Jesus. By being together, Jesus was able to open the scriptures to their eyes and to their hearts. Then they returned to the eleven disciples and others and said in **VERSE 34, *"IT IS TRUE! THE LORD HAS RISEN AND HAS APPEARED TO SIMON."***

How did they recognize the Lord? By the way He broke the bread. By being together in the past they noticed the particular way that Jesus broke bread. This would not have been noticed if they had not been together in the past.

JOHN 4:1–42 tells the story of the Samaritan woman at the well. After He talked with the Samaritan woman, she introduced Jesus to the townspeople. **VERSES 40–42, *SO WHEN THE SAMARITANS CAME TO HIM, THEY URGED HIM TO STAY WITH THEM, AND HE STAYED TWO DAYS. AND BECAUSE OF HIS WORDS MANY MORE BECAME BELIEVERS. THEY SAID TO THE WOMAN, "WE NO LONGER BELIEVE JUST BECAUSE OF WHAT YOU SAID; NOW WE HAVE HEARD FOR OURSELVES, AND WE KNOW THAT THIS MAN REALLY IS THE SAVIOR OF THE WORLD."***

This offer of hospitality was very unusual since the Jews and Samaritans despised each other. From Jesus' acceptance of their offer for hospitality and His two day stay, they believed in Jesus as the Savior. Without the offer of hospitality, they would have missed their chance to be with their Savior.

3 JOHN 1–8 tells us the example of Gaius. He was faithful to his faith. He walked and talked the faith. He would open his home to strangers, fellow Christians as they traveled and shared the gospel. He did all this for the name of Jesus. This way the travelers did not have to give money to pagans (non-Christians). By doing this Gaius and the travelers worked together. [9]

Even Paul mentions this person (or one with a same name) and speaks of his hospitality. **ROMANS 16:23** says Paul and the whole church were guests of his hospitality. Paul, later in **1 CORINTHIANS 1:14,** mentions that Gaius is one of the followers he personally baptized.

Hospitality is showing others our love or rather the love of the Lord through us. Showing our desire to share what the Lord has given us with others. This love comes from the Lord to us through the Holy Spirit.

We are to be like Him, and to do this we must show His love to others. [10]

QUESTIONS ON HOSPITALITY

1. What does hospitality mean to you?

2. How does **1 PETER 4:9** apply today? Or does it?

3. Why does he say not to grumble about being hospitable?

4. How important is a perfectly clean house? Is it important when you visit someone else's home?

5. What if you never open your own home to others? What is the big deal?

6. What benefits come from hospitality?

7. When people have been hospitable to you, how did you feel?

8. What times in the Bible remind you about hospitality?

9. What is keeping you from being the same type of person?

10. What is keeping you from being hospitable?

CHAPTER THREE

INSTRUCT

ROMANS 15:14, *I MYSELF AM CONVINCED, MY BROTHERS, THAT YOU YOURSELVES ARE FULL OF GOODNESS, COMPLETE IN KNOWLEDGE AND COMPETENT TO INSTRUCT ONE ANOTHER.*

There seems to be little if any difference between the directions to instruct and the directions to teach. Are they not one in the same? On the internet there are pages of articles written on the subject. To instruct is to tell someone what you know and direct them to follow that knowledge in the exact way you have laid it out. It is like following instructions on how to put something together. **[1]**

Teaching is to let someone know why and how to put it together using these instructions. As an example, an instructor might tell us that every time we add 2 plus 2, we are to put down the answer 4. A teacher would take the time to explain how to arrive at that answer, sometimes by using an illustration. The teacher is telling us the answer, and also telling and showing us how to arrive at the answer.

Instructions on putting things together do not tell us reasons for doing things in a particular order, but we find out when we ignore the instructions. (Am I the only one that does this?) But once we understand the instructions, then we know why things must be done in a specific way. By making the mistake, this is a teaching moment. **[2]**

So, in the Biblical sense, the instructions that come from the Scriptures tell us exactly how to act or what to do or not do. Then the teacher will teach us why, when and how we do what the instructions say.

One illustration of this would be **MARK 2:23–3:6.** Jesus was being questioned by the Pharisees on honoring the Sabbath. In the first example, they knew the instructions were not to work on the Sabbath, yet they saw Jesus' disciples picking heads of wheat to eat. To them this was work on the Sabbath. The teacher, Jesus, said to them, *"THE SABBATH WAS MADE FOR MAN, NOT MAN FOR THE SABBATH. SO THE SON OF MAN IS LORD EVEN ON THE SABBATH."* Later in chapter three when they bring a man with a shriveled hand to see if Jesus will heal on the Sabbath, Jesus asked them, *"WHICH IS LAWFUL ON THE SABBATH: TO DO GOOD OR TO DO EVIL, TO SAVE LIFE OR TO KILL?"* Then He healed the person.

Yes, the instructions said to not work on the Sabbath, but as Jesus said we were given these instructions for our own good. They are for us. A lot of people would work seven days a week if they did not observe the Sabbath. Jesus was taking the instructions and then teaching them the reasons for the instructions. This was a teaching moment with them, but they did not like what they were being taught. Since He was not following the instructions to the letter, they began to plot to kill Him.

Instructions from an instructor give us direction on a subject, then a teacher makes sure we understand the material and how to apply it to our daily lives.

My parents instructed me to not swear. My teacher, my grandfather, gave me reasons not to swear. Even to the point of telling me I should not have the words in my vocabulary. He said if the words are in your mind, they will come out at the wrong time, so it is better not to even have them in your mind. He said people with limited vocabulary use swear words to try to express themselves, and it is not necessary. He also gave me a benefit from not swearing—the example to others including my children. He was right.

So, in the Biblical sense, the instructions that come from the Scriptures tell us exactly how to act or what to do. The teachers, Paul for an example, teach us the why, the how and the when we are to do what we are instructed.

We are instructed to love the Lord with all our heart, mind and soul. We are taught by teachers, particularly Jesus, on how to do this. Thus, by loving the Lord we then want to keep His commandments. Not just because of instructions, but from the grace we have received.

Jews had plenty of instructions on what they must do or not do to be a good Jew, a religious person. These were called the Laws of God. Follow this law and do this but don't do that. I am sure for the Jews their entire religion seemed to be made up of rules and laws. Then along came the ultra-religious Jews, and they added more rules and laws so it got to be unbearable on what they had to do to have salvation—to be righteous and right with God. Many tried to follow the laws. Some followed part of the time. Some just followed the religious special days and feasts laid out in the Old Testament. Some, the religious, followed them all, all of the time. Paul says in **PHILIPPIANS 3:6B,** *AS FOR LEGALISTIC RIGHTEOUSNESS, FAULTLESS.* He was a Pharisee to the point he saw himself as perfect. Then he "met" Jesus on the road to Damascus and found out there was more to being religious than following the law. This was Paul's revelation.

The Teacher, Jesus, had come into the world. He lived out the instructions, the law. When He did this, we came to understand the purpose of the law. He said to love our neighbors, and then by His actions we see what that means. He talked to the Samaritan woman at the well even though she was rejected by all the other Jews. He healed the Roman officer's daughter when the Jews hated the Romans. He showed compassion on his fellow Jews and put it into action. So, He gave instructions, and then taught by actions.

If we truly love the Lord and want to follow His instructions, it is no longer a task. It is no longer just a list of do's and don'ts, a list of instructions; instead it is now the love of our Lord that gives us a desire to follow His commands.

An easy way to understand this is to look at ourselves as the children of God, which we are. Just like we feel about our children, He wants the best for us. The Lord gives us instructions to help us have the best life possible. Why? Because He loves us. We do the same for our children. But there is a right way to give instructions to our children. In **EPHESIANS 6:4,** Paul tells us, *FATHERS, DO NOT EXASPERATE YOUR CHILDREN; INSTEAD, BRING THEM UP IN THE TRAINING AND INSTRUCTION OF THE LORD.* [3]

Yes, we are to train and instruct our children, but we must also give them teaching. They must know why they should or should not do certain things. The answer "because I said so" only lasts to a certain age. First of all, going back to **ROMANS 15:14,** to instruct, we are to be knowledgeable and competent to instruct others. Do we know what we are talking about when we give our children spiritual guidance and instructions? Are we knowledgeable? Do we follow the same instructions that we are giving our children, or are we saying, "Do as I tell you not what I do"? This is not how Christ gave us instructions. If we want our kids to have ownership in the instructions we give them, then we must have the same ownership. It is one thing to be obedient to religious principles; it is another to have ownership of these principles and instructions. It is more important to have ownership of religious instructions than just obeying what we have been told to do.

When we give instructions, we need to teach our children why they need to follow those instructions. It should not be from the fear of disobeying, but for the benefits there are because they followed them. The benefit of being more Christ-like, of keeping the Lord's commands because we love Him. Also, an understanding of missing the consequences that go with disobedience. [4]

Our children cannot reach heaven by just following instructions and doing things a certain way. They must know why they are following the instructions; then it becomes personal to them.

As a child, then later as a teen, I followed the religious instructions given to me that would show I was a Christian. But to me they were only instructions. I did not own them. I was following instructions to please others, and in my mind this would please God.

A saying goes like this, "If it walks like a duck, and quacks like a duck, it is a duck." This is not how it always works. I walked like a Christian, I talked like a Christian, but I was not a Christian. I had no ownership of what instructions I was following or why I was doing them. If I was trying to please my earthly father, it made sense. But to please my heavenly Father, I had to first commit to Him, to be reborn. Salvation comes from grace not our puny works. Living right will not get me into Heaven, no matter how good I am. It was not until I accepted the Lord that it made sense. If I loved the Lord, I desired to do His commandments out of love, not because of instruction. [5]

Following all the Christian principles and instructions does not make us a Christian. It is a commitment we all must make on our own. It is not rules that were set up by others.

To become a Christian, we must first accept the Lord as our Savior, then gain the knowledge of what the Bible teaches. Listen to our teachers, be it in Sunday School, on radio or TV, a pastor or a friend; but most of all follow the teachings in the Bible. If someone is not teaching from the Bible, run away. Follow the teachings out of love, not duty.

Is all of this easy? No, but the Lord has left us His helper, the Holy Spirit. He comes into our lives to help us follow what the Lord instructs. He will guide us in our Christian living. But we must be sensitive to His teachings and to the love He brings into us to help us follow what the Lord wants in our lives. Once we understand what the Lord desires in our lives, we can take that knowledge and become competent to instruct others.

The Pharisees gave instructions, lots of them; they knew the law, but Jesus said in **MATTHEW 23:27–28,** *"WOE TO YOU, TEACHERS OF THE LAW AND PHARISEES, YOU HYPOCRITES! YOU ARE LIKE WHITEWASHED TOMBS, WHICH LOOK BEAUTIFUL ON THE OUTSIDE BUT ON THE INSIDE ARE FULL OF DEAD MEN'S BONES AND EVERYTHING UNCLEAN. IN THE SAME WAY, ON THE OUTSIDE YOU APPEAR TO PEOPLE AS RIGHTEOUS BUT ON THE INSIDE YOU ARE FULL OF HYPOCRISY AND WICKEDNESS."* They were free to give out instructions concerning the law, but they did not love the Lord. Don't let this be you.

It is okay to instruct others, but we should make sure we are following the instructions in a manner the Lord would approve for our lives. To give instructions we must be knowledgeable on the subject. We must then present the instructions in such a manner that the person would understand what the instructions are and the reasons behind the instructions. We must do this in love, and desire to help our brothers become closer to the Lord.

We need to be both instructor and teacher, but there are times we need to acknowledge the difference and act accordingly. Some of us are better instructors and some of us are better teachers. [6]

QUESTIONS ON INSTRUCT

1. What does it mean to you to instruct someone? To teach someone?

2. Do you think there is a difference between instructing and teaching someone?

3. What did your parents do to exasperate you as a child? Did you do the same thing as a parent?

4. Were you an instructor or a teacher?

5. Does this describe you?

6. What guidelines can help you be a better teacher versus an instructor?

CHAPTER FOUR

TEACH

COLOSSIANS 3:16A, *LET THE WORD OF CHRIST DWELL IN YOU RICHLY AS YOU TEACH AND ADMONISH ONE ANOTHER WITH ALL WISDOM.*

Webster's definition: *to impart information or skill to (a person) or about (a subject, etc.) to put forward as a fact or a principle; Christ taught forgiveness, taught that we must forgive our enemies.*

Teachers in our lives can be very influential, so this is a vital part of being involved in one another's lives.   [1], [2], [3]

According to **COLOSSIANS 3:16,** we are to teach one another. But many of us might say, "I am not a teacher, it is not my gift." How do we teach someone, and how do we know what to teach?

Paul cannot be talking to everyone since teaching is a gift. What if a person does not have the gift of teaching? Does he really want everyone to be a teacher? Absolutely!

One of the reasons the Bible was given to us is to teach all Christians the lessons of the Lord. In school I was given a book on algebra, but if I never opened it or studied the material, I would never get any wisdom from the book. To learn from the scriptures, we must put in study time. We must want to know what is in the book. **ROMANS 15:4,** *FOR*

EVERYTHING THAT WAS WRITTEN IN THE PAST WAS WRITTEN TO TEACH US, SO THAT THROUGH ENDURANCE AND ENCOURAGEMENT OF THE SCRIPTURES WE MIGHT HAVE HOPE. The scriptures are relevant to us today. It is not a dead book, in reality the Bible is a living entity that is to be living in us. Without the knowledge of the Bible it limits in each of us the ability to teach.　　　　**[4], [5]**

1 TIMOTHY 3:14–15, *ALTHOUGH I HOPE TO COME TO YOU SOON, I AM WRITING YOU THESE INSTRUCTIONS SO THAT, IF I AM DELAYED, YOU WILL KNOW HOW PEOPLE OUGHT TO CONDUCT THEMSELVES IN GOD'S HOUSEHOLD, WHICH IS THE CHURCH OF THE LIVING GOD, THE PILLAR AND FOUNDATION OF THE TRUTH.* Paul is very direct in this letter to Timothy. He is giving them no excuses for not presenting themselves as people of the Lord. He is teaching them how to be Christ-like in their actions.

Later in **2 TIMOTHY 3:14–17,** he expects them to continue in their Christ-like life according to scripture. *BUT AS FOR YOU, CONTINUE IN WHAT YOU HAVE LEARNED AND HAVE BECOME CONVINCED OF, BECAUSE YOU KNOW THOSE FROM WHOM YOU LEARNED IT, AND HOW FROM INFANCY YOU HAVE KNOWN THE HOLY SCRIPTURES, WHICH ARE ABLE TO MAKE YOU WISE FOR SALVATION THROUGH FAITH IN CHRIST JESUS. ALL SCRIPTURE IS GOD-BREATHED AND IS USEFUL FOR TEACHING, REBUKING, CORRECTING AND TRAINING IN RIGHTEOUSNESS, SO THAT THE MAN OF GOD MAY BE THOROUGHLY EQUIPPED FOR EVERY GOOD WORK.*　　　　**[6]**

When the Lord returned to heaven, He did not leave us alone and helpless. He gave us the Holy Spirit and inspired the Scriptures to give us guidance in our day to day living. Now, it is up to us to open the book and use the scriptures to direct us and to teach others. To be a teacher we must be willing to pass on what we know or have studied. A teacher is passing on information. Lessons can be learned from a good teacher, a studied friend and from a Bible preaching pastor. By reading the scriptures and studying the Bible we can learn the ways of the Lord. A good study Bible is a huge help for us to learn.

Make sure the preachers are using the Holy Scriptures in their teaching, not just their opinion. We cannot teach using only our opinions or "I think." We must be qualified to teach, not just shooting from the hip. Paul tells Timothy in **2 TIMOTHY 2:2** to pass on what he has heard *TO RELIABLE MEN WHO WILL ALSO BE QUALIFIED TO*

TEACH OTHERS. We learn, we pass it on to others, who learn, and they pass it on to others. Paul says in **TITUS 2:1,** *YOU MUST TEACH WHAT IS IN ACCORD WITH SOUND DOCTRINE.*   **[7], [8]**

But there is a caveat that goes along with being a teacher. It is to be taken very seriously. **JAMES 3:1,** *NOT MANY OF YOU SHOULD PRESUME TO BE TEACHERS, MY BROTHERS, BECAUSE YOU KNOW THAT WE WHO TEACH WILL BE JUDGED MORE STRICTLY.* Why is this so? A teacher is not only to teach the Lord, he is to lead his life in such a way that others can see the Lord in his actions, his life examples. When we accept the responsibility of teaching, we also accept the stricter judgment that follows. **[9]**

Paul goes on to say in **TITUS 2:7,** *IN EVERYTHING SET THEM AN EXAMPLE BY DOING WHAT IS GOOD. IN YOUR TEACHING SHOW INTEGRITY, SERIOUSNESS AND SOUNDNESS OF SPEECH THAT CANNOT BE CONDEMNED, SO THAT THOSE WHO OPPOSE YOU MAY BE ASHAMED BECAUSE THEY HAVE NOTHING BAD TO SAY ABOUT US.* What a testimony it would be if all teachers lived like this. All Christians, particularly teachers, are to live like Billy Graham. Nothing bad can be said about him. He is an example of Christ. Even the people who opposed him could find nothing bad to say. Let this be a desire of all of Christians. To be a Christian teacher does not mean just in a class or congregational setting.
[10]

Teaching means we are imparting knowledge on to others about a subject of which we have experience or knowledge to teach. We must be growing Christians; we cannot teach if we are not growing Christians. The Lord expects us to grow in wisdom and knowledge.

In **HEBREWS 5:11–14,** the author says *WE HAVE MUCH TO SAY ABOUT THIS, BUT IT IS HARD TO EXPLAIN BECAUSE YOU ARE SLOW TO LEARN. IN FACT, THOUGH BY THIS TIME YOU OUGHT TO BE TEACHERS, YOU NEED SOMEONE TO TEACH YOU THE ELEMENTARY TRUTHS OF GOD'S WORD ALL OVER AGAIN. YOU NEED MILK, NOT SOLID FOOD. ANYONE WHO LIVES ON MILK, BEING STILL AN INFANT, IS NOT ACQUAINTED WITH THE TEACHING ABOUT RIGHTEOUSNESS. BUT SOLID FOOD IS FOR THE MATURE, WHO BY CONSTANT USE HAVE TRAINED THEMSELVES TO DISTINGUISH GOOD FROM EVIL.* As Christians we must continue to grow. If not, we are only babies in our learning, we cannot teach others.   **[11]**

We know that a teacher is one who is willing to pass on what he knows or has studied. We as Christians must be willing to pass on what we have been taught to others. Why is it important to pass on this information? Many new Christians have not been exposed to many principles and doctrinal knowledge that an experienced Christian has learned over time. If someone has learned the principle of being a servant, a new Christian might not understand this principle and why it is important to all Christians. The experienced person must expose the new Christian to the teachings of Christ on this subject. We have learned that we must live as a servant to others. Where did this information come from? It came from Jesus, as our example, and Bible study. **PHILIPPIANS 2:7A** says Jesus *MADE HIMSELF NOTHING, TAKING THE VERY NATURE OF A SERVANT.* Then **GALATIANS 5:13B** tells us to *SERVE ONE ANOTHER IN LOVE,* thus it is important to teach this principle to others. This is just one example of how important it is to teach others how Christ lived His life and expects us to live ours.

Jesus wants and expects us to follow his teaching. **JOHN 14:23–24,** *JESUS REPLIED, "IF ANYONE LOVES ME, HE WILL OBEY MY TEACHING. MY FATHER WILL LOVE HIM, AND WE WILL COME TO HIM AND MAKE OUR HOME WITH HIM. HE WHO DOES NOT LOVE ME WILL NOT OBEY MY TEACHING. THESE WORDS YOU HEAR ARE NOT MY OWN; THEY BELONG TO THE FATHER WHO SENT ME."* Jesus is telling his disciples how important it is to follow his teachings. We are to follow his teachings because we love him.

But to follow his teachings, we must know them. **2 THESSALONIANS 2:15,** *SO THEN, BROTHERS, STAND FIRM AND HOLD TO THE TEACHINGS WE PASSED ON TO YOU, WHETHER BY WORD OF MOUTH OR BY LETTER.* We must also use the attitude by which Paul taught others. He taught them with love in his heart and wanted nothing more from them than to love the Lord and for them to have the desire to follow the Lord's teachings.

A big key to teaching is to let the Holy Spirit lead our teaching. As a Sunday school teacher, I can attest to this. If I allow the Holy Spirit to enter into my teaching, it is amazing what happens in the class. My teaching does not come from my knowledge but from the Holy Spirit. He knows the mind of God and uses me to pass on the knowledge. In **LUKE 12:12,** Jesus tells the disciples that when they defend themselves while speaking the words of God that *"FOR THE HOLY SPIRIT WILL TEACH YOU AT THAT TIME WHAT YOU SHOULD SAY."* Jesus also said in **JOHN 14:26,** *"BUT THE COUNSELOR, THE HOLY*

SPIRIT, WHOM THE FATHER WILL SEND IN MY NAME, WILL TEACH YOU ALL THINGS AND WILL REMIND YOU OF EVERYTHING I HAVE SAID TO YOU. We must rely on the Holy Spirit to direct our words when we teach others. Spend time in prayer seeking His help, then be open when He moves in the classroom.

As Christians we are to take advantage of, "teaching moments." When does a teaching moment present itself? It can come at any time from many areas. It comes from observation. When you see a child doing something that is going to harm them, you step in to teach them. Sometimes a new Christian does not think what he is doing has an effect on his Christian life. Here is an example. In the Bible we are taught not to take the Lord's name in vain, but it does not teach us about some of the other swear words we hear today. A new Christian may not realize what they say can take away from their Christian testimony. It is hard to listen to someone talking to you about his Christian life when his everyday language is "salty." People start to wonder if Christ really is in his life. He might not realize, as a new Christian, that his language needs to reflect Christ. I had a very good Christian friend; a strong devoted mature Christian in most areas of his life, but in the area of his language he was still a child. His language remained "salty." A non-Christian friend asked me, "How can he claim to be a Christian and still talk like that?"

His language affected his testimony and he never realized it. That is an example of a teaching moment.

When we observe someone getting into certain situations or doing something that is just not right, it can lead into a teaching moment. It could be our friend's becoming too close to someone of the opposite sex. It looks innocent, but it can lead them astray. This is a teaching moment.

Sometimes it is from our own personal experiences. Been there, done that, really regretted it. This is a time we can say to someone, "Let me talk to you about my own experience in what you are going through. I do not want you to experience the same regrets that I have. I do not want you to get burned like I was." Or "When I was going through the same thing you seem to be going through, I really handled it wrong. Let me tell you what I learned in the process, if you would allow me to do that."

It is always best to ask permission when we start teaching someone else. We are not to just jump in and say something like, "Let me tell you what you are doing wrong." But rather,

"Would you allow me to talk to you about an area I have noticed in your life that you might not have even noticed?" **[12]**

A teaching moment might come from seeing someone else in the same situation that another friend went through. "I don't want you to go through the same problem my friend went through because they did not know what to do, so with your permission let me help and guide you through this situation."

Another teaching moment can come from our concern that what is happening to someone is just not right. "Are you sure this is the right thing to do?" "Is this what God wants in your life?" "Have you talked to the pastor concerning what is happening in your life?"

All of these areas must come from the Holy Spirit giving us direction to speak up, the feeling that we must say something. During these times, the Holy Spirit will give us the right words on what to say, but we must listen to Him. Learn to rely on Him during times of teaching moments. The Holy Spirit works through us with love. Allow the Holy Spirit to guide and teach one another in love. Don't forget the final words in **COLOSSIANS 3:16, *IN WISDOM.*** We are to teach others with wisdom. We must show sound judgment, be knowledgeable, be wise, be well informed, and we must listen to the Holy Spirit speak and then do all these things in love. By doing all these things we are qualified to be teachers. Be the kind of teacher that others will remember in coming years. **[13], [14]**

QUESTIONS ON TEACH

1. What teachers in your public education were the most influential? Why?

2. What spiritual teacher was the most influential? Why?

3. What made either of these two teachers special to you?

4. What is so important about the teachings of the Bible and of Jesus?

5. Do you agree that a person must have Biblical knowledge to teach?

6. Explain this verse. What does "God-breathed" mean?

7. What is wrong with a person teaching by their opinions?

8. Where does "sound doctrine" come from?

9. Why is there such a strict judgment on teachers?

10. Who has taught you to act as a Christian? Was this done by words or by actions? Are you trying to do the same as that person did?

11. What is so wrong to continually be on "baby food"?

12. Why should we ask someone if we may teach them something? How would we react when someone tried to teach without asking first?

13. What is your spiritual appetite? Has it changed over the years? What made it change? How can this make us better teachers?

14. Why would we think we cannot teach?

CHAPTER FIVE

ADMONISH

COLOSSIANS 3:16A, *LET THE WORD OF CHRIST DWELL IN YOU RICHLY AS YOU TEACH AND ADMONISH ONE ANOTHER WITH ALL WISDOM.*

What exactly does admonish mean? [1]

First, let's look at what it does not mean. It does not mean:

To browbeat
To beat down
To berate publicly
To set someone straight
To yell at someone
To ridicule someone

Admonish really means to advise someone. To urge them in a serious manner so they will look at what they are doing and then change their ways. This is to be done mildly, but firmly with great love. The person that is admonishing someone is giving advice and/or a warning.

Admonishing one another needs to be tied to teaching one another. Why tie these two together? Admonishment without teaching takes on the feeling of:

Pickiness
Complaining
Nosiness
Being out of line
Getting into someone's personal business
Stirring up anger

When this happens, people have some of the following reactions.

Butt out.
Who do you think you are?
What are you, some kind of "goody-goody"?
What gives you the right to tell me I am wrong?
I don't tell you how to live your life, so don't try to tell me how to live mine.   [2]

If done incorrectly, it is like a coach saying to a player, "don't do it that way," but never telling the player the correct way to do what he wants.

I can relate to this. When I started my freshman year in college, I decided to try out for the basketball team even though I had never played any organized basketball all through my twelve years of school. I had been too shy to try out for the team even though I had played lots of pickup basketball. I had the athletic ability, but I did not have the "team ability." So, when the coach said, "Don't do it that way," I was at a loss on what else to do. I needed coaching. The coach stepped in and said, "that won't work, but let me give you a better way to do what is needed." His coaching allowed me to be better and make the team.

That was admonishment with teaching, which is what our brothers in Christ need. A lot of new Christians do not have the "team skill," and are looking for positive coaching.   [3]

Within the local church, a good pastor is one who admonishes his congregation from time to time through his sermons. They are not directed at one person, but to all the congregation. But many times it will strike home to the one that is not in the Lord's will. Surely this has happened to many of us.   [4]

At the same time of the admonishment, there must be a teaching for a better way to live our lives. We are not to take offense since it is for our own good. We are to appreciate the person who admonishes us. We all need constructive criticism at various times in our lives.

1 THESSALONIANS 5:12 gives us this advice, *NOW WE ASK YOU, BROTHERS, TO RESPECT THOSE WHO WORK HARD AMONG YOU, WHO ARE OVER YOU IN THE LORD AND WHO ADMONISH YOU.* Why should we respect people telling us to change our ways? They are: [5]

Doing it for our own good.
Helping us to be more Christ-like.
Helping us to grow as a Christian.
Keeping us on the right path.

The person giving us the admonishment has probably been there before. He knows the consequences of our actions.

This area of admonishment can easily be related to marriage. My spouse might talk to me about an area in my life that I am not handling in the right way. There are two actions that will make this admonishment more effective. One, it must be said in such a way that it is not just critical of me, but in a way that shows my spouse is trying to help me. If the beginning comment is said in the wrong way, I will stop listening and just get upset with my wife. But two, I must receive the admonishment in the way it was given, by not taking offense. Accept the message, but do not shoot the messenger. This holds true when we admonish others that are not our spouses.

This area of admonishing and teaching was very important to Paul. He actually tells the Colossians the reason for admonishing and teaching. **COLOSSIANS 1:28** says *WE PROCLAIM HIM, ADMONISHING AND TEACHING EVERYONE WITH ALL WISDOM, SO THAT WE MAY PRESENT EVERYONE PERFECT IN CHRIST.* Paul is saying the goal is to be perfect in the Lord's eyes. Is this possible? No, even Paul struggles with this. *(See Chapter 13.)* But if we don't have a goal to be perfect, then we will never strive for perfection even though we know it cannot be achieved.

Yet because we are saved, we are seen as perfect. When God looks at us, He sees we are covered by the blood of Christ. He sees us as righteous and perfect in His sight. We need to see ourselves as imperfect Christians struggling to be perfect. We must strive for perfection.

Paul in **PHILIPPIANS 2:12B** says to *CONTINUE TO WORK OUT YOUR SALVATION,* telling us our salvation is an ongoing work in process.

Are we growing in the Lord?
>   If not, we should be.

Are we closer to the Lord this year versus last year?
>   If not, why not?

Are we stronger Christians?
>   What have we done to strengthen our relationships with the Lord?

Are we weaning ourselves from baby food?
>   If not, we need to.   [6]

We need admonishment so we can look at ourselves and see what we need to change in our lives to come closer to the Christians we are striving to be. If we are not growing, we are becoming lukewarm in the sight of God. This is not what is expected of us. God does not like lukewarm Christians.

Attitude and tone of voice is everything when we admonish someone.

Don't be offensive.
Don't judge.
Admonishment must be done with love.
Use admonishment as a teaching moment.
Admonish with wisdom.
>   Know what we are talking about.
>   If we are not sure, say nothing.

When does admonishment take place? Before we admonish anyone, we need to talk it over with the pastor to make sure he is on board. Maybe he is already counseling this person on the same subject. Have we checked out the facts or is it just gossip? Have we seen the issue firsthand? Have we spent time in prayer to insure we are doing the right thing? Is God on board with what we want to do? Are we listening to the Holy Spirit?   [7]

Before we admonish someone, we need to ask ourselves these questions. Am I sure I am the right person? Am I too personally involved? Do I have any personal agenda? Can I admonish with love? Have I thought about how I can have a teaching moment, or am I just going to set them straight? The admonisher must be someone that is respected and can admonish with love in his or her heart; love that the receiver can feel and see. Not everyone can admonish in a correct manner and when it is done wrongly it can have very poor results.   [8]

If we are the one being admonished, listen to the admonishment, listen to the teaching that must come with it, and then consider changes in our Christian lives that will bring us closer to the Lord. The key here is listening. Do not get defensive. Are there changes that need to be made? Promise to pray about the teaching. It is a daily battle, but we need to fight to become better, more perfect Christians. **[9]**

We also have someone living within us that brings admonishment to us when we need it. As we live our day to day lives, the Holy Spirit is talking to us to help us become more Christ-like.

He continues to direct us in the ways of the Lord.
He admonishes us when we get out of line.
He also teaches us the ways of the Lord.
He acts as our guide.
He gets us going in the right direction.
He knows the way of the Lord.
He corrects us when we are out of line.
He brings us back in line with the Lord's teaching.

The key here, are we listening? The Holy Spirit is our GPS, God's Personal Spirit. **[10], [11]**

QUESTIONS ON ADMONISH

1. What does the word admonish mean to you?

2. What are your feelings when someone admonishes you?

3. Can you relate to the basketball admonishment? In what way?

4. Do you want the pastor to admonish you in sermons? If so, why?

5. Do you respect someone that admonishes you? Why or why not? What if it is your spouse?

6. How did you answer these questions?

7. Have you seen admonishment done badly? Have you seen admonishment done properly? What was the difference from one to the other? What where the results of both?

8. In your opinion, who should admonish others?

9. Where does most of your admonishment come from?

10. Do you see admonishment in a better light?

11. Why do we accept admonishment at our jobs, but not in our faith?

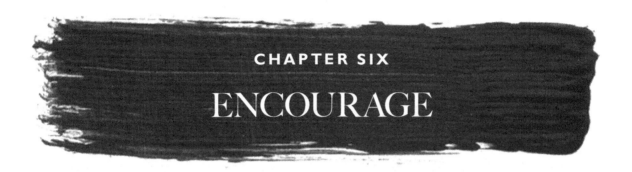

CHAPTER SIX
ENCOURAGE

1 THESSALONIANS 5:11, *THEREFORE ENCOURAGE ONE ANOTHER AND BUILD EACH OTHER UP, JUST AS IN FACT YOU ARE DOING.* **[1]**

Paul uses the word *encouragement* in all but two of his letters. He saw it as important that Christians would encourage each other as they go through life, through their day to day living. He encouraged people to stimulate others in their Christianity and to urge them to a higher plane, to a closer relationship with the Lord. **[2]**

But how can we encourage one another? Paul says in **1 THESSALONIANS 4:18,** *THEREFORE ENCOURAGE EACH OTHER WITH THESE WORDS.* As always, we need to see what the word *therefore* is there for. In the previous verses, **VERSES 13–17,** Paul was talking about the second coming of the Lord, that when He comes again, we will be caught up with the Lord to spend eternity with Him. Why is this encouraging to us today? Our home is not on this earth because it is only a temporary place, with temporary problems. He was encouraging them with the hope of the resurrection we all have. These words can and should encourage us today. What words are we to use for encouragement? **[3]**

Paul reminds us that we have the scripture to encourage us. **ROMANS 15:4,** *FOR EVERYTHING THAT WAS WRITTEN IN THE PAST WAS WRITTEN TO TEACH*

US, SO THAT THROUGH ENDURANCE AND THE ENCOURAGEMENT OF THE SCRIPTURES WE MIGHT HAVE HOPE. [4]

How do the scriptures give us encouragement? They do in various ways.

The history of our faith
The faith of others
The happiness it brings in our reading
The wisdom it teaches
The love the Lord has for us all
That God keeps His promises and does not lie
A place to turn to in times of trouble
The directions it gives to us for all areas of our lives
Seeing the struggles of others and how they held true
The hope it gives us
The assurance of our inheritance with the Lord and eternal life with Him
The knowledge and understanding of the Father, the Son and the Holy Spirit

For us to be encouraged by the Bible, we must read it. Of course, it is best for us to do this daily, but if you miss a day, get back to the Word. Encouragement is there for the taking. Scriptures can bring great comfort in a troubled world. **2 TIMOTHY 3:16A,** *ALL SCRIPTURE IS GOD-BREATHED.*

Encouragement also comes to us from sound doctrine. **TITUS 1:9,** *HE MUST HOLD FIRMLY TO THE TRUSTWORTHY MESSAGE AS IT HAS BEEN TAUGHT, SO THAT HE CAN ENCOURAGE OTHERS BY SOUND DOCTRINE AND REFUTE THOSE WHO OPPOSE IT.* What doctrine from the Bible encourages us? And what exactly is doctrine? A doctrine is a principle, or a set of principles held by a religious group. It is a basic truth or law that is used on a basis of reasoning or a guide to action or behavior. A code of right conduct. We can hold to these doctrines to become encouraged because of the truth that they hold.

As examples:

The sovereignty of scriptures. The Bible is God inspired and is the Word of God.
    Nothing is to be added or subtracted from the Bible.
God, Jesus and the Holy Spirit form the Holy Trinity.

All have sinned and come short of the Glory of God.

Jesus died for our sins. He arose on the third day. By His resurrection, all His followers will be resurrected and spend eternity with God in heaven.

No one will enter heaven except by accepting Christ as Lord. There is no other way.

When we repent and accept the Lord's grace, the Holy Spirit enters into us and we become sons and daughters of God. Our inheritance is heaven. The Holy Spirit is our constant companion.

These few doctrines should give us encouragement. We can lean on these doctrines. All of these are promises from God to us. **[5]**

We receive encouragement from the Holy Spirit. **ACTS 9:31B** tells us that churches are ***STRENGTHENED; AND ENCOURAGED BY THE HOLY SPIRIT.*** The Holy Spirit was working through the Christians that made up the body of believers. If the Holy Spirit was doing it then, He can and will do it now. We need to ask the Holy Spirit to work in our churches today. Many times we sell the work of the Holy Spirit short. It is amazing what the Holy Spirit can do within the church body if allowed and if invited to take over.

ROMANS 15:5 tells us we receive encouragement from God. ***MAY THE GOD WHO GIVES ENDURANCE AND ENCOURAGEMENT GIVE YOU A SPIRIT OF UNITY AMONG YOURSELVES AS YOU FOLLOW CHRIST JESUS.*** Paul speaks of God and Jesus giving us eternal encouragement and hope. **2 THESSALONIANS 2:16–17,** ***MAY OUR LORD JESUS CHRIST HIMSELF AND GOD OUR FATHER, WHO LOVED US AND BY HIS GRACE GAVE US ETERNAL ENCOURAGEMENT AND GOOD HOPE, ENCOURAGE YOUR HEARTS AND STRENGTHEN YOU IN EVERY GOOD DEED AND WORD.*** All this encouragement comes from the grace we have received from God. It is nothing we have earned or deserve but is a gift from the Lord. Every time we think of our salvation we should be encouraged.

This type of encouragement never ends.

We now have the Holy Spirit dwelling in us.

Our rewards from the Father are coming.

We are now adopted children of God.

The Lord will never leave us. That is His promise.

The Lord helps us through times of hardship.

We see examples of Paul's written encouragement to others:

ACTS 11:23, *WHEN HE ARRIVED AND SAW THE EVIDENCE OF THE GRACE OF GOD, HE WAS GLAD AND ENCOURAGED THEM ALL TO REMAIN TRUE TO THE LORD WITH ALL THEIR HEARTS.* Paul encouraged others to remain true to the Lord.

ACTS 14:22, *STRENGTHENING THE DISCIPLES AND ENCOURAGING THEM TO REMAIN TRUE TO THE FAITH. "WE MUST GO THROUGH MANY HARDSHIPS TO ENTER THE KINGDOM OF GOD," THEY SAID.* Paul and others encouraged them to remain true during tough times.

Paul wrote of his encouragement to the early church. **1 THESSALONIANS 2:10–12,** *YOU ARE WITNESSES, AND SO IS GOD, OF HOW HOLY, RIGHTEOUS AND BLAMELESS WE WERE AMONG YOU WHO BELIEVED. FOR YOU KNOW THAT WE DEALT WITH EACH OF YOU AS A FATHER DEALS WITH HIS OWN CHILDREN, ENCOURAGING, COMFORTING AND URGING YOU TO LIVE LIVES WORTHY OF GOD, WHO CALLS YOU INTO HIS KINGDOM AND GLORY.*

He directed Titus to encourage others on how they live their lives for Christ. **TITUS 2:6–7A,** *SIMILARLY, ENCOURAGE THE YOUNG MEN TO BE SELF-CONTROLLED. IN EVERYTHING SET THEM AN EXAMPLE BY DOING WHAT IS GOOD.*

We are reminded to encourage each other daily to keep us from sinning and unclear thinking. **HEBREWS 3:13,** *BUT ENCOURAGE ONE ANOTHER DAILY, AS LONG AS IT IS CALLED TODAY, SO THAT NONE OF YOU MAY BE HARDENED BY SIN'S DECEITFULNESS.* In other words, never stop encouraging one another. Be proactive in your encouragement to others. Go out of your way to encourage others. This is the Lord's command.

Our words can encourage people. I don't know about you, but an "atta boy" will keep me going for weeks. Sometimes words of encouragement are all someone needs to continue the work of the Lord. When we serve, there are times we can get discouraged. We all know someone who has labored faithfully for many years, doing the same work, be it a teacher, a nursery worker, a trustee, a prayer warrior, a pianist, a greeter, or any other position in the church body. We can take people who are faithful for granted. When was the last time they heard "Good job, we appreciate what you are doing for the Lord"? Look around the church and see who might need an encouraging word. We are to make the effort to encourage others. It cost nothing but it does wonders for all who receive the encouragement.

We can encourage one another today with words in many ways: a letter, a note, an email, or a text that we send. Most of these only take a minute to write but can really affect someone. **ACTS 15:30–31** tells us how the people were encouraged by a letter in Bible times. *THE MEN WERE SENT OFF AND WENT DOWN TO ANTIOCH, WHERE THEY GATHERED THE CHURCH TOGETHER AND DELIVERED THE LETTER. THE PEOPLE READ IT AND WERE GLAD FOR ITS ENCOURAGING MESSAGE.* My church, at times, receives a letter from a missionary that we support, and when it is read within the body, it gives us all encouragement for what is going on as God works in other areas of the world.

My church had postcards in the pews that were titled "encouragement cards." They were used in a variety of ways to send someone a note on a variety of subjects. As an example:

Encouragement to a teacher for a lesson delivered
Encouragement to the pastor on what his message meant
Encouragement to someone that is going through hard times
Encouragement to someone who is struggling with a problem
Encouragement to someone for a loss of something, be it a job, a pet, a loved one
Encouragement to let someone know you are praying for them
Encouragement to someone in a leadership capacity
Encouragement to the choir or a soloist for a song that was meaningful
Plus, many other areas   [6]

Sending someone an encouragement card always gives me a good feeling. Receiving one is "gold." They always seem to come at a perfect time. It only takes a quick moment to encourage someone with a note, but the results can be wonderful. We are still reading letters that Paul wrote many centuries ago and they still bring us encouragement today.

What else encourages people? Sometimes it is just seeing an old friend. We go through a tough time and then run into a friend from the past. Our spirits are lifted. This is exactly what happened to Paul on his trip to Rome. Paul was a prisoner and was shipwrecked. He finally arrived in port on a new ship and was taken to Rome. Then he was met by some fellow Christians. **ACTS 28:15,** *THE BROTHERS THERE HAD HEARD THAT WE WERE COMING, AND THEY TRAVELED AS FAR AS THE FORUM OF APPIUS AND THE THREE TAVERNS TO MEET US. AT THE SIGHT OF THESE MEN PAUL THANKED GOD AND WAS ENCOURAGED.* These men made an effort to come, and look at the result it had on Paul. We too can be encouraged by a complete stranger, a family member, a friend or someone from our church. Paul realized how he could be encouraged by a visit from someone, so he would send men to encourage the growing churches. [7]

EPHESIANS 6:21–22, *TYCHICUS, THE DEAR BROTHER AND FAITHFUL SERVANT IN THE LORD, WILL TELL YOU EVERYTHING, SO THAT YOU ALSO MAY KNOW HOW I AM AND WHAT I AM DOING. I AM SENDING HIM TO YOU FOR THIS VERY PURPOSE, THAT YOU MAY KNOW HOW WE ARE, AND THAT HE MAY ENCOURAGE YOU.*

1 THESSALONIANS 3:2, *WE SENT TIMOTHY, WHO IS OUR BROTHER AND GOD'S FELLOW WORKER IN SPREADING THE GOSPEL OF CHRIST, TO STRENGTHEN AND ENCOURAGE YOU IN YOUR FAITH.*

2 TIMOTHY 4:2, *PREACH THE WORD; BE PREPARED IN SEASON AND OUT OF SEASON; CORRECT, REBUKE AND ENCOURAGE—WITH GREAT PATIENCE AND CAREFUL INSTRUCTION.*

We encourage others by our faith. Paul gives us an example in **ROMANS 1:11–12,** *I LONG TO SEE YOU SO THAT I MAY IMPART TO YOU SOME SPIRITUAL GIFT TO MAKE YOU STRONG—THAT IS, THAT YOU AND I MAY BE MUTUALLY ENCOURAGED BY EACH OTHER'S FAITH.* How does this work? Have we ever observed other Christians going through difficult times in their lives? Ever noticed how they reacted and how they remained close to the Lord? It encourages us so that in the future we can handle things better in our difficult times. By others living their lives close to the Lord during trying times, we are encouraged that we can do the same. Many times, we do not realize that others might be observing how we live our lives. This should remind us that it is important how we live our daily Christian lives. We can also share with others our faith. This gives them encouragement that they can make it through life during turbulent times. When others are persecuted and they rejoice in the Lord, it should give us encouragement that the Lord is giving them strength. Paul is our example for this. He was in prison and yet he continued to praise the Lord and preach the gospel. He lived out his faith even while he was in chains. No matter what, he continued the mission he was sent out to do. Paul was encouraged by others' faith as well. **1 THESSALONIANS 3:7,** *THEREFORE, BROTHERS, IN ALL OUR DISTRESS AND PERSECUTION WE WERE ENCOURAGED ABOUT YOU BECAUSE OF YOUR FAITH.* **[8]**

We are encouraged by coming together weekly. **HEBREWS 10:25** tells us *LET US NOT GIVE UP MEETING TOGETHER, AS SOME ARE IN THE HABIT OF DOING, BUT LET US ENCOURAGE ONE ANOTHER—AND ALL THE MORE AS YOU SEE THE DAY APPROACHING.* This also is a "one another," but it fits in with this area of encouraging one another so well that it needs to be addressed here. Why does meeting together encourage people? Hearing the word of God in itself is encouraging. The speaker/teacher/pastor brings to our attention how we can be more Christ-like in our day to day living. They bring us instructions from the Word. It is encouraging to know what changes we need to make and how to do them. A speaker encourages us by telling us the things of God. **1 CORINTHIANS 14:31,** *FOR YOU CAN ALL PROPHESY IN TURN SO THAT EVERYONE MAY BE INSTRUCTED AND ENCOURAGED.* As we share with our friends what the Lord has laid on our hearts and all He has done for us, it gives others encouragement. **[9]**

Just being with other Christians is encouraging. We can share what good things are happening in our lives and also the heartache we might be going through. It allows us to rely on our friends to help us pray in difficult times. Encouraging words to others might be what they need at this point in their lives. When we are in a church service worshiping God with our voices and our minds, troubles seem to go away. They feel so insignificant in front of the almighty God. Our lives are uplifted as songs of praise, prayers and thanksgiving are raised to God. Sometimes we hear testimonies. We hear the teaching of God's Word. Just the smiles and greetings we receive from our friends are encouraging. Do not give up the fellowship of believers, we all need each other. **[10]**

But why would Christians need encouragement? What discourages us in our day-to-day lives? Here are some areas that discourage us in our daily living:

Continuous frustration with our family
Differences between our spouse and ourselves

Kids
In-laws and other family members
Bills
Job stress
Health issues
Lack of sunny days
Too busy
People let us down
Can't lose weight
A messy desk
Too many hours at work
Not enough hours at home
Just day-to-day living   [11]

As a Christian I get discouraged by some of the following:

It seems like I am too busy for God.
I don't do what I am supposed to do.
I keep doing what I don't want to do.
I can't find time for my devotions (or make the time).
I have a total lack of prayer time.
Two-faced Christians frustrate me.
Listening to other Christians grumble frustrates me.
I don't understand God's plan for me.
I just don't understand the Bible at times.
I don't feel I am growing in the Lord.
Why does this all happen to me? Am I being punished?
Why do such bad things keep going on in the world?   [12]

With all of this discouragement in our lives, it is no wonder we need encouragement. We need to be aware of what could be going on in our Christian brothers' lives. But isn't encouragement a gift? Yes, it is a gift. We are told in **ROMANS 12:8A** speaking about gifts, ***IF IT IS ENCOURAGING, LET HIM ENCOURAGE.*** We can probably think of someone with this gift. They always seem so upbeat and going out of their way to exhort others in their faith, by counseling people through difficult times, sending out notes that always seem to come at the right time, or telling people what a good job they are doing in the service of the Lord. But we are not to let the people with the gift of encouragement be the only ones to help others through their down periods. We are all to be encouragers.

When are we to encourage one another? Paul says in **2 CORINTHIANS 7:4,** *I HAVE GREAT CONFIDENCE IN YOU; I TAKE GREAT PRIDE IN YOU. I AM GREATLY ENCOURAGED; IN ALL OUR TROUBLES MY JOY KNOWS NO BOUNDS.* Paul was encouraged by the news of the faith of the Corinthians. He needed to hear about their faith to give him encouragement. We can each encourage one another by looking at the bright side of others and passing it on. If someone seems discouraged, that is the time to give them encouragement.

We need to be aware as people are getting ready for changes in their lives. **ACTS 18:27A** gives us an example, *WHEN APOLLOS WANTED TO GO TO ACHAIA, THE BROTHERS ENCOURAGED HIM.* This could be a Christian taking a new job, a person going off to college, or someone getting married or moving out of their parent's home. Times like this can be traumatic and for some very scary. Be aware to offer words of encouragement.

Another time when people need encouragement is during a dramatic change in their life, such as a family member has died, or a person loses his job. Paul speaks to this in **ACTS 27:33–36.** The crew and passengers of the ship they were on have all survived a shipwreck. *JUST BEFORE DAWN PAUL URGED THEM ALL TO EAT. "FOR THE LAST FOURTEEN DAYS," HE SAID, "YOU HAVE BEEN IN CONSTANT SUSPENSE AND HAVE GONE WITHOUT FOOD—YOU HAVEN'T EATEN ANYTHING. NOW I URGE YOU TO TAKE SOME FOOD. YOU NEED IT TO SURVIVE. NOT ONE OF YOU WILL LOSE A SINGLE HAIR FROM HIS HEAD." AFTER HE SAID THIS, HE TOOK SOME BREAD AND GAVE THANKS TO GOD IN FRONT OF THEM ALL. THEN HE BROKE IT AND BEGAN TO EAT. THEY WERE ALL ENCOURAGED AND ATE SOME FOOD THEMSELVES.* Not all these people were Christians, yet Paul gave them encouragement.

Some need encouragement during times of feeling inadequate. As a personal note, I can identify with this. When I started the process to put on paper what I had been directed to do, I felt very inadequate. Once I started and had written four or five chapters, I felt overwhelmed. I needed encouragement that I was going in the right direction and what I was doing was going to be accepted. This was a different feeling for me as in the past I was not one that really would seek out encouragement from others. Thank goodness friends noticed this feeling of unworthiness I was going through and gave me the encouragement I needed at just the right time. Thank you, my friends.

Some of us need to be encouraged to share our faith with others. **1 THESSALONIANS 5:14,** *AND WE URGE YOU, BROTHERS, WARN THOSE WHO ARE IDLE, ENCOURAGE THE TIMID, HELP THE WEAK, BE PATIENT WITH EVERYONE.* This could be a new Christian or someone that is just shy. Be alert and encourage them in their faith.

We all need to take a look at ourselves and see how we can better encourage others. Look back at the ways people can be encouraged.

By hearing about the faith of others
From getting an "atta boy"—an encouraging word
Through the reading or hearing of scripture
From the sound doctrine we can rely on
From the Holy Spirit within us, but we must listen
By reflecting on the gift of grace that has been freely given
Through contact with others via notes, email, tweets, etc.
Through the contact of someone from the past
By seeing the living faith in others
By being part of a worship service or just by being with other Christian friends
A simple hug to show the love and encouragement we feel

Never give up encouraging others. **[13]**

QUESTIONS ON ENCOURAGE

1. How would you go about encouraging a fellow Christian? Give an example of how someone has encouraged you.

2. Why would Paul mention encouragement so many times in his letters?

3. Are you encouraged by what **1 THESSALONIANS 4:18** says?

4. **ROMANS 15:4** says scripture can encourage us. What scriptures have encouraged you?

5. Explain the encouragement of sound doctrine.

6. Have you received written encouragement? What would you add to this list?

7. Are you thinking of someone? If so, make the effort to contact them.

8. How has someone's faith encouraged you?

9. How has a Christian speaker given you encouragement?

10. What gives you the biggest boost from attending church?

11. What in this list of discouragements affect you the most? Add to this list.

12. What in this list of Christian discouragements affect you the most? Add to this list.

13. What ideas have you thought of that you will be doing to encourage others?

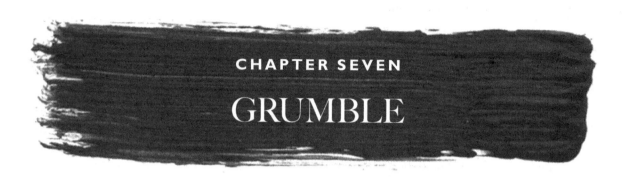

CHAPTER SEVEN
GRUMBLE

JAMES 5:9A, *DON'T GRUMBLE AGAINST EACH OTHER, BROTHERS.*

How many times as a parent have we heard our kids grumbling about something?

> Maybe a chore they were asked to do
>> "Do I have to do the dishes?"
> Grumbling about a sibling
>> "He's touching me."
>> "She's looking at me."
> About the food they don't want to eat
>> "Isn't there something else for supper?"
>> As fathers or mothers, how do we like it?

Yet as Christians we grumble among ourselves and we even grumble about each other. How do we think our heavenly Father likes this?   [1]

When I see the word *grumble*, I think of my pastor, Dr. James Smith, and a sermon he gave about grumbling. The sermon was from **NUMBERS 14.** After the Jews had crossed the Red Sea on dry land they grumbled to Moses about the lack of water to drink. They felt God had brought them into the desert to die. They were ready to return to Egypt. Pastor Smith focused on the Greek word for grumble. He told the congregation that the word sounded like what it meant. The word was *gongudzo; phonetically* it is *gone-guud-zo.*

God got tired of all the grumbling and told them that they had only been in the desert for forty days, but because of their grumbling they would wander for forty years, and all over the age of twenty, except Caleb and Joshua, would die and not enter the promise land. Later in **NUMBERS 16,** God killed 14,700 people with the plague because of their grumbling. It was evident that God did not tolerate grumbling.

Jesus got tired of hearing it as well. In **JOHN 6:35,** Jesus is talking to a crowd of Jews and tells them, *"I AM THE BREAD OF LIFE. HE WHO COMES TO ME WILL NEVER GO HUNGRY, AND HE WHO BELIEVES IN ME WILL NEVER BE THIRSTY."* He is telling them who He is and of His promises. In **VERSE 41,** they are grumbling about what He had said. In **VERSE 43** Jesus replies, *"STOP GRUMBLING AMONG YOURSELVES."*

Just like we get tired of hearing grumbling, Jesus is no different. He gets tired of it as well. Like Father, like Son. This is not how we are to act. We are to build each other up, not tear each other down. Building one up one another is part of Paul's directions to Christians. *(See Chapter 8.)*

In what ways does this happen in the local church? What grumbling do we hear or even say ourselves?

Why are they singing that song again?
Doesn't anyone dust around here?
Why are they changing the order of the service?
Why doesn't the pastor wear a tie every Sunday?
Did you see that dress she was wearing?
Someone actually wore shorts to church.
Someone needs to be in charge of sharpening the pew pencils.
It's too dark in here.
It's too light in here.
Why does he feel this is his pew? Did he buy it?
Why does everyone sit in the back of the church?
Why do we have so many burned out light bulbs?
Why doesn't the choir sing every Sunday, even in the summer? [2]

None of these should be a part of the church of Jesus Christ. We are His bride. None of these areas of grumbling bring praise to God.   [3]

Notice, all of these things are focused on one person. ME!

> I want it my way.
> It is not what I want.
> I disagree.

If we were visitors to a church and we overheard grumbling like this, would we want to come back? I doubt it.

Are any of these reasons to grumble? Possibly, but they are mighty petty complaints. Wouldn't it be better to take these complaints to someone that is in charge of the areas we complain about? A dusty church, go to the head trustee. Changes in the order of the service, go to the pastor. The choir not singing every Sunday, go to the music director. Just grumbling aloud to anyone that can hear us gives a poor representation of us all and our church. We are trying to elevate our standing within the body. I had a boss that had the rule that no one could just come to him with a complaint. If I came to complain, he expected me to have the solution to fix the problem. If we had that rule within the church, complaining and grumbling would probably just go away.

We hear grumbling at home and at our job; we sure don't want or expect to hear it in the Lord's house. It just does not belong. Grumbling is a long way from unity, praise and worship.

Grumbling can definitely hurt the church.   [4]

> It can bring about divisions and cliques within the body.
> It can hurt people's feelings.
> It can start arguments.

My friend, J. D., said as a teacher he would avoid the teacher's lounge. Why, I asked? He answered that all they did in the lounge was grumble and gripe, and he did not want to be a part of it so he would just avoid the area. If someone comes to your church and hears others grumbling, this could easily be their reaction. They just won't come back. Do not be one of the "grumblers or gripers."

JAMES 1:26, *IF ANYONE CONSIDERS HIMSELF RELIGIOUS AND YET DOES NOT KEEP A TIGHT REIN ON HIS TONGUE, HE DECEIVES HIMSELF AND HIS RELIGION IS WORTHLESS.*

In this passage, James is talking about a person who follows all the religious observances, goes to church every week, prays and tithes; yet because of his sharp tongue, his "religion" is worthless. It takes away all the good he is trying to do or has done. James realizes what a tongue can do within the church and the hurt it can bring. **[5]**

This "religious" person is one of these people we see today who lets his tongue get away from his brain. He shoots first then asks questions, or thinks, later. The words come out of his mouth without any forethought.

We need to think before we speak. Let our thoughts pass through our brain before we speak or grumble about something. Think of the consequences or hurt our words might bring.

Sticks and stones can break my bones, but words can never hurt me. I was taught this as a child by my parents, when someone said bad things about me. I did not disagree with my parents often, but in this case they were wrong. Words do hurt, and they can hurt for a long, long time. Some of the things that were said to me in my youth still haunt me today. When we grumble, others are hurt, whether on purpose or not. So, watch our tongues. Again I say, think before we speak. **[6]**

James goes on to say in **JAMES 3:5–6,** *LIKEWISE THE TONGUE IS A SMALL PART OF THE BODY, BUT IT MAKES GREAT BOASTS. CONSIDER WHAT A GREAT FOREST IS SET ON FIRE BY A SMALL SPARK. THE TONGUE ALSO IS A FIRE, A WORLD OF EVIL AMONG THE PARTS OF THE BODY. IT CORRUPTS THE WHOLE PERSON, SETS THE WHOLE COURSE OF HIS LIFE ON FIRE, AND IS ITSELF SET ON FIRE BY HELL.*

James is saying the use of our tongues for evil comes straight from Satan. If we give the control of our tongues over to the Holy Spirit, many words that hurt would never be spoken aloud.

> Both God and Jesus hate grumblers.
> It is not Christ-like to grumble.
> Control your tongue.

Think before you speak.
Control your grumbling and complaining.
Do not let Satan have control over your tongue.

Instead of grumbling we are to build up one another. Every time we grumble against others, we are judging them against our standards, not God's.

Watch your tongue. Quit grumbling! [7]

QUESTIONS ON GRUMBLE

1. Do you ever hear grumbling in the church? What do you do about it? Are you one of the "grumblers"?

2. Add to this list of grumbling in the church. Don't they seem silly and petty?

3. What must the Lord think about all this grumbling?

4. How does this hurt the church? Why is there so much grumbling in the church? How does this bring about divisions and cliques? Why is this so harmful?

5. Do you agree? Have you seen this?

6. Do you have control over your tongue? If not, why not? If you do, how did you gain control?

7. What principles do you take from this lesson? How would your church impact your community if everyone quit grumbling?

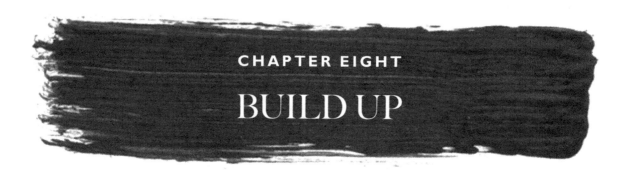

CHAPTER EIGHT
BUILD UP

1 THESSALONIANS 5:11, *THEREFORE ENCOURAGE ONE ANOTHER AND BUILD EACH OTHER UP, JUST AS IN FACT YOU ARE DOING.*

What does it mean to build up a Christian brother? What is involved? How do we go about building each other up? [1]

To answer these questions, first we must divide them into three parts.

1. Building up ourselves
2. Building up others
3. Building up the church

Why is it important that we need to build up ourselves before we build up others, thus building up the church? We cannot build up others as Christians if we are not mature built-up Christians. Once we are mature Christians, we can then lead by example to others. Can you image a rookie in sports trying to build up the older veteran? As we become mature Christians, is it just a matter of growing old? No, it is a matter of gaining knowledge and experience. The mature Christian must have a firm foundation, one he can lean on when he builds up others.

Where does this foundation come from? As Christians our foundation comes from the Word of God. Our foundation is found in the Bible. We must have a foundation given us from previous apostles and prophets. The knowledge is there for the taking. It is up to each of us to apply ourselves to gaining this knowledge and then using it to help build up others. We have the words of past saints, and we have their examples of how they lived their lives for the Lord.

To gain this knowledge, do you have a good Bible class that you go to each week? Be it Sunday morning or a small group or even a mid-week study. Take advantage of the teaching of others to help you get built up in the Word. As a Sunday school teacher I must do my due diligence in study so I can bring the Word of God to others to edify them, to make them interested in the Bible, and to open their eyes to Biblical truths to help them live their lives.

Do you own a good study Bible? They are indispensable in learning more about the Lord. Does your pastor teach the word? Is he building you up? Do you have someone you can turn to when you don't understand what you are studying or reading? Do you spend time during the week in study and reading the Word? Are you in communication with the Lord? Are you in prayer? All of these areas add to building up yourself. Ask the Holy Spirit to open your eyes and to help you understand as you listen or read. [2]

This foundation in our Christian life is key, but the real key is the cornerstone the foundation is resting on. Jesus must be the cornerstone to our knowledge.

Just what is a cornerstone? It is the first thing builders put in before they start to build. All measurements come off of the cornerstone, thus the cornerstone must be straight and true. If not, the rest of the foundation is worthless. Who is our cornerstone? **EPHESIANS 2:19–21** says *CONSEQUENTLY, YOU ARE NO LONGER FOREIGNERS AND ALIENS, BUT FELLOW CITIZENS WITH GOD'S PEOPLE AND MEMBERS OF GOD'S HOUSEHOLD, BUILT ON THE FOUNDATION OF THE APOSTLES AND PROPHETS, WITH CHRIST JESUS HIMSELF AS THE CHIEF CORNERSTONE. IN HIM THE WHOLE BUILDING IS JOINED TOGETHER AND RISES TO BECOME A HOLY TEMPLE IN THE LORD.*

Jesus must be the base of all we are leaning on. All else will fall down around us. Do not try to build up yourself by reading so called spiritual books that do not teach Jesus as the Christ. Some books are excellent if they are rooted in Jesus. But there are many that want to deceive people. Our cornerstone can only be Jesus, all others are poor substitutes. **COLOSSIANS 2:6–7,** *SO THEN, JUST AS YOU RECEIVED CHRIST JESUS AS LORD, CONTINUE TO LIVE IN HIM, ROOTED AND BUILT UP IN HIM, STRENGTHENED IN THE FAITH AS YOU WERE TAUGHT, AND OVERFLOWING WITH THANKFULNESS.*

How do we build up ourselves? **JUDE 20,** *BUT YOU, DEAR FRIENDS, BUILD YOURSELVES UP IN YOUR MOST HOLY FAITH AND PRAY IN THE HOLY SPIRIT.* Be strong in the faith, pray, receive good teaching and knowledge, and be overflowing with thankfulness. [3]

The next step after building up ourselves is to start building up others. The people we are going to help build up must be receptive to our initiatives. They must want to grow in the Lord.

Remember as we strive to help someone build up themselves in the faith that they are an ongoing project. They will not "be there" overnight. Becoming strong, experienced Christians involves an ongoing increase in spirituality in their lives. Building up others, and ourselves for that matter, does not happen quickly. It takes time. When we drive by a new building that is being erected, we watch the progression it makes. It is a step by step build. It seems slow but it is done in a proper manner. There is no rush so there will be no errors in the building. [4]

Do not expect perfection from the person immediately. Were you a mature Christian immediately?

Be patient.
Encourage the believer.
Challenge the believer.
Help them exercise their gifts for use within the body of Christ. [5]

A slow steady growth is important. If we as Christians are not growing, then we are becoming stagnant and lukewarm in our faith. The Lord despises this.

Here is a great example of someone building up other Christians. We had a great Christian in our church who knew he had a terminal illness. He was one of the few Sunday school teachers in our church at the time. He made it his goal to build up and mentor one of the younger men to become a teacher, his replacement. He took the person aside and showed him how to study, how to use references, how to put together a lesson. He spent time with him showing him how to prepare a lesson. How to lean on the Lord for help. How to depend on the Holy Spirit. After his death, his legacy lives on. This same gentleman took me, as a young Christian, under his wing to teach me how to become a church leader, lessons that stay with me to this day. His teaching has allowed me to also pass on to others the responsibilities and rewards of being a church leader as I mentor others.

If you ask most any pastor, they will give you a name of someone that mentored them when they first started out in their ministry. Who in your church do you see as someone you could help build up? [6]

Why do all this building up? It is not to make us smarter, although that is not a bad result. It is so we together can build up the church. The Bride of Christ. The House of God. **1 PETER 2:4–5** says *AS YOU COME TO HIM, THE LIVING STONE—REJECTED BY MEN BUT CHOSEN BY GOD AND PRECIOUS TO HIM—YOU ALSO, LIKE LIVING STONES, ARE BEING BUILT INTO A SPIRITUAL HOUSE TO BE A HOLY PRIESTHOOD, OFFERING SPIRITUAL SACRIFICES ACCEPTABLE TO GOD THROUGH JESUS CHRIST.* [7]

We are that living stone, part of the glorious body of the church of the Lord. Jesus is a living stone. The stone designates endurance, strength and His everlastingness. He is the one we can rely on as our foundation, our security and our protection. He is a living stone because He will last forever. We also are living stones. We will last forever thanks to our foundation, Jesus. We as Christians do not have a temple where we are to go to worship like the Jews did. Instead we are part of the temple of God. We are the stones upon which the church is being built. We make up a spiritual house of God. Thus, we are living stones, ongoing, not the dead material of the temple. We are the priests who offer spiritual sacrifices, our bodies, our souls and lives unto the Lord.

The church of the Lord is still being built today. We, as the living stones, are to continue to build up the church. We build up ourselves to build up others to build up the church. It is a continual process. Each of us is expected to be part of this process. As part of the stones that build up the church, we should not want to be a little, weak, stone. Our goal is to be a stone of consequence that is being built up and growing all the time.

Are we building up others so they can build up the church, or are we really living stones? The Lord expects us, the living stones to continually work to build up His church. He gives us gifts just for this reason. **1 CORINTHIANS 14:12,** *SO IT IS WITH YOU. SINCE YOU ARE EAGER TO HAVE SPIRITUAL GIFTS, TRY TO EXCEL IN GIFTS THAT BUILD UP THE CHURCH.* The Holy Spirit gives us special gifts for the sole purpose of building up the church, not just for our personal satisfaction. It is up to each of us to use them properly.

Building up one another is key to the continuation of the growth of the church of the Lord. Are we doing our part? [8]

QUESTIONS ON BUILD UP

1. What does it mean to build up yourself?

2. Why so much emphasis on the Bible?

3. **JUDE 20** says we can build ourselves up. How have you done this?

4. Why is this so important?

5. Why is this key?

6. What is the difference between encouragement, strengthen and building up?

7. Explain this verse.

8. What do our gifts have to do with the church?

CHAPTER NINE

SPUR ON

HEBREWS 10:24, *AND LET US CONSIDER HOW WE MAY SPUR ONE ANOTHER ON TOWARD LOVE AND GOOD DEEDS.* [1]

My pastor, Dr. Jim Smith, helped me better understand this concept of spurring one another on by translating the words "spur on" into the Greek. He informed me the Greek word for "spur on" is *parakaleo*. This word often details the work of the Holy Spirit who, by the way, is often called "the Paraclete."

Parakaleo has four distinct meanings.

The first meaning is "to exhort or to urge." It can be the "loving kick in the pants" that is needed to get someone going. This meaning of *parakaleo* comes to mind when I think of spurring someone on. What immediately comes to mind when you think of spurs? Cowboys and their horses. Why does a cowboy use his spurs? Sometimes it is to urge the horse to continue on even if the horse is getting tired; to keep it going, not letting it stop. The cowboy is pushing the horse to do more than the horse thinks is possible. How does this work for us as Christians to spur one another on toward love and good deeds? [2]

Is it up to someone to give us a jolt to keep us going? Don't we all at some time need a kick in the pants to do something as obvious as to love our Christian brothers and to do good deeds?

Speaking for myself, that would be a big fat YES! We all can get complacent in our day to day lives concerning our relationships with others. We get caught up in self. It is not natural to love someone unconditionally. It is not natural for us to do good deeds. We want others to love us and to do good deeds for us. We need spurred, or stimulated, to not give up. We need spurred to push us further into loving others and doing good deeds for them. Not allowing us to quit and reminding us we are not done and will never be done in our relationships with our Christian brothers. Others can see the potential we have, and they must at times prod us on. This is very prevalent in the life of teachers. They have students that need spurred on to reach the potential the teachers see in them. Mothers and fathers spur their children on to get them to grow in their abilities. We as Christians need to spur others on to reach their potential. But we need to do this in a way that is not offensive.   [3]

The second meaning of *parakaleo* is to intercede. It can be like a lawyer speaking on our behalf. How do we intercede for our brothers in Christ? The best way is through prayer. We are speaking to the Lord on their behalf. Are we praying for our brothers to grow in the Lord? To become closer to Him? We should be. When we are doing this, we are interceding for the person. We are calling on God to come into their lives and spur them on to a closer relationship with the Lord. We also can be praying for them to be going in the right relationship with the Lord if we think they are going astray. By praying we are interceding for others to get them to change direction. At times it might take a soft word or direction for them to see their error. Like the cowboys and their horses who wander off and need to be spurred to get back on the right path. Thus, we intercede for others to get them to change direction. Who is this someone? Sometimes it is a church leader, a spouse, a friend or just a fellow Christian. We are seeking the Holy Spirit to give our friends direction, to intercede in their lives for their benefit to bring them into a closer relationship with the Lord. A good verse is **1 JOHN 2:1, *MY DEAR CHILDREN, I WRITE THIS TO YOU SO THAT YOU WILL NOT SIN. BUT IF ANYBODY DOES SIN, WE HAVE ONE WHO SPEAKS TO THE FATHER IN OUR DEFENSE— JESUS CHRIST, THE RIGHTEOUS ONE.*** Jesus comes along side of us to intercede between the Father and ourselves. He is our advocate. He pleads for us to the Father. The Paraclete here is Jesus.

Parakaleo also has the meaning of giving comfort. When we think of comfort, we should be thinking of the Holy Spirit, who in various places in the Bible is called the Comforter, the Counselor. **JOHN 16:7, *"BUT I TELL YOU THE TRUTH: IT IS FOR YOUR GOOD***

THAT I AM GOING AWAY. UNLESS I GO AWAY, THE COUNSELOR WILL NOT COME TO YOU; BUT IF I GO, I WILL SEND HIM TO YOU." The Holy Spirit is also spoken of the same way in **JOHN 14:16–18, 25–26.** The Holy Spirit comes along side of us when we need comforted. He reminds us that the Lord is in control and he exhorts us during these bad times to keep us keeping on. This is our example of how we are to be a comforter and a counselor to others when they need our help.

The last meaning of *parakaleo* is to come along side when others need assistance mentally, physically, emotionally or spiritually. There are times I am not good at this. I either don't recognize the help that someone needs or just don't want to get involved. So a spur is used to direct us to be more loving, to incite us to action, to stimulate our energy in these areas. I have felt the spur on more than one occasion from my spouse as she reminds me that life is not just about me. The truth of the matter is I needed the spur. I was going in the wrong direction. I was only thinking of self and not giving help to others. Is it pleasant to be spurred? NO! But it is necessary. I needed the correction in my life.

Don't we all need spurred at times to show a loving and helpful spirit to others? I do. Remember, helping others is an action we take, not just words.

Notice the command is given to spur others on to loving and doing good deeds to each other. It is not a blank slate for us to just ride each other in all areas of their lives. This would be called nagging, and no one likes that. It is when someone needs assistance or help. We must keep our eyes open for the opportunity to help or assist others. We are like the horse that needs a spur to urge it on. We are to spur others on to do good deeds and to be involved in the lives of their fellow Christians. We are not to hurt others when we do this just like a cowboy does not use his spurs to hurt the horse. We are to spur others on with love, not sharp words. We must use gentle reminders, in love. We, ourselves, need to be spurred to be more passionate about love and good deeds to others. Sometimes it takes someone more objective to see what we ourselves cannot see in our own lives. **[4]**

We are called on to do good deeds to one another. *(See Chapter 48.)* Why then do we need to be spurred on to do good deeds? Because it takes an effort to do this. Without the Holy Spirit giving us direction, doing good deeds for others is just not a part of our everyday lives. We must never quit doing good deeds for others. This is why we need to be spurred on in this area. **[5]**

A spur can be used by the cowboy to get a horse started. At times it is just a matter of getting us started on the right path on loving others, on doing good deeds to others. Once started we can go on our own.

Remember, as we spur others on it must be done with love and not in an unkind manner. To spur someone on with love, we must love them first. We do not have the right to spur someone on if we do not love them. We all can use a gentle reminder to love and to do good deeds for others and this is what the writer of Hebrews is pointing out to us. Make sure love is involved when you spur others on. Never spur someone out of anger, nor nag or exasperate a Christian brother. [6]

QUESTIONS ON SPUR ON

1. Explain this verse.

2. What does it mean to you?

3. Has anyone had to spur you on? At church? At home? At work?

4. Why does it mention love in the verse at the beginning of the chapter **(HEBREWS 10:24)?**

5. Why does it mention good deeds?

6. How can we spur others on without crossing a line? What is the correct way to spur others on?

CHAPTER TEN

POINT OUT

1 TIMOTHY 4:6, *IF YOU POINT THESE THINGS OUT TO THE BROTHERS, YOU WILL BE A GOOD MINISTER OF CHRIST JESUS, BROUGHT UP IN THE TRUTHS OF THE FAITH AND OF THE GOOD TEACHING THAT YOU HAVE FOLLOWED.*

What is Paul talking about when he says we are to point out "these things"? This verse must be taken in context. Look at the preceding verses. **1 TIMOTHY 4:1–2,** *THE SPIRIT CLEARLY SAYS THAT IN LATER TIMES SOME WILL ABANDON THE FAITH AND FOLLOW DECEIVING SPIRITS AND THINGS TAUGHT BY DEMONS. SUCH TEACHINGS COME THROUGH HYPOCRITICAL LIARS, WHOSE CONSCIENCES HAVE BEEN SEARED AS WITH A HOT IRON.* Paul is saying if we see a brother that is abandoning the faith, or following false teachers, then we are to point out his errors in doctrine and teaching. He is also saying to Timothy, that you, Timothy, have been brought up in the truth from the good teaching you are following, so you will know the differences from what is being taught. **[1]**

How do we go about knowing when someone is teaching falsely? How can we tell when some other Christians are abandoning their faith? Even if we know the teaching is wrong, do we have the right to speak up? Aren't we starting to judge and meddle in others' faith?

If our child was being led astray, wouldn't we speak up? Of course, so we, as more spiritual discerning, need to speak up. It is not judging if we are letting them know the errors of their ways if they start to follow false teachings. Paul is saying we are obligated to step in when others are being led astray. How do we know when to do this? How do we know it is false teachings? How do we know when others are lying to our Christian brothers?

There are many warnings in the Bible about false teachers coming to deceive us. We must be grounded in our faith and have knowledge of Christian doctrine so we can tell when someone is teaching in error to the Scriptures. It cannot be in our opinion, but actual facts based on the Bible. In other words, know the Bible and what it teaches. **[2]**

How does Paul handle things when he receives word that a church is listening to false teaching? Does he go about berating them? Does he yell at them or tell them how dumb they are? We see the answer to this in **COLOSSIANS.** Epaphras, probably the founder and pastor at the church of Colossae, goes to see Paul while he is in prison and lets Paul know that there are false teachers in the church trying to pull away the believers that Epaphras brought to the Lord. Paul writes to the church and points out what the false teachers are trying to teach is wrong. While doing this, he also lets them know that Epaphras brought the real Gospel to them, and there is nothing to add to it. This book, **COLOSSIANS,** is a key book when looking for lessons on pointing out false teachers, since this is the main reason for the letter that Paul wrote to them.

How does he go about doing this? First, he starts out by praising what he has heard about their faith. **COLOSSIANS 1:4, *BECAUSE WE HAVE HEARD OF YOUR FAITH IN CHRIST JESUS AND OF THE LOVE YOU HAVE FOR ALL THE SAINTS.*** Paul understands it is a lot easier for someone to accept correction if he shows appreciation first. Remember this lesson!

Here are the positive statements he says to them:

1. They are holy. **VERSE 2**

2. They are faithful. **VERSE 2**

3. Paul has even heard of their faith. **VERSE 4**

4. Paul has even heard of their love for the saints. **VERSE 4**

5.   He knows their faith and hope is stored up for them in heaven. **VERSE 5**

6.   Paul knows they have heard the word of truth, the gospel. **VERSE 5**

7.   The gospel is bearing fruit and growing among them. **VERSE 6**

8.   Paul knows they understand God's grace in all its truth. **VERSE 6**

9.   They have love in the Spirit. **VERSE 8**

Then Paul warns them about deceivers coming at them from different directions. Some, if not all of these, are the same ways people try to deceive us today. Be ready to point out to others if they are being persuaded by any of these today.

Some were teaching that Jesus is only a go between. He is not the end all. Islam teaches that Jesus was just a prophet. Some say He was a good teacher. Others see Him as an angel. [3]

Paul refutes this in **COLOSSIANS 1:15–16,** *HE IS THE IMAGE OF THE INVISIBLE GOD, THE FIRSTBORN OVER ALL CREATION. FOR BY HIM ALL THINGS WERE CREATED: THINGS IN HEAVEN AND ON EARTH, VISIBLE AND INVISIBLE, WHETHER THRONES OR POWERS OR RULERS OR AUTHORITIES; ALL THINGS WERE CREATED BY HIM AND FOR HIM.* Paul is saying since He was the creator, nothing can be higher than Him. He is not a copy but God. Everything and everybody that came after Him, was created by Him. **COLOSSIANS 2:9–10** says *FOR IN CHRIST ALL THE FULLNESS OF THE DEITY LIVES IN BODILY FORM, AND YOU HAVE BEEN GIVEN FULLNESS IN CHRIST, WHO IS THE HEAD OVER EVERY POWER AND AUTHORITY.* Never let anyone depreciate Jesus to something He is not. He is the Son of God, the Christ and part of the Trinity. If we ever hear others say something different, point it out that they are wrong. The other part of this that is important is Jesus was and is both man and God. He was and is God in the flesh. He had and has the fullness of God in Him. (See **COLOSSIANS 1:19**.) Also note in **COLOSSIANS 2:10** that Jesus is over every power and authority. *Everyone* and *Everything*!

Some were teaching that we can rely on our own wisdom and the wisdom of others. **COLOSSIANS 2:4** says this: *I TELL YOU THIS SO THAT NO ONE MAY DECEIVE YOU BY FINE-SOUNDING ARGUMENTS.* Then in **VERSE 8** he goes on to say

SEE TO IT THAT NO ONE TAKES YOU CAPTIVE THROUGH HOLLOW AND DECEPTIVE PHILOSOPHY, WHICH DEPENDS ON HUMAN TRADITION AND THE BASIC PRINCIPLES OF THIS WORLD RATHER THAN ON CHRIST. Head knowledge alone will not bring us closer to the Lord. Many so-called Bible scholars on TV give bad information. They only have head knowledge, not Jesus in their hearts giving them spiritual wisdom. Always compare the information that others bring with the Bible. There are other words for "fine-sounding arguments." A few are: smooth talk, enticing words, beguiling speech. All of these sound good but check them out. Deceptive philosophy can also mean Astrology, séances or mediums. This area is exploding today with many mediums having their own TV shows and books and are being accepted as truthful. If we have fellow Christians getting involved with any of the above, point out the errors of their ways.   **[4]**

Others were teaching that there is secret knowledge that is needed to be a true Christian. In biblical times these people were called Gnostics. Today I see them as intellectual snobs. Paul refutes this in **COLOSSIANS 2:2–3,** *MY PURPOSE IS THAT THEY MAY BE ENCOURAGED IN HEART AND UNITED IN LOVE, SO THAT THEY MAY HAVE THE FULL RICHES OF COMPLETE UNDERSTANDING, IN ORDER THAT THEY MAY KNOW THE MYSTERY OF GOD, NAMELY, CHRIST, IN WHOM ARE HIDDEN ALL THE TREASURES OF WISDOM AND KNOWLEDGE.* Today we have books and TV personalities saying they have "secrets of the Bible" or "the Bible code." Do not be deceived; Paul says all wisdom and knowledge is in Jesus. Think about it, why would God hide information that only a select few think they know the answers? They will only give this wisdom if we join their group and get initiated. They might do good works, but they do not have spiritual secrets. Jesus says in **JOHN 14:6,** *"I AM THE WAY AND THE TRUTH AND THE LIFE. NO ONE COMES TO THE FATHER EXCEPT THROUGH ME."* There is no other way to salvation except through Jesus. People look for other ways, but He is the only way. When people say they have a better interpretation of the Bible, be very careful. If they say that teachings from other books are closer to the truth than the Bible, beware. People would rather read New Age books believing they have more to offer than the Bible. They are just dead wrong. If someone wants to grow closer to the Lord, it is simple. His must pray that the Holy Spirit would open his eyes and mind as he continues to study the Bible. In the 1960s and 1970s, the Beatles went to India to study under a Maharishi to get mystical spiritual enlightenment. The only thing they found was drugs. All spiritual wisdom and knowledge are from the Lord. If fellow Christians are going astray and getting caught up in New Age material or looking for knowledge of God in the wrong area, we must point out that only true knowledge about God can come through the study and knowledge of Christ that will come to us through the study of the Bible and with the Holy Spirit's help in our discernment, no other way. **[5]**

Recently we have seen more and more about angel worship. People see them as heavenly beings to be worshiped, and look to them as their mediator between themselves and God. Many TV productions have angels in their shows. Angels are not for worship. **REVELATION 22:8–9, *I, JOHN, AM THE ONE WHO HEARD AND SAW THESE THINGS. AND WHEN I HAD HEARD AND SEEN THEM, I FELL DOWN TO WORSHIP AT THE FEET OF THE ANGEL WHO HAD BEEN SHOWING THEM TO ME. BUT HE SAID TO ME, "DO NOT DO IT! I AM A FELLOW SERVANT WITH YOU AND WITH YOUR BROTHERS THE PROPHETS AND OF ALL WHO KEEP THE WORDS OF THIS BOOK. WORSHIP GOD!"*** Jesus is our high priest; we need no other person or angel to open our presence to God. Paul says in **COLOSSIANS 2:18, *DO NOT LET ANYONE WHO DELIGHTS IN FALSE HUMILITY AND THE WORSHIP OF ANGELS DISQUALIFY YOU FOR THE PRIZE. SUCH A PERSON GOES INTO GREAT DETAIL ABOUT WHAT HE HAS SEEN, AND HIS UNSPIRITUAL MIND PUFFS HIM UP WITH IDLE NOTIONS.*** Some religions have leaders who claimed to have been visited by angels and then directed to start a church since all the other churches were wrong. When people give us claims like this and then start changing the Bible to glorify themselves, run away, no matter how good it sounds. Point out to others that angels are not to be worshiped, they are servants to God, the same as us. **[6]**

Be careful of people who say they speak for the Lord. God gives this warning in **JEREMIAH 23:30–32, *"THEREFORE," DECLARES THE LORD, "I AM AGAINST THE PROPHETS WHO STEAL FROM ONE ANOTHER WORDS SUPPOSEDLY FROM ME. YES," DECLARES THE LORD, "I AM AGAINST THE PROPHETS WHO WAG THEIR OWN TONGUES AND YET DECLARE, 'THE LORD DECLARES.' INDEED, I AM AGAINST THOSE WHO PROPHESY FALSE DREAMS," DECLARES THE LORD. "THEY TELL THEM AND LEAD MY PEOPLE ASTRAY WITH THEIR RECKLESS LIES, YET I DID NOT SEND OR APPOINT THEM. THEY DO NOT BENEFIT THESE PEOPLE IN THE LEAST," DECLARES THE LORD.*** Do not believe people when they say they speak for God. He opposes this vehemently. Point out to fellow Christians when we see them believing others who say they have had the Lord speaking directly to them. Yes, God can and does speak directly to people today, but what they say and do must match Biblical truths. God cannot contradict Himself.

Be very careful of false teachers who promote self-denial as the only way to Heaven. This is legalism. Works alone are not the way to Heaven. Self-righteousness is not the way to Heaven, if it was, Heaven would only have the Pharisees there. All this self-denial is simply for our false humility. "Look how good I am, I deserve to be in Heaven." Do not let others judge or set up a list of rules and regulations. We are saved by grace and grace alone. Yes, this grace gives us freedom in the Lord, but with this freedom comes responsibility. Some have taught, or are still teaching, diet restrictions, Sabbath day rules, self-denial of the flesh, no marriage or having or using any luxury. The Law was given for us to realize we need a Savior and point us to Christ. He is the one and the only way to make us holy before the Lord. Beware of false teachers teaching works and self-denial. Paul says in **COLOSSIANS 2:20–22,** *SINCE YOU DIED WITH CHRIST TO THE BASIC PRINCIPLES OF THIS WORLD, WHY, AS THOUGH YOU STILL BELONGED TO IT, DO YOU SUBMIT TO ITS RULES: "DO NOT HANDLE! DO NOT TASTE! DO NOT TOUCH!" THESE ARE ALL DESTINED TO PERISH WITH USE, BECAUSE THEY ARE BASED ON HUMAN COMMANDS AND TEACHINGS.* [7]

There are many other areas of false teachings. Satan is a deceiver so beware.

Paul did give the Colossians the following advice in **COLOSSIANS 2:6–7,** *SO THEN, JUST AS YOU RECEIVED CHRIST JESUS AS LORD, CONTINUE TO LIVE IN HIM, ROOTED AND BUILT UP IN HIM, STRENGTHENED IN THE FAITH AS YOU WERE TAUGHT, AND OVERFLOWING WITH THANKFULNESS.*

We must stay rooted in the Lord. If we are to point out to others when they are going astray, then we must be grounded in our Bible knowledge. How do we stay rooted? Be in the Word of God. Study the Bible. **HEBREWS 4:12** says *FOR THE WORD OF GOD IS LIVING AND ACTIVE. SHARPER THAN ANY DOUBLE-EDGED SWORD, IT PENETRATES EVEN TO DIVIDING SOUL AND SPIRIT, JOINTS AND MARROW; IT JUDGES THE THOUGHTS AND ATTITUDES OF THE HEART.* Our defense and offense against Satan is the Bible. In **EPHESIANS 6:17B** it is called *"THE SWORD OF THE SPIRIT, WHICH IS THE WORD OF GOD."* Without the knowledge of the Bible we cannot know if a teacher is true or false. The Lord is relying on us to know what is true or false and to point it out to other Christian brothers. **2 TIMOTHY 3:16–17,** *ALL SCRIPTURE IS GOD-BREATHED AND IS USEFUL FOR TEACHING, REBUKING, CORRECTING AND TRAINING IN RIGHTEOUSNESS, SO THAT THE MAN OF GOD MAY BE THOROUGHLY*

EQUIPPED FOR EVERY GOOD WORK. Know the Bible, spend time in study. The Bible is our offense and our defense. Before we point out to others the errors of their ways, have Biblical backup. Not our opinions, not words from other books, not our feelings, not traditions or philosophy, nothing of human origin, just Biblical truths to point out the errors that will harm their Christian lives and their fellowship with the Lord.

Being in fellowship with other Christians also helps us be rooted in the Lord. We are not Christians so we can serve alone. We are part of the body of Christ, His church. There is strength and safety in numbers. Be a part of a church body. **[8]**

We are to be faithful in prayer. Prayer is our contact with the Lord. We are to be seeking His guidance so we know His directive. The Holy Spirit will alert us to false teachings so be ready to point out to others where teaching is going astray. We are not to judge others, but we need to warn others when they are being deceived.

We need all of these areas for us to be rooted in the Lord. Without any of them, we will be undernourished, thus not capable to help others in their problem times. We need to stay strong so we can be guardians of the truth—basing our comments on the Word of God. **[9]**

The end of **REVELATION** carries a warning from John. **REVELATION 22:18–19,** *I WARN EVERYONE WHO HEARS THE WORDS OF THE PROPHECY OF THIS BOOK: IF ANYONE ADDS ANYTHING TO THEM, GOD WILL ADD TO HIM THE PLAGUES DESCRIBED IN THIS BOOK. AND IF ANYONE TAKES WORDS AWAY FROM THIS BOOK OF PROPHECY, GOD WILL TAKE AWAY FROM HIM HIS SHARE IN THE TREE OF LIFE AND IN THE HOLY CITY, WHICH ARE DESCRIBED IN THIS BOOK.* Do not take away words, or add to any of the scripture, there are penalties involved.

Most false teachers want the emphasis on them versus Jesus. They try to build themselves up to replace Jesus. They think making Him smaller will make them larger. Some false religious leaders tell of visions they have received from angels or from dreams. They say they have been told to add to or change the Bible and that their church is the only church. From the verses in **REVELATION 22:18–19,** John warns that this is wrong. Paul gives warnings to us about angels in disguise when talking about false apostles. **2 CORINTHIANS 11:13–15,** *FOR SUCH MEN ARE FALSE APOSTLES, DECEITFUL WORKMEN,*

MASQUERADING AS APOSTLES OF CHRIST. AND NO WONDER, FOR SATAN HIMSELF MASQUERADES AS AN ANGEL OF LIGHT. IT IS NOT SURPRISING, THEN, IF HIS SERVANTS MASQUERADE AS SERVANTS OF RIGHTEOUSNESS. THEIR END WILL BE WHAT THEIR ACTIONS DESERVE. [10]

Paul warned the Galatians that false witnesses were trying to sway them from the true gospel. **GALATIANS 1:6–9,** *I AM ASTONISHED THAT YOU ARE SO QUICKLY DESERTING THE ONE WHO CALLED YOU BY THE GRACE OF CHRIST AND ARE TURNING TO A DIFFERENT GOSPEL—WHICH IS REALLY NO GOSPEL AT ALL. EVIDENTLY SOME PEOPLE ARE THROWING YOU INTO CONFUSION AND ARE TRYING TO PERVERT THE GOSPEL OF CHRIST. BUT EVEN IF WE OR AN ANGEL FROM HEAVEN SHOULD PREACH A GOSPEL OTHER THAN THE ONE WE PREACHED TO YOU, LET HIM BE ETERNALLY CONDEMNED! AS WE HAVE ALREADY SAID, SO NOW I SAY AGAIN: IF ANYBODY IS PREACHING TO YOU A GOSPEL OTHER THAN WHAT YOU ACCEPTED, LET HIM BE ETERNALLY CONDEMNED!*

If you are looking for a new church, here are some key areas to look for:

1. Scripture being read publicly.

2. A Bible-based message, not someone's opinion.

3. A message from the leader that can be applicable for the help of the congregation as they lead their daily lives and try to be more Christ-like.

4. The message should open up the Word of God for those in the pews as the leader teaches.

5. Music through hymns or spiritual songs that praise the Father, Son and Holy Spirit.

6. Bring out that God is Three in One. This can come about through the message, songs or in prayer.

What was going on in Paul's day is still going on. Be vigilant and be prepared to point out to other Christian brothers the fallacy in what false teachers bring to them in another gospel besides what our Lord has given to us through the Scriptures. [11]

QUESTIONS ON POINT OUT

1. Have you ever done this?

2. Have you ever been taught something that was false? How did you react?

3. Have you heard false teachers bring this message?

4. Do you know people who have bought into this area of mediums and séances?

5. Have you recognized false teachings coming from television or movies?

6. Why this great fascination with angels, particularly on TV?

7. Why do some churches today teach so many dos and don'ts?

8. Do you feel this is important or no big deal?

9. What has made you strong in the Lord?

10. Do any particular religions come to mind?

11. Where else do people look for salvation?

CHAPTER ELEVEN

JUDGMENT

ROMANS 14:13A, *THEREFORE LET US STOP PASSING JUDGMENT ON ONE ANOTHER.*

Anytime we see a "therefore" in the Bible, always see why (what) it is there (for).

Look back at the preceding verses to get the context of his statement. Let's look at **ROMANS 14:1–12.** In **VERSES 1–3,** Paul tells the "stronger" Christian to not pass judgment on the "weaker" Christian on disputable matters. Disputable matters would be some areas that are not clearly stated as wrong in the Bible.   [1]

Specifically in this context, "dietary restrictions" were an issue. The big issues today might be any of the following within a church: smoking, alcohol, observing the Sabbath, jewelry, attire, food, music, tattoos, or anything that is not "proper or Christian" in the judgment of the "stronger" Christian. We must consider if these issues are Biblical or man-made. These are some things that Paul would term today as "disputable matters." Differences of opinions should never cause problems between fellow believers. Maybe God is dealing with the weaker Christian on issues we see as all important.   [2]

Remember, we are saved by grace, not law. It is not by our opinions, or individual likes or dislikes, or works. It is not on trying to keep the law. Trying to keep the law leads to frustration and continual guilt instead of living by grace which brings about living for the Lord and doing His will out of love.

VERSE 4A, ***WHO ARE YOU TO JUDGE SOMEONE ELSE'S SERVANT? TO HIS OWN MASTER HE STANDS OR FALLS.*** Paul says we are not to judge a servant belonging to someone else. He is not only speaking about someone's actual servant but also fellow Christians who are servants of the Lord. We are not to judge fellow Christians who are serving the Lord. They belong to Him. Only the Master is to judge the servant. *We have no say in the matter.*

VERSES 10–12, ***YOU, THEN, WHY DO YOU JUDGE YOUR BROTHER? OR WHY DO YOU LOOK DOWN ON YOUR BROTHER? FOR WE WILL ALL STAND BEFORE GOD'S JUDGMENT SEAT. IT IS WRITTEN: "AS SURELY AS I LIVE,' SAYS THE LORD, 'EVERY KNEE WILL BOW BEFORE ME; EVERY TONGUE WILL CONFESS TO GOD.'" SO THEN, EACH OF US WILL GIVE AN ACCOUNT OF HIMSELF TO GOD.*** We will be individually judged on our service to the Lord, not on what our fellow Christians do or do not do. (See also **2 CORINTHIANS 5:10.**)

Judging other Christians does not promote peace, it causes dissension. We are to be tolerant and help fellow Christians grow to be more Christ-like, not tear them down and put stumbling blocks in their way.

Further on in **ROMANS 14:17–18,** Paul tells us the kingdom of God is not about eating, drinking and rules. It is about righteous people, peace and the joy of serving the Lord. **[3]**

As men and women, we are incapable of living this type of life on our own. We rely on the Holy Spirit to give us our direction so we can be pleasing to God. We cannot live like this on our own. All of this Christ-like living comes from the Holy Spirit being in us and giving us direction. We must give the Holy Spirit control to do this. **[4]**

VERSE 19, ***LET US THEREFORE MAKE EVERY EFFORT TO DO WHAT LEADS TO PEACE AND TO MUTUAL EDIFICATION.*** Work hard to do things that lead to peace. The Lord does not want Christians to be at odds with one another, but to show the unity of the Spirit in our daily lives. Judging one another, more than anything else, will take away this peace we are to have with one another. **[5]**

The Holy Spirit will tell us if we are living Christ-led lives. Then it is up to us to follow the Holy Spirit's directions, not our own desires or, in some cases, the freedom we feel we have and want to use. Our freedom can become a stumbling block to fellow Christians. **1 CORINTHIANS 8:9–13** directs us to be cautious in how we use our freedom when we are around fellow Christians that are "weak" in the faith. Usually this is a newborn Christian, but it could be an experienced Christian who is still on baby food. Living under grace does not give us a license to live as we want. We have obligations to our fellow Christians to display a lifestyle that is "God" approved. We are to live a life of love and service. **GALATIANS 5:13, *YOU, MY BROTHERS, WERE CALLED TO BE FREE. BUT DO NOT USE YOUR FREEDOM TO INDULGE THE SINFUL NATURE; RATHER, SERVE ONE ANOTHER IN FAITH.*** [6]

Our tendency is to judge by our standards, not the Lord's. We always want to see how others measure up to "me." This makes us feel good about ourselves and makes us feel very spiritual and righteous. Of course, this is not what we are to do. [7]

Christ gives us a strong warning about this type of judgment. It says in **MATTHEW 7:1–5,** that how we judge others is the way we will be judged. Particularly in **VERSES 1–2** Jesus says, *"DO NOT JUDGE, OR YOU TOO WILL BE JUDGED. FOR IN THE SAME WAY YOU JUDGE OTHERS, YOU WILL BE JUDGED, AND WITH THE MEASURE YOU USE, IT WILL BE MEASURED TO YOU."* Are we ready for that type of judgment? What we see in a person's life that we are judging might just be a speck in his eye. Yet we have a huge board in our own eye that we are doing nothing about. If we don't want judgment in return, don't judge others.

We are only to judge ourselves to how we measure up to the Lord, not to others. We are to be Christ-like.

As James says in **JAMES 4:12, *THERE IS ONLY ONE LAWGIVER AND JUDGE, THE ONE WHO IS ABLE TO SAVE AND DESTROY. BUT YOU—WHO ARE YOU TO JUDGE YOUR NEIGHBOR?***

There always has been and always will be disputable matters within any church. It is best to avoid judging in these areas. Most of them are very subjective; subjective to our ideas of what is right and wrong for all Christians. [8]

If we encounter someone judging a fellow brother, talk to him or her about what judging can do to the church body. In most cases we are dealing with gossip or opinion. Who are we to judge our brothers? We are not to judge non-Christians as well. Weren't we as non-Christians turned off by a Christian judging us before we came to the Lord?   **[9]**

QUESTIONS ON JUDGMENT

1. What do you consider disputable matters?

2. What guide should we use today in dealing with disputable matters?

3. In **VERSES 17–18,** if the kingdom of God is not about food, drink and rules, what is it about?

4. Do you agree with **VERSES 17–18?**

5. Why do we as Christians want to judge other Christians?

6. Who do you consider the "weak Christians"? Who do you consider the "strong Christians"?

7. Whose or what standard do you use to judge others? Remember, we are not to judge others.

8. What gray areas divide the church today?

9. Why is it so key to follow the Holy Spirit's leading in this area?

CHAPTER TWELVE

STUMBLING BLOCK

ROMANS 14:13, *THEREFORE LET US STOP PASSING JUDGMENT ON ONE ANOTHER. INSTEAD, MAKE UP YOUR MIND NOT TO PUT ANY STUMBLING BLOCK OR OBSTACLE IN YOUR BROTHER'S WAY.*

What exactly is a stumbling block? It can be a person who is standing in the way of another that keeps him from reaching his goal or his full potential. Sometimes it is someone that intentionally stands in the way of a person or opposes the person. It can be something that makes someone hesitate in the pursuit of his goal. The person who is the stumbling block does not always realize what is happening, he may be unaware of being a problem. Stumbling blocks can happen in any area of our lives, but we will be addressing how it affects us as Christians. A stumbling block can also be an obstacle that will cause someone to stumble and fall. In Paul's case he is talking about someone stumbling and falling into sin. [1]

Anytime I see a "therefore" in the Bible I look back and see what it is there for. In this case, Paul has been talking about strong faith and weak faith and how the eating of food can be a stumbling block for others.

The food he is talking about can be one of three things.

1. Food that had previously been offered to idols, then was sold and eaten by others.

2. It could just be meat. Paul mentions in **ROMANS 14:2, *ONE MAN'S FAITH ALLOWS HIM TO EAT EVERYTHING, BUT ANOTHER MAN, WHOSE FAITH IS WEAK, EATS ONLY VEGETABLES.***

3. Paul can also be talking about the Jewish laws that do not allow Jews to eat particular foods. Pork products would be a prime example.

Paul says in **ROMANS 14:14A, *AS ONE WHO IS IN THE LORD JESUS, I AM FULLY CONVINCED THAT NO FOOD IS UNCLEAN IN ITSELF.*** Paul is the stronger Christian. He knows that God has okayed the eating of meat. He also knows that Peter was shown that the eating of unclean food has passed away per the Lord. Paul also knows that the meat offered to idols is not in itself wrong.

Why then does Paul refrain from eating meat at certain times? **ROMANS 14:15, *IF YOUR BROTHER IS DISTRESSED BECAUSE OF WHAT YOU EAT, YOU ARE NO LONGER ACTING IN LOVE. DO NOT BY YOUR EATING DESTROY YOUR BROTHER FOR WHOM CHRIST DIED.*** Then on to **VERSES 20–21, *DO NOT DESTROY THE WORK OF GOD FOR THE SAKE OF FOOD. ALL FOOD IS CLEAN, BUT IT IS WRONG FOR A MAN TO EAT ANYTHING THAT CAUSES SOMEONE ELSE TO STUMBLE. IT IS BETTER NOT TO EAT MEAT OR DRINK WINE OR TO DO ANYTHING ELSE THAT WILL CAUSE YOUR BROTHER TO FALL.*** Paul also knows that the person who is the stumbling block is usually the stronger Christian. [2]

Personally, my defense is should I, the stronger Christian, deny myself areas that are not sin to me? I have the right, haven't I? I have earned it by my stronger faith to do as I please so long as I do not see it as a sin. We are told not to judge other Christians, so they should not be judging me. But is this okay? Do we really have the right? Must I live my actions based on others' stumbling blocks?

It comes down to the love we must have for our brothers and for wanting the best for them as growing Christians. Today if someone is a vegetarian, it is probably not for religious reasons. It is a choice they have made. Probably the biggest stumbling block today would be the indulgence of alcohol. To some, they cannot believe a person can be a Christian and drink anything alcoholic. To others, they have no problem with drinking as long as they follow the Biblical rules of "not getting drunk." But is it wrong for some people to drink? The answer would be "yes." To others the answer would be "no." Thus to some this can be a major stumbling block. If we do not see it as wrong, we should be careful not to be a stumbling block to others. If we always try to do the right thing with love, we will not cause others to fall. [3]

We, as the stronger Christian, can educate the weaker brothers, but if they still feel certain things are wrong for them to do, then do not push the issue. For example, Paul tells Timothy to drink some wine to help his stomach. Jesus made wine and even drank wine during the sacrament of Communion. Some will say this was watered down wine, which personally I don't see that as the point. But for some it would be a sin to drink any alcoholic beverage so we must love our brothers and do the right thing. **ROMANS 14:14B, *BUT IF ANYONE REGARDS SOMETHING AS UNCLEAN, THEN FOR HIM IT IS UNCLEAN.*** Do not try to push someone to do something that might be a sin for him.

1 CORINTHIANS 8:9, *BE CAREFUL, HOWEVER, THAT THE EXERCISE OF YOUR FREEDOM DOES NOT BECOME A STUMBLING BLOCK TO THE WEAK.* Some new Christians are working out their salvation as they set the standards in their lives on how they will live Christ-like. We as the strong Christian must be careful with our freedoms not to cause them to stumble.

Paul speaks of working out our salvation in **PHILIPPIANS 2:12–13.** Here he says *THEREFORE, MY DEAR FRIENDS, AS YOU HAVE ALWAYS OBEYED— NOT ONLY IN MY PRESENCE, BUT NOW MUCH MORE IN MY ABSENCE— CONTINUE TO WORK OUT YOUR SALVATION WITH FEAR AND TREMBLING. FOR IT IS GOD WHO WORKS IN YOU TO WILL AND TO ACT ACCORDINGLY TO HIS GOOD PURPOSE.* We, as the strong Christian, continue to grow in our closeness to the Lord as we walk with Him, thus we continually make changes in our Christian lives. The *"THEREFORE"* speaks back to **VERSES 8–11** about how Jesus lowered Himself and came to earth. While here, He was obedient to the Father. He is our example. Thus, the key to **VERSES 12–13** is what it says in **VERSE 13.** We must let God work in us as we walk and talk with Him. He, through His Holy Spirit, will direct us to act in His will. This is for His good purpose. The Lord wants what is best for us. As we mature as Christians, we realize that some things we do are not in themselves sinful even though we might have been taught by our church or our parents that they were. I was raised in a fundamental Christian home and certain things were seen as wrong, thus sinful. Examples would be dancing, drinking, playing cards, going to movies and for women, no shorts or earrings. Do I follow all of these rules, laws today? No, I had to decide for myself if the Lord was telling me all of these areas are wrong in my life. A good example would be dancing. Even today, I wish I would have had lessons on how to dance. I think it is something my wife and I would and could enjoy together. Even David danced. Some areas, out of respect and love for my parents, I did not do in front of them. **[4]**

What is the point? The point is, we must grow in our salvation, and as we listen to the Holy Spirit we will be led in the right direction. We will learn to live by grace and not by rules and laws set up for us by others. That is over. We live by grace and grace alone. **[5]**

No matter what, we need to take Paul's advice given in **1 CORINTHIANS 10:31–11:1.** *SO WHETHER YOU EAT OR DRINK OR WHATEVER YOU DO, DO IT ALL FOR THE GLORY OF GOD. DO NOT CAUSE ANYONE TO STUMBLE, WHETHER JEWS, GREEKS OR THE CHURCH OF GOD—EVEN AS I TRY TO PLEASE EVERYBODY IN EVERY WAY. FOR I AM NOT SEEKING MY OWN GOOD BUT THE GOOD OF MANY, SO THAT THEY MAY BE SAVED. FOLLOW MY EXAMPLE, AS I FOLLOW THE EXAMPLE OF CHRIST.* What we do, as we live our lives on a daily basis, can and will affect others in the growth as Christians.

Notice the last areas of stumbling blocks we have studied have been over everyday actions. But there are still other areas of stumbling blocks we can be to other Christians. It is not always a person that causes the stumbling block. It can be what happens to the person that is the stumbling block. **1 CORINTHIANS 1:23, BUT** *WE PREACH CHRIST CRUCIFIED: A STUMBLING BLOCK TO JEWS AND FOOLISHNESS TO GENTILES.* How can the preaching of the crucified Jesus, being the Christ, be a stumbling block to Jews and Gentiles alike? To the Jews, anyone hung on a tree, crucified was cursed. They could not believe the Messiah would be a cursed person. This comes from **DEUTERONOMY 21:22–23A,** *IF A MAN GUILTY OF A CAPITAL OFFENSE IS PUT TO DEATH AND HIS BODY IS HUNG ON A TREE, YOU MUST NOT LEAVE HIS BODY ON THE TREE OVERNIGHT. BE SURE TO BURY HIM THAT SAME DAY, BECAUSE ANYONE WHO IS HUNG ON A TREE IS UNDER GOD'S CURSE.* So how can Jesus be the Messiah since He is a cursed man? For the Gentiles, how can Jesus, killed as a common criminal, be the Messiah? So to both groups, just the way Jesus was killed was a stumbling block to both of them. They both had a problem getting past the way He died.

Thus, it made it hard, if not impossible, for them to understand why He was crucified, and by that how He could be the Messiah.

Paul tells the strong Christians not to be a hindrance to the weak Christian. We can do this as leaders when we squelch a person's spirit. If a church leader hears an idea from a new Christian, he can be a stumbling block when he says,

> We have tried that before, and it did not work.
> Why should we make any changes, we need to stay the same?
> That will cost too much.
> We can never get the people in the church to do that.
> We can never get enough workers to do what you want.
> We are not going to do that. End of discussion.

All of these answers can be a stumbling block not only to new Christians but to the Holy Spirit and His guidance as well. Be very careful in our leadership not to put stumbling blocks in front of newer Christians, mature Christians and also to the Holy Spirit's leading. **[6]**

We should live like Paul when he says in **2 CORINTHIANS 6:3, *WE PUT NO STUMBLING BLOCK IN ANYONE'S PATH, SO THAT OUR MINISTRY WILL NOT BE DISCREDITED.*** Paul lived his life in such a way that he would not discredit the Lord. This should be the goal of all Christians. We need to search our lives and see what areas we need to get out of our lives so they will not discredit the Lord. If we have something in our lives that can be a stumbling block to other Christians, we need to get it out of our daily living.

Even a disciple could be a stumbling block. An example would be **MATTHEW 16:21, *FROM THAT TIME ON JESUS BEGAN TO EXPLAIN TO HIS DISCIPLES THAT HE MUST GO TO JERUSALEM AND SUFFER MANY THINGS AT THE HANDS OF THE ELDERS, CHIEF PRIESTS AND TEACHERS OF THE LAW, AND THAT HE MUST BE KILLED AND ON THE THIRD DAY BE RAISED TO LIFE.*** Peter had a hard time accepting this, so he went to Jesus.

MATTHEW 16:22–23, *PETER TOOK HIM ASIDE AND BEGAN TO REBUKE HIM. "NEVER LORD!" HE SAID. "THIS SHALL NEVER HAPPEN TO YOU!" JESUS TURNED AND SAID TO PETER, "GET BEHIND ME, SATAN! YOU ARE A STUMBLING BLOCK TO ME; YOU DO NOT HAVE IN MIND THE THINGS OF*

GOD, BUT THE THINGS OF MEN." Jesus saw Peter as a tool of Satan. Peter was trying to turn Jesus away from the suffering that must take place to fulfill the scriptures. Peter loved the Lord and did not want him to suffer. But he did not realize that suffering and dying on the cross must take place for grace to be possible. Jesus knew the pain and suffering He was about to go through and did not need someone telling Him not do to it, thus to Jesus, Peter was a stumbling block. Peter did not see the big picture. He was only looking at things through human perspective. He did not totally hear Jesus' words when He said that He *MUST BE KILLED.* For our salvation, He must be killed so He could defeat death.

It is not as if Peter did not know who Jesus truly was. Just a short time before this when asked by Jesus in **MATTHEW 16:15–16**, *"BUT WHAT ABOUT YOU?" HE ASKED. "WHO DO YOU SAY I AM?" SIMON PETER ANSWERED, "YOU ARE THE CHRIST, THE SON OF THE LIVING GOD."* [7]

What can we take from this? Even when we see ourselves as strong Christians, we can still be a stumbling block to others. We may need to take our time and make sure we know what we are talking about before we say it; make sure we know the Lord's will before we speak. Be aware that sometimes we can be in over our heads when we are dealing with someone on an issue.

Sometimes we can be like Peter who thought he knew what was best for the Lord. We can feel like we know what is best for our fellow Christian brothers or for that matter our children. At times people must suffer to fulfill what the Lord has in mind for them; His plans, not ours.

As we grow as Christians, we will be able to see where we are being a stumbling block to others. Listen to the Holy Spirit as He guides us through these gray areas. [8]

QUESTIONS ON STUMBLING BLOCK

1. Has someone ever been a stumbling block to you? What was the cause?

2. Have you ever been a stumbling block to someone? What do you think caused it?

3. Where is the line on pleasing someone? Is this what we are supposed to do? Are we not being hypocrites?

4. Are any of the following stumbling blocks to you? Types of music Christians listen to? Revealing clothes? How some Christians use their money? Going to casinos? Christians in politics? Are we not infringing on others' freedoms?

5. Isn't it wrong to do something in your home, but not in public?

6. Have any of the above been a stumbling block in your life?

7. Was Jesus too harsh on Peter? Can a Christian be a tool of Satan?

8. What principles do you use in gray areas?

CHAPTER THIRTEEN

ACCEPT

ROMANS 15:7, *ACCEPT ONE ANOTHER, THEN, JUST AS CHRIST ACCEPTED YOU, IN ORDER TO BRING PRAISE TO GOD.*

How do we keep from judging one another? We learn to accept one another, whether the person is a strong or weak Christian. We need, and we must, do this willingly in order to bring praise to God. [1]

How were we accepted by the Lord? Unconditionally!

We definitely were not perfect when we accepted the Lord. We did not become perfect overnight when we received the Lord into our hearts. We are still human, and as humans we are still able and willing to sin. Not that we want to, but we just do. Paul, in **PHILIPPIANS 3:10–14,** talks about striving for perfection but states that he has not already been made perfect.

Paul talks about the contradictory effect on his life. Look at **ROMANS 7:15–20,** particularly **VERSE 15,** *I DO NOT UNDERSTAND WHAT I DO. FOR WHAT I WANT TO DO I DO NOT DO, BUT WHAT I HATE I DO.* In this verse Paul actually sounds frustrated. He knows what he wants to do but can't seem to do it. But instead he does what he "hates to do."

Ever been this way?   **[2]**

> Lord, I want to have a great prayer life.
>> But I don't.
> Lord, I want my life to reflect you.
>> But sometimes it does not.
> I want to be a great Christian parental example.
>> But sometimes I am not.
> I want to take time for my daily devotions.
>> But I get busy or forget.
> I want to give of myself to the Lord, both time and money.
>> But I am selfish.
> I don't want to sin.
>> But I do.
> I want to accept my fellow Christian brothers.
>> But I don't.

If Paul, as a saint of God, can't seem to do what he wants to do right, then how can we as everyday Christians hope to do all that is right?

Like Paul, who says "but I do what I hate to do," we also keep going back to the same sinful addictions we had. They might be bad language, losing our temper, drunkenness, not treating our wives and kids according to Biblical directions, porn, lying, cheating or anything that we cannot seem to conquer.

VERSE 17, *AS IT IS, IT IS NO LONGER I MYSELF WHO DO IT, BUT IT IS SIN LIVING IN ME.* This verse tells us we still must battle sin in our lives even though we have been saved by grace. **VERSE 18,** *I KNOW THAT NOTHING GOOD LIVES IN ME, THAT IS, IN MY SINFUL NATURE. FOR I HAVE THE DESIRE TO DO WHAT IS GOOD, BUT I CANNOT CARRY IT OUT,* says we still have the sinful nature living in us, and then Paul restates it in **VERSES 19–20,** *FOR WHAT I DO IS NOT THE GOOD I WANT TO DO; NO, THE EVIL I DO NOT WANT TO DO—THIS I KEEP ON DOING. NOW IF I DO WHAT I DO NOT WANT TO DO, IT IS NO LONGER I WHO DO IT, BUT IT IS SIN LIVING IN ME THAT DOES IT.*

But as Christians we don't sin.

  Yeah, right!!!

We cannot have sin in us since we have the infilling of the Holy Spirit.

  Yeah, right!!!

Being sinless is impossible since we are still human.

  Only Christ was without sin.

1 JOHN 1:8 speaks to this. *IF WE CLAIM TO BE WITHOUT SIN, WE DECEIVE OURSELVES AND THE TRUTH IS NOT IN US.* As Christians we are to recognize the sins that have been shown to us by the Holy Spirit, and then we are to ask for forgiveness. **1 JOHN 1:9** states *IF WE CONFESS OUR SINS, HE IS FAITHFUL AND JUST AND WILL FORGIVE US OUR SINS AND PURIFY US FROM ALL UNRIGHTEOUSNESS.* If we were not going to sin, John would not have told us this.

What does all of this have to do with accepting one another? We judge others when they don't do what we want or expect them to do. We can't do it either. We must first learn to accept ourselves before we learn to accept others. [3]

For most of us it is hard to accept ourselves. We see all our flaws, faults and blemishes. The Lord accepts us as His sons and daughters and loves us. It is easier to accept others after we have learned to accept ourselves.

We need to accept our Christian brothers and sisters even though they do not measure up to how we think they should be. As my wife reminds me, "We need to accept people for who they are, not what we want them to be."

When we judge, and we will, we need to ask for forgiveness from the Lord and learn to accept our brothers in Christ. They have the same struggles that we have. If we cannot, as mature Christians, do what is right, how can we expect the weaker brother to be perfect? [4]

To be accepted means that Jesus accepted us willingly. He treated us as one of the family. We became His and thus His responsibility. We were no longer alone but have His Holy Spirit with us at all times.

Remember **ROMANS 15:7A** says *ACCEPT ONE ANOTHER,* but it can have another connotation other than what we have been looking into. It can also mean accepting all Christians into our church. In the song *"Jesus Loves the Little Children,"* we see that whether we're red or yellow, black or white, rich or poor, Jesus loves *all* the children of the world. Thus, none of these areas make a bit of difference in God's eyes.

God does not judge or accept us by outward appearance. (See **GALATIANS 2:6**.) Why should we judge that way?

Why don't we accept others?

> We see ourselves as better than them.
>> We are all the same in God's eyes.
> We don't love them the way we are supposed to.
>> Pray for the Holy Spirit's help in this area.
> We don't think they are Christian enough.
>> Whose standards are we using?
> They are not up to our standards.
>> How do we measure up to God's standards?
> We just don't like them.
>> If we start to pray for someone daily, our hearts will soften.
> They think they are better than us.
>> Get to know them better. Spend some time together.
> My heart is not right.
>> Go to the Lord in prayer. Ask for the Holy Spirit to work in your life.　　**[5]**

Recently when my wife and I were in Florida for an extended stay, we went to a couple of churches that were new to us. The first church never even acknowledged our presence. No one spoke to us. No one shook our hands. It was a small church, so it was obvious we were visitors. We never went back.

The second church we went to was just the opposite. From the time we walked from the parking lot until the service started, we were greeted no less than seven times by seven different people. This included a greeting by the pastor as he walked the aisles prior to the start of the service. It was a very large church and it would have been easy for people to miss a new couple. But they were going out of their way to meet and greet us. We were accepted immediately.　　**[6]**

Jesus understood this area of not accepting people for who they are. He speaks to this in **LUKE 4:24** about a prophet not being ***"ACCEPTED IN HIS HOMETOWN."*** He was rejected by his own villagers. Both before and after his death many Jews could not accept Jesus as the Messiah. Our Lord knew rejection. He was not accepted.

As followers of Christ we are to welcome and accept our brothers with open arms. This is how Christ welcomes us.

Can we do anything less? [7]

QUESTIONS ON ACCEPT

1. What does it mean to accept someone willingly?

2. How much like Paul are you?

3. How hard is it to accept yourself? Why?

4. Explain judging versus acceptance.

5. What other areas keeps us from accepting others?

6. How is your church at accepting new people? How can this area be improved?

7. What does it mean to accept one another? What keeps you from accepting someone?

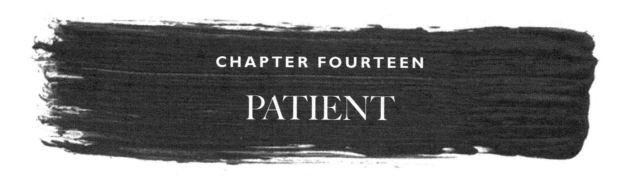

CHAPTER FOURTEEN
PATIENT

1 THESSALONIANS 5:14, *AND WE URGE YOU, BROTHERS, WARN THOSE WHO ARE IDLE, ENCOURAGE THE TIMID, HELP THE WEAK, BE PATIENT WITH EVERYONE.* [1]

This is a tough area, for me personally, to put together a lesson on patience. To say the least, I am not known to be the most patient of people. I have discovered that to get more patience, you must have patience. I am like "I want patience and I want it now." Patience does not come easily for some of us, but that is no excuse not to try to gain patience in our lives, particularly with our Christian brothers. Some people just seem so patient on the outside. What comes to mind when you think of someone having patience?

A certain calmness
Perseverance
Endurance
A person who takes the time to listen before acting
Someone wanting to help after hearing all the facts
A person who does not get upset despite what is going on around them

When we are around someone who is a patient person, it gives us assurance that everything is okay and will turn out alright. The patient person gives calmness to others. The patience just naturally rubs off. But not everyone is like this. What do you think of when you reflect on a person with a lack of patience? [2]

Yelling
Jumpy, nervous
Irritation
Intolerant
Someone not getting their way
Someone that is close to losing it
Someone not able to wait without showing their emotions

Which person would you rather be around? If this person was a boss, would you want to work for him? If this was a leader within the church body, would you want to serve with him on a committee or an activity? We need to take a hard look; which one is us?

What does the Bible have to say about patience? Patience is part of the fruit of the Holy Spirit. When we become Christians, the Holy Spirit enters us to bring us the fruit of the Spirit. He produces certain traits within us. Patience is something we are to have as Christians. Patience does not just automatically happen. We as Christians must help it to grow in our lives. All fruit needs to be cultivated.

We are told that **1 CORINTHIANS 13** is the love chapter. The first characteristic of love is patience per **VERSE 4A,** *LOVE IS PATIENT.* Our best example of love and patience is God. We see how much in **2 PETER 3:9,** *THE LORD IS NOT SLOW IN KEEPING HIS PROMISE, AS SOME UNDERSTAND SLOWNESS. HE IS PATIENT WITH YOU, NOT WANTING ANYONE TO PERISH, BUT EVERYONE TO COME TO REPENTANCE.* To me this is the ultimate show of patience. Here we are as sinners, who God doesn't even want to look at, yet He is patient with us and wants to save us. Not just a few of us, but everyone so He patiently gives us time to come to Him. It is the type of patience we, as humans, are not even familiar with as we live out our own lives day to day. [3], [4]

Paul uses himself as an example of the Lord's patience. **1 TIMOTHY 1:15–16,** *HERE IS A TRUSTWORTHY SAYING THAT DESERVES FULL ACCEPTANCE: CHRIST JESUS CAME INTO THE WORLD TO SAVE SINNERS—OF WHOM I AM THE WORST. BUT FOR THAT VERY REASON I WAS SHOWN MERCY SO*

THAT IN ME, THE WORST OF SINNERS, CHRIST JESUS MIGHT DISPLAY HIS UNLIMITED PATIENCE AS AN EXAMPLE FOR THOSE WHO WOULD BELIEVE ON HIM AND RECEIVE ETERNAL LIFE. Paul was hunting down and killing Christians, yet Jesus showed his patience until the correct time in God's infinite wisdom to confront Paul. As Paul says, even for the worst of sinners, God is patient so that none may perish.

God shows patience toward us. How are we at showing patience toward God?   [5]

> When God does not move fast enough in our opinion
> When we need help now, not when God wants to
> When God is not doing what we want, when we want
> When God is allowing bad things to happen to us or our family and friends
> When God seems to be letting us go through difficult times
> When things are just not going right in our lives

We are told to be patient in times of affliction. **ROMANS 12:12, *BE JOYFUL IN HOPE, PATIENT IN AFFLICTION, FAITHFUL IN PRAYER.*** Affliction, pain and misery are just part of what we go through while on this earth. We will continue to deal with them until we are called home to Heaven. Until then, we are told to be patient. Why are we to show patience when dealing with problem areas that are affecting our lives? What does patience teach us during times like this? We are being taught to rely on the Lord. We are being taught that try as we might we have no control over areas of our lives. This is when we are taught to lean on the Lord. These are the learning experiences that teach us we do not know the Lord's timing; thus we must wait upon the Lord.   [6]

In **PSALM 40:1–3,** David tells the benefits of waiting patiently on the Lord. While David waited on the Lord, the Lord lifted him ***OUT OF THE SLIMY PIT, OUT OF THE MUD AND MIRE;*** then David said ***HE SET MY FEET ON A ROCK AND GAVE ME A FIRM PLACE TO STAND. HE PUT A NEW SONG IN MY MOUTH, A HYMN OF PRAISE TO OUR GOD.*** David goes on to tell the benefits of his waiting patiently. He said ***MANY WILL SEE AND FEAR AND PUT THEIR TRUST IN THE LORD.*** David was saying that not only did being patient help him during times of trouble, his example of being patient and waiting on the Lord brought others to the Lord and helped them to put their trust in God as well. By us depending on the Lord, we become examples for others.   [7]

Where does this lack of patience come from? For some of us it just seems to be part of our makeup. We want things done now and done the way we want it. We see ourselves as knowing what is best. But this shows our ego, our feeling of we know what to do under all circumstances. When it is put like this, it really shows how egotistical we are. We think we know better than God. Since He won't do anything, we will. We are not giving the Lord the chance to do things on His own timing. We are not willing to turn areas of our lives over to Him. We are not allowing the Holy Spirit to have control of our lives.   [8]

Another area that affects the lack of patience in our lives is the society we are in. Today's society teaches us it is wrong to wait on anything.

> We complain when we have to wait on a microwave to heat up our food.
> We want fast food, not slow food.
> We spend lots of money to make our computer react faster by microseconds.
> We want instant gratification on everything.
> Our televisions shows must be wrapped up in 30–60 minutes.
> We now have speed dating, drive through weddings and funerals, quickie divorces, faster cars, instant news, minute rice, instant oats, instant coffee and instant communication: email, tweets, twitter, texting, cell phones and apps.   [9]

This list could go on and on. All of these things came about because we are impatient. Our attitude is "if you can't keep up, get out of the way."

But how does patience apply to dealing with "one another"?   [10]

Another word for patience is "bear with." In **COLOSSIANS 3:13,** we are told to *BEAR WITH EACH OTHER AND FORGIVE WHATEVER GRIEVANCES YOU MAY HAVE AGAINST ONE ANOTHER. FORGIVE AS THE LORD FORGAVE YOU.* Our Christian brothers mess up and do not do things right. We, who are the stronger Christians, need to have patience as they grow into their Christianity. If a Christian brother wrongs us, be patient with him. If he does not see things the same way, be patient with him, bear with him.

I struggle having patience with my immediate family, much less my friends, particularly if they wrong me. My reaction is simply to stay away from them, to forget them. But this is not what we are taught. We must show patience and forgive them, and then try to straighten things out.

How do we do this? It is so against our nature. **EPHESIANS 4:2** is the answer. *BE COMPLETELY HUMBLE AND GENTLE; BE PATIENT, BEARING WITH ONE ANOTHER IN LOVE.* This is the kind of love the Lord has shown to us. We can develop this type of love for people we find unlovable. To others, we might be the unlovable person. We cannot have this kind of love without the intervening of the Holy Spirit in our lives. We must allow the Holy Spirit to develop in us the fruit of the Spirit. We cannot love in this manner without the Holy Spirit's direction. Be patient and let Him give us the help we need to love others.

How are we to deal with our frustrating brothers? **ROMANS 15:1,** *WE WHO ARE STRONG OUGHT TO BEAR WITH THE FAILINGS OF THE WEAK AND NOT TO PLEASE OURSELVES.* We see weak Christians and we want to give up on them. We want to stay away from them, we are unable to forgive them or even want to. Remember, at one time we were the weaker Christians. It can be just as difficult to bear with our mature Christian friends who are pushy and self-righteous. Be careful this is not us. Again, we are to deal with these brothers in love.

Usually patience, or the lack of, is prevalent when we are not getting our own way, when we are being selfish. But we are not to put ourselves first. In **LUKE 22:42,** Jesus prays while in the garden *"FATHER, IF YOU ARE WILLING, TAKE THIS CUP FROM ME; YET NOT MY WILL, BUT YOURS BE DONE."* We must strive to live Christ-like. We need to show the patience of Christ in our lives and not just be concerned about our own feelings, about getting our own way. **COLOSSIANS 3:12** tells us to clothe ourselves with patience. We are to put it on in the morning. It is to be part of our attire. If we expect patience from others, we are to show patience.

One of the key areas of patience is waiting on the Lord's return. Until His return we will continue to live in a broken, sinful world. We will feel frustrated with the injustice of everyday problems. But we are to be patient, since the Lord is in control. James tells us to be like farmers. I can relate to this since I love to garden. **JAMES 5:7–8,** *BE PATIENT, THEN, BROTHERS, UNTIL THE LORD'S COMING. SEE HOW THE FARMER WAITS FOR THE LAND TO YIELD ITS VALUABLE CROP AND HOW PATIENT HE IS FOR THE AUTUMN AND SPRING RAINS. YOU TOO, BE PATIENT AND STAND FIRM, BECAUSE THE LORD'S COMING IS NEAR.* After a garden is planted, harvest cannot be rushed. While on earth we are to prepare the soil for the seed, the Word of God, to start to grow. We cannot allow ourselves to be impatient, it can affect our entire time here on earth. Remember, the Lord is coming again but will return when the harvest is ready and not until then. His timing is perfect, unlike ours. **[11]**

QUESTIONS ON PATIENT

1. How are you at showing patience towards others? At work? At home? In daily life? At church? When is your lack of patience at its worst?

2. What are your symptoms when you lack patience?

3. What does it mean when it says "love is patient"?

4. Why would this be true?

5. Are you patient with the Lord? What enables you to be patient with the Lord? What prevents it?

6. What qualities have you developed during times of trouble and frustration in your life?

7. Has someone showing patience and relying on the Lord influenced you? Explain the comfort it gave you.

8. Does this describe you? What must you do to change your lack of patience?

9. What else would you add to this list?

10. What is your answer to this question?

11. What can you do personally to gain and develop patience with your Christian brothers? Do you really want to?

CHAPTER FIFTEEN

PROVOKING

GALATIANS 5:26, *LET US NOT BECOME CONCEITED, PROVOKING AND ENVYING EACH OTHER.* [1]

Webster defines provoke as: *to make angry, to arouse to a feeling of action, to irritate or annoy.*

Looking in the NIV concordance the word *provoke*, is only used one time in the New Testament. It is used multiple times in the Old Testament. In the Old Testament, almost every occasion it was used was when the Jews provoked God. **2 KINGS 17:17–18A,** *THEY SACRIFICED THEIR SONS AND DAUGHTERS IN THE FIRE. THEY PRACTICED DIVINATION AND SORCERY AND SOLD THEMSELVES TO DO EVIL IN THE EYES OF THE LORD, PROVOKING HIM TO ANGER. SO THE LORD WAS VERY ANGRY WITH ISRAEL AND REMOVED THEM FROM HIS PRESENCE.* The Jews provoked God, and it resulted in God's anger coming down on them. He did not want to see them. They had provoked Him so much, that He wanted them out of His sight. God later said to Isaiah about the Jews in **ISAIAH 65:3,** *A PEOPLE WHO CONTINUALLY PROVOKE ME TO MY VERY FACE, OFFERING SACRIFICES IN GARDENS AND BURNING INCENSE ON ALTARS OF BRICK.* The Jews went against God's laws and He responded with anger. They knew what God expected of them, but they did not do it and went against His laws. [2]

It seems like a simple thing. We need to know what provokes our fellow Christian brothers, and then we should not do it. Sounds easy, but it is not. I know what provokes my spouse and I still do it even after many, many years of marriage. As an example, I am notorious for not closing doors behind me. I am working in the kitchen making dinner and I open a drawer to get out a measuring spoon. I don't close the drawer. I get into a cupboard to get a measuring cup or some spice and I don't shut the door. It continues on until most of the drawers and doors are open including the microwave. When my wife comes into the room, I notice what I have done. Too late! Sometimes she lets it go, then there are other times it provokes her to anger. In this case, it is deserved. It is not that I don't know what irritates her, I am just too busy to care or notice. In this case I am definitely in the wrong. I deserve the anger. I provoked her. [3]

But how does this work with other Christians? Do I know what might provoke a fellow Christian? Sometimes I do. Not all Christians agree on all doctrines, and I can provoke an argument just by getting them "fired up" on a certain subject. It is up to me to avoid this issue with my Christian brothers. Sometimes in my Sunday school class someone wants to provoke me to get me aroused on a certain subject. A teacher must be careful, or he can divide the class. Lively discussion is one thing, provocation is another. This happened in Jesus' time. **LUKE 11:53** (King James version), *AND AS HE SAID THESE THINGS UNTO THEM, THE SCRIBES AND THE PHARISEES BEGAN TO URGE HIM VEHEMENTLY, AND TO PROVOKE HIM TO SPEAK OF MANY THINGS.* Why would they do this? **LUKE 11:54** (NIV), *WAITING TO CATCH HIM IN SOMETHING HE MIGHT SAY.* If he spoke wrongly, they could kill him. The perfect time to get someone to say something provoking is when they are being provoked. They are aroused and will spout off. We must be careful when this happens to us.

We can gossip about a brother and this will provoke him if it gets back to him. And it usually does. In this case we need to keep our mouths shut. It can happen if we treat a brother with disrespect or look down on him. If we betray a secret this can also provoke someone. All of these actions will provoke a person to anger or action of some sort.

We can also provoke a friend by taking sides in a disagreement among other friends. In most cases it is best if we just don't get involved. When we take either side in an argument, we have already alienated one side or the other. Why put ourselves in this position?

Another way we provoke people is by what we say. Filters are a trouble area for me. Sometimes I speak, and the thought has not gone through my brain but instead directly to my tongue. Usually the wrong thing comes out in the wrong way. I get the "wife" look, deservingly so. I have provoked her by what I said. I have possibly also provoked a friend by my smart, sarcastic mouth. I never want to hurt a friend, but I do it. I have also provoked some negative feelings in my friend's mind. It is usually something that is out of line, or I am putting myself first, both of which can provoke others. When I put myself first, this means my friend is second. This can provoke anyone.

We can provoke others when we are intolerant of their opinions. We see this continually in the political world. When a Republican and a Democrat get into a discussion, both want to talk over the other person. Why? Because they know they are so right, and they don't want to hear what the other person is saying. We must be careful of this by learning to listen and not form opinions as they are talking to us. This is hard to do no matter who we are, but it is key to not provoking others. We must be careful of being so strongly opinionated on a subject that we don't even want others' opinions. James says in **JAMES 1:19–20**, *MY DEAR BROTHERS, TAKE NOTE OF THIS: EVERYONE SHOULD BE QUICK TO LISTEN, SLOW TO SPEAK AND SLOW TO BECOME ANGRY, FOR MAN'S ANGER DOES NOT BRING ABOUT THE RIGHTEOUS LIFE THAT GOD DESIRES.* Our words and actions can push our brothers away from a righteous life. We must be careful with our words, attitude and actions and not do this. **MATTHEW 5:22A**, *BUT I TELL YOU THAT ANYONE WHO IS ANGRY WITH HIS BROTHER WILL BE SUBJECT TO JUDGMENT.* When we provoke our brothers to anger, we are setting them up for judgment. Keep this in mind when we aggravate our brothers in Christ. We are to be slow to anger, but we are also to be slow to anger others by our provocations. [4]

The King James version also gives us this verse, **EPHESIANS 6:4**, *AND, YE FATHERS, PROVOKE NOT YOUR CHILDREN TO WRATH: BUT BRING THEM UP IN THE NURTURE AND ADMONITION OF THE LORD.* There are many ways we can provoke our children, and I am sure I have done them all. We provoke them when we hover over them and do not let them mature or accept them as mature people. We can provoke them when we push them over and above what they can tolerate, or we just lay unrealistic expectations on a child. Kids get provoked when we have double standards from one child to another or if we are always finding fault. We can provoke our children when we compare them to others, or we can be too legalistic. By provoking our children to anger, we push them away. This is not the way we are to raise our children. [5]

How do we keep from provoking others? Most all the areas above are within our power to avoid, with a little effort on our part. Most of the time we provoke someone is when we say something to arouse them. Think before we speak. Paul, in the verses prior to **GALATIANS 5:26,** had been talking to the Galatians about living in the Spirit. He says in **GALATIANS 5:16,** *SO I SAY, LIVE BY THE SPIRIT, AND YOU WILL NOT GRATIFY THE DESIRES OF THE SINFUL NATURE.* When we provoke others, we are probably not living our lives in the Spirit. We are living our lives for ourselves, our sinful nature. We are to give ourselves to the Spirit, not to our sinful nature. This is not a one-time thing. We must constantly give up "self." **[6]**

The best way to not provoke others is by our love. The King James version says in **1 CORINTHIANS 13:5** when it is speaking about love, that it *DOTH NOT BEHAVE ITSELF UNSEEMLY, SEEKETH NOT HER OWN, IS NOT EASILY PROVOKED, THINKETH NO EVIL.* Thank goodness for this! Because of my wife's love for me, she is not provoked easily. This holds true for my Christian brothers. Because we love them, they do not provoke us easily, and we do not provoke them easily. Most all provocation comes from being self-seeking. By knowing this, we must learn to put others first. If we do this, we will not seek to provoke others. It is not easy, but if we truly love our brothers, it will go a long way in not provoking others.

Love your brothers and keep from provoking them. Love is the key! **[7]**

QUESTIONS ON PROVOKING

1. What does this mean to you?

2. Why was God so provoked? Was He right?

3. If we know what provokes someone, why do we continue to do it?

4. In what ways have you provoked another Christian brother? What ways have they provoked you?

5. How does this apply to you? What ways have you provoked your children?

6. Why do Christians provoke each other?

7. What must you do in your life to keep you from provoking others?

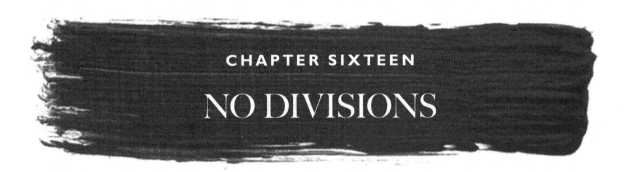

CHAPTER SIXTEEN

NO DIVISIONS

1 CORINTHIANS 1:10, *I APPEAL TO YOU, BROTHERS, IN THE NAME OF OUR LORD JESUS CHRIST, THAT ALL OF YOU AGREE WITH ONE ANOTHER SO THAT THERE MAY BE NO DIVISIONS AMONG YOU AND THAT YOU MAY BE PERFECTLY UNITED IN MIND AND THOUGHT.* [1]

Can a church ever achieve this? A home cannot get everyone on the same page. Neither can a classroom. Why would Paul see this as so important? To be united together in *MIND AND THOUGHT* gives the church the opportunity to achieve all the glory that the Lord has in mind for the church. But what kinds of division is Paul speaking about?

There are two types Paul might bring to their attention, and ours as well—the divisions of the churches themselves and the divisions of the people within each church body.

When it comes to the divisions within the churches, Paul had an issue even when the churches first started. There was disagreement within the beginning churches. One of the first recorded disagreements came in the Corinthian church. To understand this fully read **1 CORINTHIANS 1:10–3:23.** Let's look at the condensed version. The division is about whom they follow. Paul continues in **1 CORINTHIANS 1:11–13,** *MY BROTHERS, SOME FROM CHLOE'S HOUSEHOLD HAVE INFORMED ME THAT THERE ARE QUARRELS AMONG YOU. WHAT I MEAN IS THIS: ONE OF YOU SAYS, "I*

FOLLOW PAUL"; ANOTHER, "I FOLLOW APOLLOS"; ANOTHER, "I FOLLOW CEPHAS"; STILL ANOTHER, "I FOLLOW CHRIST." IS CHRIST DIVIDED? WAS PAUL CRUCIFIED FOR YOU? WERE YOU BAPTIZED INTO THE NAME OF PAUL? He goes on to tell them all of these people are mere men, servants of the Lord. Paul points out that some men plant, some water, some reap, but the harvest is based on the foundation of Jesus Christ. These arguments happen in today's churches as well. One pastor leaves and people divide the congregation to follow the old pastor. Don't both men bring the Word of God? Don't both men base their beliefs on the foundation of Christ? Why then divide ourselves for mere men? The church is not about the leaders, it is about Jesus Christ. Do not get caught up in the leaders of the church, they will come and go, but get caught up in Jesus Christ. He is the head of the church, not men. If the church is not bringing the message of Christ crucified, then go elsewhere. A church trying to serve two leaders will not move forward. It will be in chaos and divisions will happen. **[2]**

Another division Paul tried to correct comes from **1 CORINTHIANS 11:17–24.** The division was over how communion was taken and/or how people were treating others during communion and the fellowship meal that preceded it. He realized the problem would take more than a few words so he said in **1 CORINTHIANS 11:34B, *AND WHEN I COME I WILL GIVE FURTHER DIRECTIONS.*** Even today there are divisions over communion. Who is to take it, who meets the requirements, how often to have communion and even the sacraments themselves pose problems? Is real wine to be used and must it be unleavened bread? One of the main keys of communion is preparing ourselves for the sacredness of the moment. As Paul says, we must judge ourselves whether we should take communion. Divisions like these must be settled by the heads of the local church, then once settled all others must fall in line and not create problems that will create divisions. **[3]**

A major division within the first church came about because there were both Jews and Gentiles accepting the Lord. The Jews felt that for the Gentiles to be accepted into the church, they must follow all the Jewish laws and traditions including the food they ate, and also, they must be agreeable to circumcision. The Gentiles felt they were Christians, not Christian Jews. Read the full account in **ACTS 15:5–21.** Looking at **VERSES 10–11,** Peter says to the group, *"NOW THEN, WHY DO YOU TRY TO TEST GOD BY PUTTING ON THE NECKS OF THE DISCIPLES A YOKE THAT NEITHER WE NOR OUR FATHERS HAVE BEEN ABLE TO BEAR? NO! WE BELIEVE IT IS THROUGH THE GRACE OF OUR LORD JESUS THAT WE ARE SAVED, JUST AS THEY ARE."* When it came to eating food sacrificed to idols, Paul gives them this answer in **1 CORINTHIANS 8:8,** *BUT FOOD DOES NOT BRING US NEAR TO GOD; WE ARE NO WORSE IF WE DO NOT EAT, AND NO BETTER IF WE DO.* Do things like this work to divide churches today? Absolutely! Once people are saved, many churches come across as if there is a list of things to do and not to do. Most of it is not biblical, just tradition. No movies, no jewelry, no dancing, no drinking, no smoking, how to keep the Sabbath and many other areas so people can judge if we are truly Christians. Yes, we are to live our lives as Christ would have us live, but our lives are not to be a list of rules and traditions or we are just regressing to what the Pharisees would have others do.

We have areas like this today:
Dancing
Going to movies
Wearing jewelry
Tobacco use
Working on Sunday
Musical instruments in the worship service
The use of drums or guitars in the service
Wearing shorts to a church service
The use of alcohol
The type of music within the church service
Which hymnal to use
What Bible version to use
Women in leadership capacities [4]

Many churches have divided over just a few of the above areas that are mentioned. Most of these would have been viewed as stumbling blocks in Paul's time. He writes to the church in Rome to answer some of their issues over food that was served to idols and the Sabbath. **ROMANS 14:12–13A,** *SO THEN, EACH OF US WILL GIVE AN ACCOUNT OF HIMSELF TO GOD. THEREFORE LET US STOP PASSING JUDGMENT ON ONE ANOTHER.* Replace the thought of eating food served to idols with one from the list above. Do not become a part of a church that is setting up areas for judging each other. We are only to be judged by the Lord, not man.

Divisions within a church can come from many different areas, and from different people. **ROMANS 16:17,** *I URGE YOU, BROTHERS, TO WATCH OUT FOR THOSE*

WHO CAUSE DIVISIONS AND PUT OBSTACLES IN YOUR WAY THAT ARE CONTRARY TO THE TEACHING YOU HAVE LEARNED. KEEP AWAY FROM THEM. What would this be? It would be teachings that are anything different than what comes from the Bible, in other words, what some individual would be teaching, from what they think or feel should be the rules. What does Paul have to say about them? **VERSE 18,** *FOR SUCH PEOPLE ARE NOT SERVING OUR LORD CHRIST, BUT THEIR OWN APPETITES. BY SMOOTH TALK AND FLATTERY THEY DECEIVE THE MINDS OF NAIVE PEOPLE.*

To expound on this:

These people are not following the Lord's teachings.

They serve what they want, what feeds them personally.

They are doing things for their own desires.

They are smooth talkers.

They deceive the minds of the followers who are not in tune with correct teachings.

They deceive the minds of people that are naive or easily turned.

Do you recognize anyone like this in today's Christian media? If they are not teaching Christ's resurrection which brings us grace, run away no matter how smooth the talk or how good it sounds. We must know the teachings of the Bible so we are not naive. People like this want to satisfy their appetites which usually has something to do with their wallets.   **[5]**

Paul tells us some people do not want the true doctrine and will leave it. **2 TIMOTHY 4:3–4,** *FOR THE TIME WILL COME WHEN MEN WILL NOT PUT UP WITH SOUND DOCTRINE. INSTEAD, TO SUIT THEIR OWN DESIRES, THEY WILL GATHER AROUND THEM A GREAT NUMBER OF TEACHERS TO SAY WHAT THEIR ITCHING EARS WANT TO HEAR. THEY WILL TURN THEIR EARS AWAY FROM THE TRUTH AND TURN ASIDE TO MYTHS. VERSE 10A* goes on to say *FOR DEMAS, BECAUSE HE LOVED THIS WORLD, HAS DESERTED ME AND HAS GONE TO THESSALONICA.* Paul is not upset that Demas has left him to go another way, Paul is upset that Demas turned his love toward the world and all that is in it. But what is the warning here?   **[6]**

1.   Some people within the church do not want to hear the truth. They want to listen to what they want to hear whether it is doctrine and truth or not. They will promote an unsound doctrine.

2.   Not only do they not want to hear the truth, they will turn away from it.

3.   They in turn will gather around the teachers telling them what they want to hear, to hear what satisfies their sinful desires. (See **ISAIAH 30:9–11**.)

4.   They will turn to myths, or doctrine that is not true.

5.   Some will leave the church because of their love for the world and its pleasures. Example: Demas.

Some people are just divisive. They stir up controversies within the church body. Paul tells us in **TITUS 3:9–11** how to handle such people. *BUT AVOID FOOLISH CONTROVERSIES AND GENEALOGIES AND ARGUMENTS AND QUARRELS ABOUT THE LAW, BECAUSE THESE ARE UNPROFITABLE AND USELESS. WARN A DIVISIVE PERSON ONCE, AND THEN WARN HIM A SECOND TIME. AFTER THAT, HAVE NOTHING TO DO WITH HIM. YOU MAY BE SURE THAT SUCH A MAN IS WARPED AND SINFUL; HE IS SELF-CONDEMNED.* In every church it seems we have people that want to stir things up over some type of controversy. There are some areas we will never have answers for while here on earth. Some think they have the answers but others will disagree. Areas like pre-tribulation versus post-tribulation, eternal security versus free will, methods of baptism, which Bible translation the church and the pastor are to use. Others are foolish, how many angels will fit on the head of a pin. What is Paul telling us about these arguments?   [7]

1.   Avoid such people that bring up controversial areas. Why? They are warped and sinful.

2.   The person is self-condemned.

3.   These areas are unprofitable and useless.

4.   Give them two warnings then have nothing to do with them.

Do not let people like this take over the church. As a Sunday School teacher over the years there always seems to be someone wanting to direct the lesson into some area where the Bible does not give a definitive answer and there are people with strong beliefs on both sides. All this does is divide the church for no reason. Open discussion is one thing, but when the discussion turns personal, that is another. Do not pick on someone's beliefs. Be aware of other's feelings. Just because we think we are right does not make it so. This is what the Lord would have us do. If your mother believed you should not have playing cards in the house, would you give her a hard time? Would you quarrel or make fun of her? No, you would be sensitive to her beliefs even if you did not agree with them. Act the same with your fellow Christians.   **[8]**

GALATIANS 3:26–28 points out we are all brothers in Christ. *YOU ARE ALL SONS OF GOD THROUGH FAITH IN CHRIST JESUS, FOR ALL OF YOU WHO WERE BAPTIZED INTO CHRIST HAVE CLOTHED YOURSELVES WITH CHRIST. THERE IS NEITHER JEW NOR GREEK, SLAVE NOR FREE, MALE NOR FEMALE, FOR YOU ARE ALL ONE IN CHRIST JESUS.*

1.   Neither Jew nor Greek. Some equivalents today would be American or foreign, black or white. We are all the same in the Lord's eyes. Do not discriminate or allow divisions to happen in the church because of this issue. God is color blind and nationality blind. This must be a non-issue.

2.   Slave or free. Business owner or blue-collar worker. Rich or poor. We are to have no divisions because of economic issues.

3.   Male or female. Do not discriminate within the body because of the sex of a person.   **[9]**

Speaking about being one in Christ, Paul says in **EPHESIANS 2:19,** *CONSEQUENTLY, YOU ARE NO LONGER FOREIGNERS AND ALIENS, BUT FELLOW CITIZENS WITH GOD'S PEOPLE AND MEMBERS OF GOD'S HOUSEHOLD.* The last thing the Lord wants is divisions among the believers, but it is easy to see why divisions happen. A slightly different take on certain scriptures and suddenly there is a new church. Sometimes people just do not get along. No matter what causes the division, we should all get along since we are all brothers and sisters in Christ. Today there are at least 33,000 denominations. It is key that every Christian does his or her part to keep divisions out of the church. This is key to the local church. Lean on our local leaders to get rid of divisions. Go directly to them if we have an issue with someone else and their teachings. Watch out for those who try to divide the church and speak out boldly against them. Divisions within the body take up too much time. Time to be better used elsewhere. Do not allow a division to start. We need to do our best to bring unity to the local body. Yes, a church can have diverse people, but they still should not have disunity. The Lord wanted His church, His bride to be united. We are all in Christ.   **[10], [11]**

QUESTIONS ON NO DIVISIONS

1. How important is this to Paul? Notice the word *appeal*.

2. Do divisions happen today over certain leaders? Can this be eliminated?

3. Why do we have divisions over the sacrament of communion? It seems so simple.

4. Have you seen divisions over any of these areas? What would you add?

5. What "smooth talk" and "flattery" have you heard? How did you recognize it for what it was?

6. Explain "itching ears." Does this still happen today?

7. What are your comments on **TITUS 3:9–11?**

8. Have you ever seen someone causing divisions within your church? How did it play itself out? Is it always on purpose?

9. How do you interpret **GALATIANS 3:26–28** in today's society?

10. What usually causes divisions within the local churches? What part can we each play to keep from having divisions within the body?

11. Do outsiders away from the church recognize divisions happening within the body? How does this affect the local church?

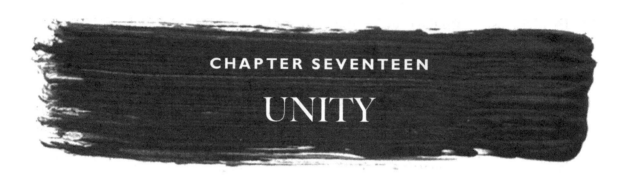

CHAPTER SEVENTEEN
UNITY

ROMANS 15:5-6, *MAY THE GOD WHO GIVES ENDURANCE AND ENCOURAGEMENT GIVE YOU A SPIRIT OF UNITY AMONG YOURSELVES AS YOU FOLLOW CHRIST JESUS, SO THAT WITH ONE HEART AND MOUTH YOU MAY GLORIFY THE GOD AND FATHER OF OUR LORD JESUS CHRIST.* [1]

We are united by one spirit. This "spirit of unity" Paul is talking about is the Holy Spirit. When we become Christians, the Holy Spirit enters each of us. Thus, we become united together. But even in Peter and Paul's days there were divisions and contentions between these two great saints. Paul writes in **COLOSSIANS 3:11,** *HERE THERE IS NO GREEK OR JEW, CIRCUMCISED OR UNCIRCUMCISED, BARBARIAN, SCYTHIAN, SLAVE OR FREE, BUT CHRIST IS ALL, AND IS IN ALL.* Yet we know they disagreed and there was contention between the Christian Jews and the Gentile Christians. Peter and Paul agreed to disagree. Peter ministered and preached to the Jews, and Paul to the Gentiles. Both had many, many converts. They also agreed that outward appearance and social standing meant nothing.

This is key to being a Christian. We are all the same to God once we become a Christian, we now have Christian brothers and sisters of all colors, of all ethnicity, of all social standing, rich or poor, educated or uneducated, long or short hair, tattooed or not tattooed, young or old, attractive or unattractive, liberal or conservative. None of these areas should separate us from being united together in Christ, in one body.   [2]

Why is this so important? When we all get to Heaven, we will all be together as one big family. So, should it be here on earth, united together, by the Holy Spirit.

It is key to remind ourselves to have unity, not uniformity. Uniformity means

> No one is different.
> We all think alike.
> Everyone agrees totally on everything.

This is not what God wants or expects, plus it is impossible. What God wants from unity is the attitude of working together for the same goal. The body of Christ, the Church.

It does not mean we all agree on minor points in doctrine. We can still be united but have disagreements. We are to get past these disagreements and remain united, knowing we can agree to disagree. Unity means having

> The same goals
> The same savior
> The same enemy   [3]

My church has a written purpose of mission. Maybe yours does as well. Do you know what it is? Does the church body seek this mission when you come together? Are you united in the mission's purpose?   [4]

My church's Mission Statement is: *To exist to know, love, and worship God; and to win, build, and equip followers of Jesus Christ.* This statement is of no value unless everyone is united to fulfill the purpose. My church must be unified in this purpose or else it is just words on paper and thus worthless.

Notice my church says it does not exist for

> Entertainment
> Self-satisfaction

Personal promotion
Being a social club
Sitting on the sideline watching and not being involved

All are to be involved and active for the mission of the church—united.

Why is unity stressed so hard? What is the big deal about Christians getting along? In **JOHN 17:23,** Jesus prays *"I IN THEM AND YOU IN ME. MAY THEY BE BROUGHT TO COMPLETE UNITY TO LET THE WORLD KNOW THAT YOU SENT ME AND HAVE LOVED THEM EVEN AS YOU HAVE LOVED ME."* [5]

We need to be examples to the world just what Christianity is all about. It breaks my heart to see fussing within the church body. To see fellow Christians not getting along. After all we are the Bride of Christ. [6]

Who would want to attend a church that is having internal issues? Paul realizes this when he writes in **PHILIPPIANS 4:2–3,** *I PLEAD WITH EUODIA AND I PLEAD WITH SYNTYCHE TO AGREE WITH EACH OTHER IN THE LORD. YES, AND I ASK YOU, LOYAL YOKEFELLOW, TO HELP THESE WOMEN WHO HAVE CONTENDED AT MY SIDE IN THE CAUSE OF THE GOSPEL, ALONG WITH CLEMENT AND THE REST OF MY FELLOW WORKERS, WHOSE NAMES ARE IN THE BOOK OF LIFE.* Notice the key word Paul uses at the beginning, he "pleads" with them. Paul has received word of two women, fellow workers in the church, that were fussing. He wanted it taken care of immediately. He knew the longer the disagreement went on the less chance of unity within the local church. The situation would do nothing but fester. This same thing can happen in churches today. Two people within the church body disagree. What's the big deal? People take sides and then it is not just two people in a disagreement, it is the whole church body. This can go on for years and the church never heals. In this case Paul would have been happy if they had agreed to disagree. We're never told what the argument was all about. All we know is two fellow Christians, fellow workers, do not agree.

He wanted them to come to their senses over this disagreement.
It was not a matter of their Christianity, but of their pride.
He did not want personal interests to control the situation.
He wanted them to do any and everything in their power to keep dissention out of the church.

He wanted them to resolve the problem whatever it was.
He asked the church to help them with this problem.

Within the church there is common ground.

The common ground within the church body is the Lord.
We are to be proactive to settle disagreements within the body.
As the church body we are to be proactive to keep disagreements from festering.
Do not sit back and allow the body to disintegrate in front of us.

He asked the church to "help these women." Notice he calls on one person, yokefellow, a person who was yoked together with these women. He wants him involved, *now*. God does work in and through fellow Christians even when they disagree.

Paul in **PHILIPPIANS 2:1–2** says in a rhetorical way, *IF YOU HAVE ANY ENCOURAGEMENT FROM BEING UNITED WITH CHRIST, IF ANY COMFORT FROM HIS LOVE, IF ANY FELLOWSHIP WITH THE SPIRIT, IF ANY TENDERNESS AND COMPASSION, THEN MAKE MY JOY COMPLETE BY BEING LIKE-MINDED, HAVING THE SAME LOVE, BEING ONE IN SPIRIT AND PURPOSE.* In other words, "since you have," the following should occur:

We should be like minded.
We will have the same love.
We will be one in spirit and purpose.
We are to do nothing out of selfish ambition or vain conceit.
We are, in humility, to consider others better than ourselves.
We don't look after our own interest, but the interest of others and the whole.   [7]

Then he says we are to have the attitude of Jesus Christ. We know what that was. His attitude was that of a servant.

Lack of unity happens the most when people want their own way.

When they see their values as number one.
When they have their own agenda.
When they see themselves as better than anyone else.

This cannot happen within the church body and still have the unity that the Lord wants us to have.

How is this unity possible? How can we all be unified? How can a church be in unity with all its members when my household of two or more cannot get along on a day to day a basis? How about yours? This unity that the Bible speaks about can only happen through the love that the Holy Spirit brings to us as individuals. Each of us through our own power cannot love each other the way the Holy Spirit enables us to do in His power.   **[8]**

COLOSSIANS 3:12–14 gives us a list of virtues and guidelines for holy living, how to get along. Notice in **VERSE 14** what the *key* is and what ties it all together, *AND OVER ALL THESE VIRTUES PUT ON LOVE, WHICH BINDS THEM ALL TOGETHER IN PERFECT UNITY.*   **[9]**

Paul is saying we are to "put on love." This takes an action on our part.

> We must be willing to put it on.
> We must have the desire to put it on.
> We must put it on and leave it on.
> We are to do this on a daily basis.

It is up to us to make the effort for the purpose of peace within the body. We cannot just expect unity to happen, it will not. We are all to be putting forth the effort to make all this happen. What makes up the body is all the Christians all over the world. It is all the believers.

This type of love does not come naturally to any of us. This is the love for our Christian brothers that the Holy Spirit instills in us when we accept the Lord. But it still takes an effort. It is up to us to make that effort. **EPHESIANS 4:3,** *MAKE EVERY EFFORT TO KEEP THE UNITY OF THE SPIRIT THROUGH THE BOND OF PEACE.*

Paul tells us about the body in **1 CORINTHIANS 12:12–14,** *THE BODY IS A UNIT, THOUGH IT IS MADE UP OF MANY PARTS; AND THOUGH ALL ITS PARTS ARE MANY, THEY FORM ONE BODY. SO IT IS WITH CHRIST. FOR WE WERE ALL BAPTIZED BY ONE SPIRIT INTO ONE BODY—WHETHER JEWS OR GREEKS, SLAVE OR FREE—AND WE WERE ALL GIVEN THE ONE SPIRIT TO DRINK. NOW THE BODY IS NOT MADE UP OF ONE PART BUT MANY.*

ONE UNIT=UNITY.

We cannot be part of something and not be working together. If someone on a sports team is going their own way, it affects the whole team. If a quarterback calls for a play to go to the right and one player thinks it would be better if he went left, the whole play does not work. The team must be like-minded and have one purpose for it to be successful. Everyone must be working together. What if you had one leg wanting to go left and the other wanting to go right, how would that work out? It would not. You would get nowhere. This is the same for the body of Christ. All in the body need to be working together. Why? **EPHESIANS 4:25B,** *FOR WE ARE ALL MEMBERS OF ONE BODY.* We are members of one team. The team of Jesus Christ.

ROMANS 12:4–5, *JUST AS EACH OF US HAS ONE BODY WITH MANY MEMBERS, AND THESE MEMBERS DO NOT ALL HAVE THE SAME FUNCTION, SO IN CHRIST WE WHO ARE MANY FORM ONE BODY, AND EACH MEMBER BELONGS TO ALL THE OTHERS.*

We are one body yet made up differently. We each have a gift (or gifts) to use for the good of the body. Make an effort to keep unity within the church, not only the one you attend but the church body as a whole. Whatever we do should be good for the body. We are one. **ROMANS 15:5–6** says we are to be one with our heart and with our mouth. When we speak, remember we are speaking for all. **[10]**

QUESTIONS ON UNITY

1. Explain unity in your own words.

2. Do any of these give you a problem? Why?

3. Do you agree with differences explained between unity and uniformity? How would you explain the differences?

4. Does your church have a mission statement? What is it?

5. Why is it so important to Jesus for Christians to show unity to the world?

6. Do churches do this? Does your church do this? In what ways?

7. Is it possible for Christians to agree to disagree and still have unity?

8. What can you do in your church to promote unity?

9. How does love work to bind us together in unity?

10. By having different gifts, how does this work within a church to promote unity?

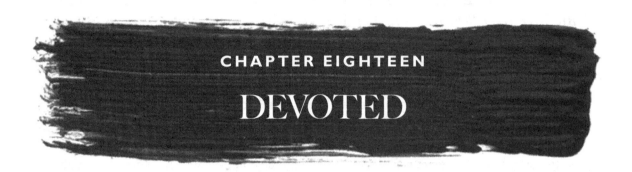

CHAPTER EIGHTEEN

DEVOTED

ROMANS 12:10A, *BE DEVOTED TO ONE ANOTHER IN BROTHERLY LOVE.*

Devoted: *loyal or loving* [1]

In the New Testament, believers are told to devote themselves to many things. But in only one place does it tell us as Christians to be devoted to one another. [2]

Paul tells Timothy in **1 TIMOTHY 4:13,** *UNTIL I COME, DEVOTE YOURSELF TO THE PUBLIC READING OF SCRIPTURE, TO PREACHING AND TO TEACHING.* He wants Timothy to be loyal in praying in public, to preach, teach and read scriptures in public. Not just when he feels like it, but to be loyal and devoted to following Paul's direction.

To the church in Colosse, **COLOSSIANS 4:2A,** he says *DEVOTE YOURSELVES TO PRAYER.* We need to take this advice today. Praying for our church family shows we are loyal and devoted to them.

When Paul writes in **TITUS 3:8B,** he says *BE CAREFUL TO DEVOTE THEMSELVES TO DOING WHAT IS GOOD,* and then in **VERSE 14A** he further states *OUR PEOPLE MUST LEARN TO DEVOTE THEMSELVES TO DOING WHAT IS GOOD.*

We must be loyal, devoted in doing good to one another. (*See Chapter 48.*)

In the early church, according to **ACTS 2:42,** ***THEY DEVOTED THEMSELVES TO THE APOSTLES' TEACHING AND TO THE FELLOWSHIP, TO THE BREAKING OF BREAD AND TO PRAYER.*** This is a lesson for us to devote ourselves to spending time with our fellow Christians. For us today, when he says ***DEVOTED THEMSELVES TO THE APOSTLES' TEACHING,*** it is referring to what we now have in the scriptures. We need to be loyal in spending time reading and studying the word. We need to have communion together and to pray together. This can all come about in a Sunday morning service.

By looking at the early church, this should give us an idea on how we are to devote ourselves to one another. [3]

If I care about someone, like my spouse, I try to show my love for her and my devotion and loyalty to her. How can I do this? Here are some thoughts:

I am concerned about her life; so concerned that I keep her in my constant prayers.
I want to spend time with her and treat her in a way that she recognizes my love for her.
This is not a one-time deal. It is a lifetime commitment, not only in public, but also in private.
I must treat her with respect; not just when I feel like it, or when I think she is being nice to me.
I am to devote myself to doing good things for her.

I want the best Christian life for her as well as myself, so I try to be around fellow Christians and to be in the Word. As a Christian husband I am to be devoted to my wife. I am to love her just as much as I love myself. How do I love myself? I take care of all parts of my makeup: physical, mental and emotional. By taking care of myself in this manner, I need to take care of my wife the same way. I am also to forsake all others because of my love and devotion. [4]

This is the same devotion Christ expects of me:

First, devoted to Him, and Him alone
Second, devoted to my wife and family
And third, devoted to my Christian brothers

To say we are devoted to someone but not show it is false advertising. It is not what we really believe. The same way I show my devotion to my spouse is the same way I am to show devotion to my fellow Christians.

Devotion to one another should cause us to have the following actions in our life. We are to show loyalty in the following manners:

We will be there when we are needed.
We will stand with them as they go through life.
We will be steadfast in our loyalty.
We will pray for them.
We will encourage them to be in the Word.
We will love them with unconditional love.
We will spend time with them.
We will do good deeds for them.
We will encourage them to do good deeds in service of the Lord.
We will encourage them during good times and bad.

Are we loyal to our Christian friends? Are we showing love to our Christian friends? If so, this is devotion, and this is what we are commanded to do. [5]

QUESTIONS ON DEVOTED

1. What does devoted mean to you?

2. Whom are you devoted to?

3. What does it mean to be devoted to your Christian friends?

4. How do you show your devotion to your spouse? To your family? To the Lord?

5. How do you show devotion to your Christian brothers?

CHAPTER NINETEEN

FELLOWSHIP

1 JOHN 1:7, *BUT IF WE WALK IN THE LIGHT, AS HE IS IN THE LIGHT, WE HAVE FELLOWSHIP WITH ONE ANOTHER, AND THE BLOOD OF JESUS, HIS SON, PURIFIES US FROM ALL SIN.*

Webster defines fellowship as: *friendly association with others, companionship. A number of people associated together, a society, a membership of this. A community. A partnership.* [1]

Before we look at what is *fellowship of the believers*, let's look at what is *fellowship with the Lord.*

1 CORINTHIANS 1:9, *GOD, WHO HAS CALLED YOU INTO FELLOWSHIP WITH HIS SON JESUS CHRIST OUR LORD, IS FAITHFUL.*

Since we have answered the call, we have fellowship with the Lord.

> We have associated with Him.
> We have come together for a common purpose.
> We are called Christians.
> We are now a part of the kingdom of God.
> We have a partnership with the Lord.
> We have a partnership with all other Christians.

We have membership in a special group.
We share things together.
We learn and grow in the Lord. [2]

If we share, what do we share? We share Christ and each other. We share in the unity of the body of Christ.

Since we are partners with the Lord, what do we get out of this union? Paul explains it in **PHILIPPIANS 3:10–11,** *I WANT TO KNOW CHRIST AND THE POWER OF HIS RESURRECTION AND THE FELLOWSHIP OF SHARING IN HIS SUFFERINGS, BECOMING LIKE HIM IN HIS DEATH, AND SO, SOMEHOW, TO ATTAIN TO THE RESURRECTION FROM THE DEAD.* Paul is saying since we have been part of Christ's suffering and death, thus we too will have the same power of resurrection as Him, eternity with the Lord.

Paul also speaks to this in **ROMANS 6:4–5,** *WE WERE THEREFORE BURIED WITH HIM THROUGH BAPTISM INTO DEATH IN ORDER THAT, JUST AS CHRIST WAS RAISED FROM THE DEAD THROUGH THE GLORY OF THE FATHER, WE TOO MAY LIVE A NEW LIFE. IF WE HAVE BEEN UNITED WITH HIM LIKE THIS IN HIS DEATH, WE WILL CERTAINLY ALSO BE UNITED WITH HIM IN HIS RESURRECTION.*

Why quote all these verses? They show us our dividend, our reward for being part of the fellowship with the Lord. We are with Him and reap the reward of eternal life; our reward for being a member of the "church." We are now citizens of the kingdom of God.

John states in **1 JOHN 1:3–4,** *WE PROCLAIM TO YOU WHAT WE HAVE SEEN AND HEARD, SO THAT YOU ALSO MAY HAVE FELLOWSHIP WITH US. AND OUR FELLOWSHIP IS WITH THE FATHER AND WITH HIS SON, JESUS CHRIST. WE WRITE THIS TO MAKE OUR JOY COMPLETE.* [3]

John is saying not only do we have fellowship with the Lord, we have fellowship with each other, and this makes us joyful.

What is included in this fellowship and how does it come about? First, we have fellowship with the Holy Spirit. Paul, as he is ending his letter in **2 CORINTHIANS 13:14,** states *MAY THE GRACE OF THE LORD JESUS CHRIST, AND THE*

LOVE OF GOD, AND THE FELLOWSHIP OF THE HOLY SPIRIT BE WITH YOU ALL.

What does this mean? Since we are joined together in the fellowship of Jesus, we have fellowship with the Holy Spirit. This takes place when we become Christians.

> The Holy Spirit brings us together into one body, the church.
> We are one big fellowship for the purpose of following the Lord and doing what servants should do.
> We are to serve, honor and worship the Lord.
> To help this fellowship, the Holy Spirit gives us gifts to enhance the body. [4]

PHILIPPIANS 2:1–2A, Paul says *IF YOU HAVE ANY ENCOURAGEMENT FROM BEING UNITED WITH CHRIST, IF ANY COMFORT FROM HIS LOVE, IF ANY FELLOWSHIP WITH THE SPIRIT, IF ANY TENDERNESS AND COMPASSION, THEN MAKE MY JOY COMPLETE BY BEING LIKE-MINDED.*

Just like any other fellowship group, there are expectations. If I join a group, they expect me to attend meetings. This attendance shows I have an interest in the fellowship group. The same holds true when we become Christians. I should want to have fellowship with other believers. Be it Sunday morning service, small groups or a men's group, I need to be involved somehow. **HEBREWS 10:25A** tells the Hebrew Christians, *LET US NOT GIVE UP MEETING TOGETHER.* Do not make it a habit of skipping church but a habit of attendance. What is to be gained by giving up our only day off to be in a church? We can still be a Christian and stay at home, can't we? Yes, but why would we want to? Being with other Christians gives us encouragement. Friendships are developed. We become a part of the fellowship of believers. [5]

When writing about the church body, Paul says in **1 CORINTHIANS 12:12A,** *THE BODY IS A UNIT, THOUGH IT IS MADE UP OF MANY PARTS; AND THOUGH ALL ITS PARTS ARE MANY, THEY FORM ONE BODY.* The body is incomplete without all the parts together.

There are expectations to be a member of this group of believers. If we avoid these expectations, there should be consequences. Paul tells us in **1 CORINTHIANS 5:1–5** that a man was having sexual relations with his father's wife and the Corinthians should *PUT OUT OF YOUR FELLOWSHIP* this man. The reason? It was a blatant sin and a total disregard of grace. He was taking advantage of the Lord's grace and violating the father/son relationship. He could no longer be involved with the fellowship of believers. The man's feeling seemed to be, *I am saved so anything I do is all right.*   **[6]**

Why would Paul make such a big issue of getting the man out of the fellowship of Christians? He saw it as if they were condoning sin in their body of believers. There are expectations of this membership. Condoning sin cannot be a part of this body. We, as Christians, are not to be yoked with unbelievers. Paul says in **2 CORINTHIANS 6:14B**, *WHAT FELLOWSHIP CAN LIGHT HAVE WITH DARKNESS?*   **[7]**

Does this mean we are not to be with unbelievers? Absolutely not!
> How can we testify?
> How can we bring others to the Lord?
> How can we witness?

But we should not spend all our time with unbelievers. If we do, it would be easy to be led astray. As a past leader of a youth group, I knew it was very important to have more Christians in an outing than non-Christians to keep straying and temptation to a minimum.   **[8]**

We are to spend our main time with fellow Christians. Fellowship is the bond that unites all Christians.   **[9]**

GALATIANS 2:9 also talks about *THE RIGHT HAND OF FELLOWSHIP* that was extended to Paul and Barnabas from Peter and James as they took the gospel to the Gentiles. This was to show that they were united with the Lord as fellow Christians and united as Christian brothers. It showed a partnership as they worked together for the Lord even though they had very different ministries.

What does all this fellowship, that we are to show to one another, mean today? We are to see our fellow Christians as brothers, and we are to recognize that we are joined together as one body, one community, the body of Christ, the church. We are to spend time with our brothers in fellowship. In my church we have a big room known as the fellowship hall. I am sure other churches have a similar room. It is a place to be together with our Christian brothers.

> To eat together
> To enjoy each other's company

To encourage and show love for one another
Sometimes to cry together
To laugh together
To reminisce
To listen to concerns
To hear testimonies of what God has done and is doing in our lives   **[10]**

This is what we do as Christians in fellowship. It is special since the Holy Spirit is the one that holds us together. We can lean on each other as we deal with day to day struggles. This is why it is so important to have this fellowship and to abide in one another's company.

Look forward to the fellowship of believers. Spend time with your Christian friends. Get to know other Christians in your church so you can relate to their trials and their testimonies.

Personally, I *want* to be with my friends. I look for excuses to be together. I know their immediate families and their extended families. By doing this, they have now become my family as well. From these relationships, I know how to pray for them, and they pray for me. They give a shoulder for me to lean on and I do the same for them. We have so much in common; our love for the Lord and the love of our brothers in Christ. This is a bond that binds us together.

The great part about this fellowship is the relationships that are created over a lifetime. These relationships are held together by the Holy Spirit and will go on until we are called home.

Have you ever connected with friends that you have not seen for many years? Sometimes it is like you never parted. The Holy Spirit is the tie that binds, and we as Christians are tied together as *one with another* and with our Lord Jesus Christ.

QUESTIONS ON FELLOWSHIP

1. What does fellowship mean to you?

2. What and where is the kingdom of God?

3. Explain **1 JOHN 1:3.** Why is this so important?

4. Do you agree?

5. What benefit from fellowship do you receive from church attendance?

6. Why shouldn't we have fellowship with someone like Paul shows in **1 CORINTHIANS 5:1–5?** Has this type of issue come up within your church?

7. What does walking in the light have to do with fellowship with one another?

8. Have you seen this happen?

9. Do you agree?

10. What else comes out of our fellowship?

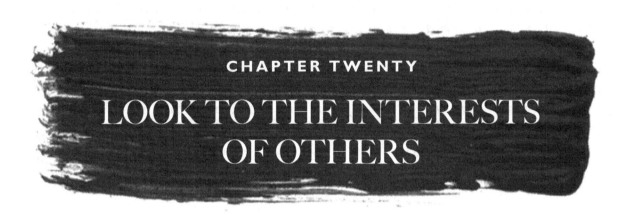

CHAPTER TWENTY

LOOK TO THE INTERESTS OF OTHERS

PHILIPPIANS 2:4, *EACH OF YOU SHOULD LOOK NOT ONLY TO YOUR OWN INTERESTS, BUT ALSO TO THE INTERESTS OF OTHERS.*

Just what is Paul telling us when he asks us to look out for the interests of others?

I don't have time for other people and what is going on in their lives. I am busy with my own life. I am busy with service to the church, choir, teaching Sunday School, my wife, my kids and grandkids, yard work, working in my garden, paying bills, and honey do list. How can I be involved with others? There is no time. Besides, if I try to look out for the interests of others, I will come across as nosy. I don't even know what it means to look out for the interests of others.

Notice the key word here—"I." We are not to live a world that is all about us and only us. We are to be a part of the lives of our Christian brothers. If we don't look out for the interests of others, we will be seen as selfish. Only looking out for ourselves. **[1]**

If we look back one verse to **PHILIPPIANS 2:3,** Paul says, ***DO NOTHING OUT OF SELFISH AMBITION OR VAIN CONCEIT, BUT IN HUMILITY CONSIDER OTHERS BETTER THAN YOURSELVES.***

First, if we are looking out for the interests of others we are not just looking inward to our own interests. The Lord does not want us to be selfish. We are to connect with others. This whole study talks about our relationship with "one another" and gives us directions on how to live our lives with our Christian brothers. It is about putting others first. We are to be Christ-like where He looked out for others even up to the point of giving His life.

If we are looking out for others' interests, we must find out what they are because life is not just about "me" or "you." For some this is hard to believe but it is true. If we consider others better than ourselves, we want to do things for them, to be a part of their lives. We want to know what they want before they even say it. We should know when it is time to celebrate a special occasion. We need to get to know our Christian brothers, know what their interests are, know about their families, how they spend their free time, how they met, how their lives are going and most of all how their Christian lives are progressing.

If we look out for the interests of others, they in turn should look out for our interests. By doing all this it makes the body more unified, which is one of the primary goals of all churches and for the Church of our Lord.

Why does looking out for the interests of others make us more unified? The church I grew up in and attend when we are in Ohio is a very diverse church. The prime reason is it is located in the town where Wright Patterson Air Force Base is located. Many people that come to church have no knowledge of the area, don't know anyone and do not know the background of the church. Some might only come for a year or two before they are off to another assignment. If I want to get to know them, there can be no hesitation on my part.

The church I attend in Florida has its own challenges. That church is very big, so it is possible to be in the background and still fit in (or hide). It is also a big "Snowbird" church, of which I am one. It is a challenge to get to know people and their interests if I don't try. I think to myself, why should I even try, we can only have a few months together. These are excuses for any of us to use to keep us from getting to know others and their interests. But they are just excuses. We cannot look out for others' interests if we do not get to know them. Be the one to break the ice. Yes, we are all called to look out for the interests of others, but some people are very shy, or want to be by themselves. It is not that we can't honor their privacy, but in most cases, it is not because they are recluses, but because they can't, won't or don't know how to open a conversation.

What interests should we know about our fellow Christians? The first step I take is to ask someone "Where are you from?" Why ask this? There are a couple of reasons. One, it is a great icebreaker. Most people want to talk about where they are from. Second, it gives me the opportunity to bring up something if I have been in their area. My wife and I have traveled within the U.S. a lot and know many restaurants and attractions. This allows conversation to flow easily. Ask about kids, why they are in the area, what do they do? All of this is just a short "getting to know you" tidbit. The next time we see that person, we now have something to talk about. We had a couple that had arrived from Hawaii and they were looking for a church. That afternoon our local paper had a big article on the island they came from. I cut it out and gave it to them on their next visit. No big deal, but they seemed to appreciate it. It all came from getting to know them on their first visit. This is just the first step to making a friend. There must be follow-ups involved. Paul is telling us to have more in common with our Christian brothers than just waving across the aisle to each other on a Sunday morning.

The second step to getting to know someone is asking about their family. Once we know that, we can ask how they are doing. This gives the other person a chance to open up a little, particularly if one of their children needs prayer.

An easy third step is asking what a person does for a living. It can give us an opportunity to send business their way if possible. This can be either from ourselves or from other friends. We can ask all kinds of questions about their job. Do they enjoy it? Are the hours long? What is the atmosphere at work? How did you get into that field? Etc. As we learn about the vocation of someone, their job might be similar to someone else within the body. Get them together, thus more people are involved with each other.

We can ask about others' hobbies. If there is mutual interest, so much the better. If we have no interest in their hobbies, there might be others within the church body that have that interest. If we know others' interests, we can hook them up with other people. If the wife quilts, hook her up with other quilters.

We can find out what they like to do with their leisure time. If they like to hike, tell them of trails in the area. If they like to eat out, tell them of good restaurants in the area and ones to avoid. Offer to go out with them. To me there is no better time to get to know someone than over a meal.

Ask what projects they are working on at their home. Offer to help, if it is appropriate, or put them in contact with someone who has gone through the same projects or a name of a reliable contractor.

Ask about their marriage and how they met. How they met the Lord, their Christian journey. Anything to get to know the person better. Notice, this all takes some of our time, but we are commanded to do this. Why? If we know something about others' lives, we will know how to pray for them and their families. We will know when to encourage them, when to build them up, when to just listen and not offer advice, when to help them in their weaknesses. By doing all of this, we hold each other accountable. It is beneficial to both parties. [2]

Speaking for my wife and myself, by doing this over our lifetime, we now have friends all over the world. A few years ago, we had a big wedding anniversary party at our home, and I invited a friend that was a business acquaintance that I knew slightly. He was very quiet and did not seem to have a lot of friends. When he arrived and saw how many people were there, he asked me if I was the mayor of the town. I took this as a compliment. Yes, we have a lot of friends, but it takes work to have a lot of friends. Do not take the responsibility lightly. If it takes opening up our homes, and we are comfortable doing it, then invite people in so we can get to know them better. Not everyone is comfortable doing this. [3]

To show a true interest in others shows them the love we have for them. As Christians, can we do anything less? This is the key to all the areas of looking out for the interests of others. As we get to know the interests of others, we will love them more and they us in turn. [4]

At a recent church party, I asked the attendees questions about some of their fellow church going friends. Questions like "Who was the quarterback of an undefeated football team?" "Who won awards for singing in state competition in a duet and a trio?" Plus, many other questions. Almost nobody knew any of the answers. If asked, would we? How well do we know our Christian friends? Their interests? Bury "self" and get to know others.

What are the benefits of knowing the interests of others?

Knowing how to pray for them.
We now have friends that can and will pray for us.
We will have friends for a lifetime.
Knowing I am following the Lord's command.
By getting to know the interests of others, we are building and unifying the Church.
It gets us away from "self."

Take time and get to know others within the church body. Don't put it off. [5]

QUESTIONS ON LOOK TO THE INTERESTS OF OTHERS

1. Explain the verse in your words. Do you think Paul is only talking about the interests within the church itself?

2. Do you know details about the lives of your Christian brothers?

3. Are you willing to open up your house?

4. Do you know the interests of your friends?

5. Are you prepared to put in the time and effort necessary to know the interests of your Christian brothers?

CHAPTER TWENTY-ONE

SHARE

ROMANS 12:13, *SHARE WITH GOD'S PEOPLE WHO ARE IN NEED. PRACTICE HOSPITALITY.*

Sharing happens in many forms. Paul gives the command to share with each other. We, as Christians, are to share with our brothers in need.

What is the main idea about sharing? The answer is in **2 CORINTHIANS 9:11–13.** *YOU WILL BE MADE RICH IN EVERY WAY SO THAT YOU CAN BE GENEROUS ON EVERY OCCASION, AND THROUGH US YOUR GENEROSITY WILL RESULT IN THANKSGIVING TO GOD. THIS SERVICE THAT YOU PERFORM IS NOT ONLY SUPPLYING THE NEEDS OF GOD'S PEOPLE BUT IS ALSO OVERFLOWING IN MANY EXPRESSIONS OF THANKS TO GOD. BECAUSE OF THE SERVICE BY WHICH YOU HAVE PROVED YOURSELVES, MEN WILL PRAISE GOD FOR THE OBEDIENCE THAT ACCOMPANIES YOUR CONFESSION OF THE GOSPEL OF CHRIST, AND FOR YOUR GENEROSITY IN SHARING WITH THEM AND WITH EVERYONE ELSE.* [1]

What are the keys to these verses?

These verses do not mean that a Christian will be made rich because they shared.
It does not mean that when you share with others you will get monetary riches back.
Sharing is not just for the rich.
We are to share with others besides our Christian brothers.
It does mean we will receive spiritual enrichment.
We need to be generous on every occasion.
Our generosity is a thanksgiving to God.
By being generous we are supplying the needs of others.
Our sharing is an outpouring of our thanks to God.
Because of our generosity, people will praise God for our obedience.
Generosity shows we are followers of Christ.
Sharing shows our obedience to the Lord.
Sharing with others shows our sincerity of fellowship with them.

Why does our giving show as a thanksgiving to God and why is that important? By giving we are showing our obedience and trust we have in God to not only supply our needs but allow us to supply others' needs. Giving is just a way of thanking God for all He has given to us. By contributing to the needs of others, it will allow others to be witnesses, they can spread the gospel. When we give to missions, we are a part of the results. **[2]**

HEBREWS 13:16, *AND DO NOT FORGET TO DO GOOD AND TO SHARE WITH OTHERS, FOR WITH SUCH SACRIFICES GOD IS PLEASED.* It pleases God when we share, and who doesn't want to please their Father? This also tells us we are not to just give out of our excess but give even if it means a sacrifice. When our giving is a sacrifice it shows that we trust God that He will provide. Sharing is not only for the rich, it is also for us that are just making a living and keeping up. We are responsible for what we have and how we share with others.

God has given us an example of how to give. **JOHN 3:16A,** *"FOR GOD SO LOVED THE WORLD THAT HE GAVE HIS ONE AND ONLY SON."* How did God give? He gave out of love. He gave what was needed for others. He did not hold back but gave to the benefit of others. He literally gave until it hurt. By God giving His son, He gave us the opportunity of new life.

By His giving, we are now His adopted sons and daughters. **COLOSSIANS 1:12B,** *HAS QUALIFIED YOU TO SHARE IN THE INHERITANCE OF THE SAINTS IN THE*

KINGDOM OF LIGHT. By His giving, we have been given hope, peace with God and a new family. Isn't it time to go back and review how we handle what the Lord has given us? Are we giving out of thanks or are we giving begrudgingly? Are we sharing at all?   **[3]**

In *A Christmas Carol*, Scrooge found out what the spirit of Christmas meant. We need to find what the spirit of sharing is all about. It is not "must I share with my brother?" But it should be "how can I help?" What is God pointing out to us to do that would give Him praise when we share? Show the love of God by giving in such a way that it would please Him.

There is a wide area of sharing. It can mean many things:

Food
Shelter
Clothing
A helping hand
Money
Time
Advice or counseling
A listening ear   **[4]**

We might even be thinking, "I have no problem sharing these things." But how about:

The TV remote
The last piece of mom's pie
Time with our spouse   **[5]**

Sharing can get very personal. Sharing is different from donation. If we give a donation it is not as personal as sharing. When we share, it is personal. We are involved in whatever we share. If we donate to the Salvation Army, we really have no connection to the gift. But if we share with someone, we see what happens to whatever we shared. When we share, the focus goes away from us to the person we affected with our gift.

Some verses give us direct instructions. In **LUKE 3:11,** John the Baptist tells the people this, ***"THE MAN WITH TWO TUNICS SHOULD SHARE WITH HIM WHO HAS NONE, AND THE ONE WHO HAS FOOD SHOULD DO THE SAME."*** Food and clothing are the essentials of life. John is not asking them to give away all their food and clothing, just what they have in excess. If someone needs clothing and we have a closet full, we are to give the excess. The same applies for food. This is called sharing. As for me, once or twice a year I clean out my closets and take the excess to Goodwill or to the Salvation Army. They both know how to distribute the clothing to the ones in need, I do not. It is amazing and sometimes embarrassing what I really have in excess. Do we have extra food? Take it to the local food bank or to a local mission. This can be done as an individual or by your church body. My church supports the local mission with gallons of milk on a monthly basis. We keep a tub for donations to the local FISH, and we also, once every two months, bring in prepared food for a dinner for the needy. If we want to share, there is some place for us to do it.

A local grocery store at Christmas has barrels for food to help the needy. We pay for the food and then drop it off in the barrels provided. A local television station has barrels for people to drop off used coats, called "coats for kids." People drop off winter coats, gloves and hats and a local dry cleaner cleans them for free, then they are donated to the ones that have a need. By taking part in these donations, our efforts clearly help the ones in need. If any community has neither of these ideas, maybe we could be the one to start it. Both are great charities for the needy.   [6]

Help is always needed. All we have to do is look around and then get involved. In this case it is not as if we are being asked to give all our possessions away, just our excess.

We are also called to share our faith. **PHILEMON 6,** *I PRAY THAT YOU MAY BE ACTIVE IN SHARING YOUR FAITH, SO THAT YOU WILL HAVE A FULL UNDERSTANDING OF EVERY GOOD THING WE HAVE IN CHRIST.* We must not think of sharing only material products. Sharing our faith might be the best thing we share. We are not to keep our faith to ourselves. It is not to be used only in the body, our local church. Our faith is not something we are to hide. If we have joy in our hearts from following the Lord, we should want to share with others what the Lord is doing for us. By sharing our faith there is no cost to us, only benefit.   [7]

Paul also gives direction to those who are rich. **1 TIMOTHY 6:17–19,** *COMMAND THOSE WHO ARE RICH IN THIS PRESENT WORLD NOT TO BE ARROGANT NOR TO PUT THEIR HOPE IN WEALTH, WHICH IS SO UNCERTAIN, BUT TO PUT THEIR HOPE IN GOD, WHO RICHLY PROVIDES US WITH EVERYTHING FOR OUR ENJOYMENT. COMMAND THEM TO DO GOOD, TO BE RICH*

IN GOOD DEEDS, AND TO BE GENEROUS AND WILLING TO SHARE. IN THIS WAY THEY WILL LAY UP TREASURE FOR THEMSELVES AS A FIRM FOUNDATION FOR THE COMING AGE, SO THAT THEY MAY TAKE HOLD OF THE LIFE THAT IS TRULY LIFE. Here the key word is *willing*. It takes a willingness to give away what in our minds is "rightfully ours." It's ours, why should we share with others? We get upset at our government when they tax us and then give it away to someone or something we don't deem deserving. We think we have already done our part to help those in need. In the book, *A Christmas Carol,* Scrooge says, "Are there no prisons, are there no workhouses?" Scrooge saw paying his taxes as adequate. His taxes went to prisons and workhouses, wasn't that enough? What more does he have to do? In his mind, he had done enough. It is very easy, in today's world, to think that by paying our taxes, we have done all we need to do, we have done our part for the needy. But for us to share, it has to be more than that.   [8]

As Christians, it should and must be different. First of all, our responsibility is to take care of our immediate family, then our extended family, then our church family and then all others. Have you talked to the pastor or to any of the deacons to see if there is a need? It is a matter of being pro-active versus reactive. My church takes a benevolence offering every time we have Communion, and then uses the fund to help the needy.

Those of us who are rich have a higher requirement of how we handle our riches. **LUKE 12:48B, *"FROM EVERYONE WHO HAS BEEN GIVEN MUCH, MUCH WILL BE DEMANDED; AND FROM THE ONE WHO HAS BEEN ENTRUSTED WITH MUCH, MUCH MORE WILL BE ASKED."*** If God has blessed particular people with riches, He is expecting more out of those so blessed. God has blessed some people in a way that they can give abundantly. They have been blessed by the Lord; thus the Lord expects them to bless others.

But I am not rich. I don't have that much. By anyone's imagination, I am not wealthy. But to others, I am seen as rich. The responsibility is upon us to take care of the ones who cannot take care of themselves.

We cannot always think of sharing as being dollars and cents. Sharing comes in many forms. It can be money or possessions, but it can also be time. Sometimes people just need someone to talk to or we need to give our time to organizations that need the help.

It can also mean sharing our family. Where I live many people come and go because of their connection to Wright Patterson Air Force Base. It is hard for people to be away from their families, probably more so for children. A small child was telling my father how much she missed her grandpa. My dad said, "While you are here, I will be your grandpa." The look on her face was precious. She was so pleased. He simply shared his love with her. He had plenty to give.

Sharing others' burdens is very important. There are areas in people's lives that are too heavy for them to carry alone. They need help dealing with their problems. Just listen and watch and then be proactive to share whatever is needed.

Sharing can involve such things as: laughter, sorrows, concerns, love, prayers, Bible studies, joy, celebrations and on and on.

We as Christians need to be aware of these needs so we can fill them. Sharing can mean anything involved with life.

Sharing for some does not come easy. Remember how it was trying to teach your child to share? They want nothing to do with it. Can't you still hear them yell, "mine." Sharing must be taught either by words or by deeds. Make sure we, as Christians, are good examples by words and by deeds, as we share with one another. Not only to our children, but to fellow Christians. **[9]**

We are commanded to share. We please the Lord when we share. Need we say more? **[10]**

QUESTIONS ON SHARE

1. Explain this verse in your words.

2. How does sharing make you feel?

3. What does God share with us? What will God share with us?

4. Add to this list.

5. Do these even count?

6. How can you do a better job of sharing?

7. When was the last time you shared your faith with someone? Does anyone have a story to share?

8. Can you relate to Scrooge?

9. How do we teach sharing to others?

10. Why is it so important for Christians to share with one another?

CHAPTER TWENTY-TWO

SPEAK WITH PSALMS, HYMNS AND SPIRITUAL SONGS

EPHESIANS 5:19, *SPEAK TO ONE ANOTHER WITH PSALMS, HYMNS AND SPIRITUAL SONGS. SING AND MAKE MUSIC IN YOUR HEART TO THE LORD.*

Doesn't this seem strange to you? Why would Paul tell people to go around singing to each other? Sounds like he expects us to live our lives as though we are in a musical or an opera. There are some people I do not want to hear singing. I heard them once, and once was enough.

Was this just for the Christians of those times? Was this just a Jewish thing or does it apply today? [1]

In the previous verses, **EPHESIANS 5:15–18,** Paul lays out the principles of a Christian life.

> Be careful how you live.
> Live as wise, not unwise.
> Make the most of every opportunity.

The days are evil.
Do not be foolish.
Understand the Lord's will.
Do not get drunk on wine.
Being drunk leads to debauchery.
Instead be filled with the Spirit.   [2]

In these verses Paul is giving directions to the Ephesians on how to live the life of a Christian. We are to live our lives in a wise manner. How do we do this?   [3]

For myself, using wisdom in my life means to stop and think what I am doing or saying before I do it. I cannot just go through life doing as "I" please, but instead I am to let the Holy Spirit lead and guide me in my daily living. We as Christians are to live our lives as the Lord leads. We need to gain knowledge and then use that knowledge for wisdom on how to live. The Ephesians, as new converts, would have no idea of what is expected of them in their new life with Christ. They did not have any examples of Christian living except for the Christian missionaries that came to speak to them. Paul lays it out for them. Paul wants them to use every opportunity to witness both by words and by their examples in the way they live.

If the days are evil, we need to show the opposite of evil. We need to show a Christ-like life. Then in **VERSE 18,** he tells them how not to live. If the days are evil, do not be part of it.

Paul tells them very plainly, "Do not get drunk." Why would Paul have to tell Christians not to get drunk? In those times the Ephesians had many festivals honoring the "god" Bacchus, the god of wine, thus drinking and getting drunk was just part of their lives. Paul is saying they needed to separate the festivals that were part of their old life as non-Christians from their lives today, which is to be filled with another spirit, the Holy Spirit. He tells them the reason for not getting drunk. It can lead to *debauchery.* A kind of old-fashioned word we do not hear today. Webster defines it as: indulgence in harmful and immoral pleasures.

We might not hear the word, but we see the effects of drunkenness. When we hear any of the following, our first thoughts are "alcohol must have been involved."

Spring break revelry
People acting out sexual immorality
Public nudity

A head on collision
A physical fight between partners
Frat parties
Wild parties
A man on a trip that involves adultery
A dumb stunt
Destruction of a hotel room by a celebrity
Anything where someone says, "Bet you've never seen this before."   [4]

These are all areas that when drinking, sin takes hold and man in his drunken condition does things he probably would not do if he were sober. People act differently when they drink. Some just get mean and hateful. Some want to come onto every woman or man in sight, while others draw away from their friends. Still others say things that they would never say if sober. Paul is saying to lead a Christian life, we must stay in control and not let the devil have a chance of controlling us. Do not let the "spirit" that is in alcoholic drinks become our controlling spirit. The Holy Spirit is to be in control of our lives. **GALATIANS 5:22–23B**, tells us the Holy Spirit brings to us the Fruit of the Spirit which includes, *LOVE, JOY, PEACE, PATIENCE, KINDNESS, GOODNESS, FAITHFULNESS, GENTLENESS AND SELF-CONTROL.* Isn't it better to be filled with the Spirit than filled with "spirits"?

What does drinking have to do with singing songs of praise? Usually if a person is drunk, they would not be singing spiritual songs or psalms. Instead they would be singing a vulgar song or thinking vulgar thoughts. Paul is telling the Ephesians to sing to the Lord. The Holy Spirit in our lives brings us joy. Let it out in a way that is pleasing to the Lord, in a way that is worshipful to Him.

Look at what Paul is saying in **EPHESIANS 5:19.** He says *SPEAK TO ONE ANOTHER WITH PSALMS.* This would be the Psalms of David. These were well known to the Jews, but Paul is writing to the Ephesians who were Gentiles. Many of the Psalms would be known to them. King David had a way with words. He was a man who loved the Lord and was loved by the Lord. He loved to write Psalms (songs) to the Lord. He or someone else would put his words to music. A different kind of music than we would think of today but still music. This is why we have so many Psalms set to music that we know and love today.   [5]

Every Sunday, churches around the world will sing Psalms that are put to music.

PSALM 8:9 *"How Majestic Is Your Name"*
PSALM 23:1 *"The Lord Is My Shepherd"*
PSALM 40:2 *"He Brought Me Out"*
PSALM 42:1 *"As the Deer"*
PSALM 48:1 *"Great Is the Lord"*
PSALM 51:7 *"Whiter Than Snow"*
PSALM 84:1 *"How Lovely Is Your Dwelling Place"*
PSALM 96:1: *"Sing to the Lord a New Song"* [6]

The Lord loves to hear these Psalms today just as He did when they were written.

We are also to speak with hymns. Most of the hymns we think about have been written in years past, but to today's congregations they have become blasé. But the words to the hymns still hold truth. Many hymns come from scripture. The Lord's Prayer and **JOHN 3:16** come to mind. Others come from a time in a person's life, be it good or bad, which causes them to put their feelings into words. They want to express their emotions. They are speaking to God in music. Such examples would be:

"Just As I Am"
"It Is Well With My Soul"
"I Am Thine O Lord"
"Take My Life"
"Great Is Thy Faithfulness"
"Rock of Ages" [7]

Horatio Spafford wrote the words to the beautiful hymn, *"It Is Well With My Soul"* (composed by Phillip Bliss) after losing his business and as he was crossing the ocean over the watery graves of his children. He expressed to God that his soul was at peace with God no matter what happened to him.

We are also to speak with spiritual songs. Spiritual songs are what might be termed contemporary music. Music of people writing their thoughts into choruses. This is music we can sing along with. Songs like:

"Give Thanks"
"Come, Now Is the Time to Worship"
"Shout to the Lord"
"Here I Am to Worship"
"Mighty to Save"
"Power of Your Love" [8]

What would a church service be without music so we can express our feelings to the Lord? This is exactly what we are doing when we sing in church. We are singing to God. We sing with many emotions, just like David when he wrote the Psalms. We sing with love, gratitude, praise, frustration, and understanding of who God is, with thanksgiving and with commitment. Make sure we have thought about the words before we sing to the Lord. Can we live out the words we are singing, or are they just words?

Some churches only sing the old hymns, and the new contemporary churches only want to sing the spiritual songs; but we have a God that loves variety. He loves to be praised with different music. Be careful of legalism and being rigid within the body, thus it seems to me we should be singing a variety of music to our Lord.

But music can be more than an outlet to praise God. Music can also be wisdom. Some of my best theological teachings as a child came to me in songs and probably stuck with me more than some of the teaching I received. See if you remember these songs and the message they bring to all of us?

"The B-I-B-L-E, yes that's the book for me. I stand alone on the Word of God, the B-I-B-L-E." Writer unknown.
"Deep and wide, there's a fountain flowing deep and wide." Written by Sidney Cox.
"Jesus loves me, this I know, for the Bible tells me so." Written by Anna B. Warner.
"Rolled away. Rolled away. Rolled away. All the burdens of my heart rolled away." Written by Walter D. Kallenbach.
"Jesus loves the little children, all the children of the world. Red and yellow, black and white, they are precious in His sight. Jesus loves the little children of the world." Written by C. Herbert Woolston.

For most of us, we can still remember the motions going along with the songs. This is the power of music. These songs are still with us today, and they have deep meaning.

But does Paul, in his writing of **EPHESIANS 5:19,** really expect us to go around singing to each other? No, I don't think so. **[9]**

If it doesn't mean that, what does it mean? I think it means we are to have a song in our heart; a song that is constantly giving praise to the Lord. We are to be constantly praising the Lord and giving Him thanks. What better way is there than having a song in our heart? If we have a spiritual song in our hearts, when we speak to our fellow Christians we will do it with a soft versus hard word—with love versus anger. **COLOSSIANS 3:16,** *LET THE WORD OF CHRIST DWELL IN YOU RICHLY AS YOU TEACH AND ADMONISH ONE ANOTHER WITH ALL WISDOM, AND AS YOU SING PSALMS, HYMNS AND SPIRITUAL SONGS WITH GRATITUDE IN YOUR HEARTS TO GOD.* This speaks to a change of attitude when we are trying to help our fellow Christians in their lives. It is hard to be angry and mistreat someone while you are singing a spiritual song. Music seems very important to the Lord and should not be looked at as just a "filler" in our church service. The Word of God can come through songs and dwell in us as well as if we are taught the word or hear it in a sermon.

EPHESIANS 5:19B says to *SING AND MAKE MUSIC IN YOUR HEART TO THE LORD.* We are to have a song in our heart that reflects our love for the Lord; just because we are not musically talented does not mean we shouldn't have, and can't have, a song in our heart. It is not just the tune but the words that can be important. **[10]**

My wife talks about waking up with a song in her head. Most times it is a spiritual song. How can we not wake up happy when we have a song on our mind that is giving praise to the Lord? We are told in scriptures to have our minds on spiritual things. Music can be a key to this. Music can bring to mind scripture or words of praise.

One of the problems with music is that it is everywhere. It is all around us, whether we are in our car, in a store, using an iPad, or playing a CD. With that being said, there are all types of music out there. Some, we or our children should not listen to. Not that we must only listen to spiritual music at all times. Surely the Lord has gifted many people with the ability to write all kinds of music, be it classical, jazz, rock, or country. **[11]**

We are to have a song in our heart. When we have a song in our heart it is going to our innermost thoughts. If it is Christian music, our thoughts are on the Lord and it is hard to be in a bad mood, hard to be stressed, and hard to let the worries of the day overcome us. Use music to remind you of the Lord and all he has done and is doing for you. **[12]**

Music in our lives can be key to many of our innermost feelings. A dear friend of mine who works in divorce care, said there are four keys to seeing if kids are doing okay after a divorce. Watch to see if the children are:

Eating
Sleeping
Playing
Singing

The bonus is, are they singing? If all of these happen, then they should be okay.

What better way to go through life that with a smile on your face, love throughout, and a song in your heart. Be joyful and give thanks to the Lord.

QUESTIONS ON PSALMS, HYMNS AND SPIRITUAL SONGS

1. Does this apply today?

2. Do these principles still apply today?

3. How would you answer this?

4. What would you add to this list?

5. Who are the Gentiles?

6. How many other songs can you think of that come from the Bible?

7. How many other hymns can you name that have meaning to you?

8. How many choruses come to your mind?

9. Does it really mean to sing to each other or talk to one another using Bible verses?

10. Do you have a song in your heart? What would that song be?

11. Do your kids know the words to today's secular music? Is that good or bad? Do kids learn from songs and then act them out?

12. Why should we do this? Does singing teach you anything?

CHAPTER TWENTY-THREE

FAITHFUL

3 JOHN 5, *DEAR FRIEND, YOU ARE FAITHFUL IN WHAT YOU ARE DOING FOR THE BROTHERS, EVEN THOUGH THEY ARE STRANGERS TO YOU.* [1]

Notice, this is not a direct "one another," but John is speaking to Christians and saying they are faithful to each other, even brothers that are strangers.

Webster defines faithful as: *being loyal, trustworthy, and conscientious.*

When a Christian wants to learn what it means to be faithful, we need to look at the faithfulness of God and the faithfulness of Jesus, so let's look at what the Bible has to say about this area of faithfulness.

DEUTERONOMY 7:9, *KNOW THEREFORE THAT THE LORD YOUR GOD IS GOD; HE IS THE FAITHFUL GOD, KEEPING HIS COVENANT OF LOVE TO A THOUSAND GENERATIONS OF THOSE WHO LOVE HIM AND KEEP HIS COMMANDS.*

PSALM 33:4, *FOR THE WORD OF THE LORD IS RIGHT AND TRUE; HE IS FAITHFUL IN ALL HE DOES.*

PSALM 100:5, *FOR THE LORD IS GOOD AND HIS LOVE ENDURES FOREVER; HIS FAITHFULNESS CONTINUES THROUGH ALL GENERATIONS.*

PSALM 117:2, *FOR GREAT IS HIS LOVE TOWARD US, AND THE FAITHFULNESS OF THE LORD ENDURES FOREVER.*

PSALM 145:13B, *THE LORD IS FAITHFUL TO ALL HIS PROMISES AND LOVING TOWARD ALL HE HAS MADE.*

What can be gleaned from these verses? How do we see God and His faithfulness?

> He is a faithful God.
> He is faithful in all He does.
> His faithfulness continues forever.
> He is faithful in His love for us and for keeping His promises.

What a wonderful God we have! He sets a wonderful example for us to follow as we are faithful to our Christian brothers. We need to be faithful to our brothers forever in all we do. We need to keep our promises to them. We are to have love for them, and this love will bring about faithfulness. We also need to be faithful to future generations of our friends. Not only to them but to their children and their children's children.   [2]

What does the Bible have to say about the faithfulness of Jesus?

HEBREWS 2:17, *FOR THIS REASON HE HAD TO BE MADE LIKE HIS BROTHERS IN EVERY WAY, IN ORDER THAT HE MIGHT BECOME A MERCIFUL AND FAITHFUL HIGH PRIEST IN SERVICE TO GOD, AND THAT HE MIGHT MAKE ATONEMENT FOR THE SINS OF THE PEOPLE.*

HEBREWS 3:2, *HE WAS FAITHFUL TO THE ONE WHO APPOINTED HIM, JUST AS MOSES WAS FAITHFUL IN ALL GOD'S HOUSE.*

REVELATION 19:11, *I SAW HEAVEN STANDING OPEN AND THERE BEFORE ME WAS A WHITE HORSE, WHOSE RIDER IS CALLED FAITHFUL AND TRUE. WITH JUSTICE HE JUDGES AND MAKES WAR.* This is speaking of Jesus.

What can be gleaned from these verses about the faithfulness of Jesus?

1. He was made like us and He was faithful to the service of God. He is our high priest, our go between. By doing this He made atonement for our sins as He faithfully gave His life for our salvation.

2. He was faithful to His father, just like Moses.

3. Jesus is called faithful and true and He will judge and also make war on the sinners who have not been faithful to Him. **[3]**

In **3 JOHN 5,** John is praising the church and telling them how proud he is of how they have taken care of strangers. Fellow Christians are passing through the area and are being taken in by their Christian brothers. This would include setting up sleeping arrangements and feeding them for as long as they stayed. They could be evangelists like Paul, missionaries, teachers or just fellow Christians going through the area. John is praising their hospitality and their faithfulness to their hospitality.

But it can mean more than this. We do know that many of the new Christians would donate money to be taken to Jerusalem, where times were tough. The Jerusalem Christians had little food or money and were being persecuted and even killed. Paul saw faithfulness in other Christians as they dug in their pockets and supported them with money. **[4]**

ACTS 24:17, *"AFTER AN ABSENCE OF SEVERAL YEARS, I CAME TO JERUSALEM TO BRING MY PEOPLE GIFTS FOR THE POOR AND TO PRESENT OFFERINGS."* Notice Paul says my people. What did he mean by that? His fellow Christians. Where did this money come from? Not from Paul himself but from people he had converted to Christianity. These groups did not know the Jerusalem Christians but were faithful and pleased to be a part of giving, so Paul could take their offering to help them out. **ROMANS 15:26, *FOR MACEDONIA AND ACHAIA WERE PLEASED TO MAKE A CONTRIBUTION FOR THE POOR AMONG THE SAINTS IN JERUSALEM.***

But Paul goes even farther in why they would send money. **ROMANS 15:27, *THEY WERE PLEASED TO DO IT, AND INDEED THEY OWE IT TO THEM. FOR IF THE GENTILES HAVE SHARED IN THE JEWS' SPIRITUAL BLESSINGS, THEY OWE IT TO THE JEWS TO SHARE WITH THEM THEIR MATERIAL BLESSINGS.*** We have an obligation to our fellow Christians to be faithful in our giving. This would include being faithful to the local church so it can do the tasks the Lord has laid on it, and also to being faithful to other areas of need like the missionaries that the church supports or local charities that the local body is involved with, such as FISH, a place to donate food for the needy. We also see faithfulness in the Old Testament, **2 CHRONICLES 31:11–12A,** *HEZEKIAH GAVE ORDERS TO PREPARE STOREROOMS IN THE TEMPLE OF THE LORD, AND THIS WAS DONE. THEN THEY FAITHFULLY BROUGHT IN THE CONTRIBUTIONS, TITHES AND DEDICATED GIFTS.* Personally, I have always seen tithes I give to be used by the local church. Other contributions and dedicated gifts of money go toward areas outside the church or a special designated area such as a building fund within the body. This would be money over and above our regular tithes. We are to be faithful in our giving. Be faithful:

As you give to your church.
As you support the youth and children's work.
In your support of missions. Paul is our example.
As others go out on work teams or on mission trips.

There will be times when we are called upon to faithfully give our own friends and fellow Christians money to help them out of a tough area. Do it with a pleasing attitude. Paul says in **2 CORINTHIANS 8:7,** *BUT JUST AS YOU EXCEL IN EVERYTHING— IN FAITH, IN SPEECH, IN KNOWLEDGE, IN COMPLETE EARNESTNESS AND IN YOUR LOVE FOR US—SEE THAT YOU ALSO EXCEL IN THIS GRACE OF GIVING.* [5]

Our faithfulness to our fellow Christians should also entail praying for our friends and their families. To pray for someone must also include knowing them in such a way that we know their prayer needs. Praying for someone shows our love for them, and it shows we are faithful in talking to the Lord about their lives. Our prayers should also include praying for their families as well. Don't you love it when someone prays for you and your family? I think we all do.

Be faithful to pray for:
Your pastor and fellow leaders within the local body.
Your fellow Christian friends.
The local prayer list.
Fellow workers in your church. [6]

When I think of faithfulness in the Bible, the friendship of David and Jonathan comes to mind. Jonathan was faithful to David even when he knew it meant giving up his right of becoming the next king. Their friendship was based on their love for each other. Jonathan was so faithful in his friendship that he betrayed his own father to tell David that Saul was going to kill him. **1 SAMUEL 20:17** tells us *AND JONATHAN HAD DAVID REAFFIRM HIS OATH OUT OF LOVE FOR HIM, BECAUSE HE LOVED HIM AS HE LOVED HIMSELF.* This is our example of how we are to be faithful to our friends.   [7]

To be faithful to someone means we are to be loyal. This is just the opposite of betrayal. Think of our wedding vows. In our promises we make, it is the underlying current of being faithful. If one person betrays the other, all the other promises go out the window. This is how it is with our faithfulness of one to another. The faithfulness we have must be constant. It must last forever. There must be no lapses in our loyalty, our commitment, and our steadfastness to our friends. We are faithful even when they irritate us, when they don't do what we expect. We should treat our friends' faithfulness just as we treat our wedding vows. They are for a lifetime.   [8]

God speaks of His loyalty and friendship to us, but He also speaks of our actions and faithfulness to Him.

We are to serve him faithfully, through loyalty in our service. **1 SAMUEL 12:24,** *BUT BE SURE TO FEAR THE LORD AND SERVE HIM FAITHFULLY WITH ALL YOUR HEART; CONSIDER WHAT GREAT THINGS HE HAS DONE FOR YOU.*

The Lord is loving and faithful but there are conditions. **PSALM 25:10,** *ALL THE WAYS OF THE LORD ARE LOVING AND FAITHFUL FOR THOSE WHO KEEP THE DEMANDS OF HIS COVENANT.* We are to follow the directions of the Lord. By following His commands, it shows we love Him.

By being faithful to the Lord, He will guard our lives. He will deliver us from wicked people. **PSALM 97:10,** *LET THOSE WHO LOVE THE LORD HATE EVIL, FOR HE GUARDS THE LIVES OF HIS FAITHFUL ONES AND DELIVERS THEM FROM THE HAND OF THE WICKED.* Our responsibility is to love the Lord.

The Lord gives us protection and guards us. **PROVERBS 2:8,** *FOR HE GUARDS THE COURSE OF THE JUST AND PROTECTS THE WAY OF HIS FAITHFUL ONES.*

On this area of faithfulness, I think Christians are given direction when the Lord gives the disciples the parable of the talents. Jesus says in **MATTHEW 25:21,** *"HIS MASTER REPLIED, 'WELL DONE, GOOD AND FAITHFUL SERVANT! YOU HAVE BEEN FAITHFUL WITH A FEW THINGS; I WILL PUT YOU IN CHARGE OF MANY THINGS. COME AND SHARE YOUR MASTER'S HAPPINESS!'"* Jesus is saying because of the servant's faithfulness, there is a reward and the servant is given more responsibility. Take this to heart. The more we are faithful, the more trust we receive from the Master. Plus, we make our Master happy. But with this trust, there is a caveat, we must prove ourselves faithful.

1 CORINTHIANS 4:2, *NOW IT IS REQUIRED THAT THOSE WHO HAVE BEEN GIVEN A TRUST MUST PROVE FAITHFUL.* [9]

We will receive a reward for our faithfulness. **REVELATION 2:10,** *"DO NOT BE AFRAID OF WHAT YOU ARE ABOUT TO SUFFER. I TELL YOU, THE DEVIL WILL PUT SOME OF YOU IN PRISON TO TEST YOU, AND YOU WILL SUFFER PERSECUTION FOR TEN DAYS. BE FAITHFUL EVEN TO THE POINT OF DEATH, AND I WILL GIVE YOU THE CROWN OF LIFE."*

Faith is not something we just talk about. It requires actions of some sort, be it praying, giving of money, suffering, being faithful in the tasks the Lord has given us, or following the Lord's commands. Be steadfast to our Christian brothers. Value their faithfulness.

HEBREWS 11:1, *NOW FAITH IS BEING SURE OF WHAT WE HOPE FOR AND CERTAIN OF WHAT WE DO NOT SEE.* Our examples of faith come from all the believers who came before us, all the way back to Adam. We must be faithful in such a way to show others we have our faith in the Lord. We believe in Him and His promises. We can count on Him. Now we must be people others can count on, steadfast and loyal.

A strange thing to me is when I looked up the word *faithful,* Webster also used this description: *the faithful, true believers (especially Muslims), and loyal supporters.*

Why would Webster's dictionary use Muslims as an example? Aren't Christians as faithful as Muslims? Evidently Christians are not seen this way. Believers, yes, totally faithful, no. This must be changed in our lives to be what the Lord has planned for us. [10]

QUESTIONS ON FAITHFUL

1. Explain being faithful.

2. What does God's faithfulness mean to you?

3. How did Jesus show his faithfulness?

4. Does this happen today?

5. Why is our faithfulness in our giving so important?

6. Why is faithfulness in praying so vital to our relationship with our Christian brothers?

7. What do you remember about Jonathan and David?

8. Have you ever had friends who have been unfaithful to you?

9. How do **MATTHEW 25:21** and **1 CORINTHIANS 4:2** apply to us today? Or do they?

10. Are you steadfast in your faithfulness to others? How do you show it?

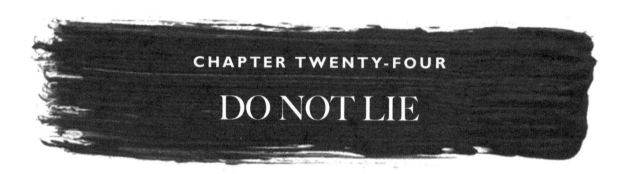

CHAPTER TWENTY-FOUR

DO NOT LIE

COLOSSIANS 3:9A, *DO NOT LIE TO EACH OTHER.*

EPHESIANS 4:25, *THEREFORE EACH OF YOU MUST PUT OFF FALSEHOOD AND SPEAK TRUTHFULLY TO HIS NEIGHBOR, FOR WE ARE ALL MEMBERS OF ONE BODY.*

Being truthful as a Christian is extremely important as we deal with others in our day to day lives. But it is essential when we interact with our Christian brothers and sisters. But why is it so important to be truthful as Christians?

When we look at the life of Christ, we see how important truth is to Him. He uses the phrase *"I TELL YOU THE TRUTH"* over twenty five times in the Bible. For example, Jesus says in **MATTHEW 8:10,** *WHEN JESUS HEARD THIS, HE WAS ASTONISHED AND SAID TO THOSE FOLLOWING HIM, "I TELL YOU THE TRUTH, I HAVE NOT FOUND ANYONE IN ISRAEL WITH SUCH GREAT FAITH."* [1]

What does it mean to us when we see this quote from Jesus in the Bible? It means we can trust what He says all the time and every time, no exceptions. This can be unlike some of our dealings with others. Telling the truth to others is critical in a relationship. If we cannot believe someone, we want no part of them since we do not know when they are telling the truth. [2]

In today's society we have become so used to putting up with people that embellish the truth or tell us what we want to hear that sometimes we forget how important it is not to lie. When we hear a politician talking, can we believe every word we are hearing? No one is gullible enough to believe everything they say, but we accept what they say because it sounds good. When we hear a used car salesman say, "It was only driven by a little old lady on Sunday," can we believe it? Absolutely not! How about the internet? We can believe everything we read on the internet, right? Wrong! It is so bad that there is a web site called Snoops.com just for fact checking. We have come to the point where we cannot even believe the evening news broadcast. [3], [4]

I don't know about your family, but in mine I could get away with some things I did wrong, but if I lied to either parent I was in big trouble. Why? Truth is important in a family relationship. We should be able to count on each other to tell the truth. This must hold true in our relationships with our Christian family. We must have confidence that we are hearing the truth from our brothers in Christ.

Think back to the beginning with Adam and Eve. When caught in their sin, God gave them the opportunity to tell Him the truth. Instead Adam first blamed Eve and then Eve blamed the serpent. "It was not my fault for what happened. He made me do it." Would we as parents believe this excuse if our children said it to us? Neither did God. He is truth and knows the truth.

Once a person tells us one lie, it is hard to believe anything they tell us from then on. It makes us wonder if they are telling the truth or a lie.

One of the comedic characters on local radio, WLW 700 AM radio out of Cincinnati, used to say, "This time, I'm being honest with you." This is how we look at people who are caught in a lie. Is this the time they are being honest with us, or was it the last time, or the next time? A relationship like this will never last. How long can a relationship last that is built on lies? Not very long at all. A marriage must be built on truthfulness. Truthfulness that is always true every time. [5]

If you had a pastor that brought messages that were not true, how long would you attend that church? If you had a good friend who lied to you, would you keep the friendship? If you dated a person and found out some of the things they told you were lies, would you continue the relationship? If you had a boss that was a habitual liar, would you ever believe anything that he told you? Have you ever been around someone that would rather tell a lie than the truth? Even when it made no difference. I worked with someone like this, and the person received no respect from anyone. Rightfully so. She could not tell the truth because the truth was not in her. She would tell a lie when it did not make a bit of difference. [6]

Jesus told of people like this in His time in **JOHN 8:42–45.** In **VERSE 44** Jesus says to the Jews, *"YOU BELONG TO YOUR FATHER, THE DEVIL, AND YOU WANT TO CARRY OUT YOUR FATHER'S DESIRE. HE WAS A MURDERER FROM THE BEGINNING, NOT HOLDING TO THE TRUTH, FOR THERE IS NO TRUTH IN HIM."* He then goes on to compare these people to Satan. *"WHEN HE LIES, HE SPEAKS HIS NATIVE LANGUAGE, FOR HE IS A LIAR AND THE FATHER OF LIES."* Here is the crux of why it is important for Christians not to lie. If Satan is the father of lies, and Jesus is the father of truth, who is our father? What is coming out of our mouths, the lies of Satan or the truth of Jesus? The truth, the whole truth, and nothing but the truth comes from God through His Son, Jesus. As Christians, we must not lie in our words and in our lives. Both are testimonies of who is our father. As followers of Christ our word must be true to our Christian brothers and all others we are acquainted with as we live our lives.

Have you ever heard the quote, "If his lips are moving, he is lying"? This is Satan.

Truth is the basis of the Christian religion. **TITUS 1:2B** says *WHICH GOD, WHO DOES NOT LIE,* and **HEBREWS 6:18B** says *IT IS IMPOSSIBLE FOR GOD TO LIE.*

Jesus, our Savior, says in **JOHN 14:6,** *"I AM THE WAY AND THE TRUTH AND THE LIFE."* When speaking about the Holy Spirit, Jesus says in **JOHN 16:13A,** *"BUT WHEN HE, THE SPIRIT OF TRUTH, COMES, HE WILL GUIDE YOU INTO ALL TRUTH.* The Trinity knows only the truth and brings the truth to us. We, as Christians, are only to speak the truth.

In **JOHN 18:37–38A,** Pilate asks Jesus if He is a king. Jesus answers, *"YOU ARE RIGHT IN SAYING I AM A KING. IN FACT, FOR THIS REASON I WAS BORN, AND FOR THIS I CAME INTO THE WORLD, TO TESTIFY TO THE TRUTH. EVERYONE ON THE SIDE OF TRUTH LISTENS TO ME."* Pilate replies, *"WHAT IS TRUTH?"* As a politician and a leader, Pilate was not used to hearing the truth. We, as Christians, know the truth. John writes in **1 JOHN 2:21,** *I DO NOT WRITE TO YOU BECAUSE YOU DO NOT KNOW THE TRUTH, BUT BECAUSE YOU DO KNOW IT AND BECAUSE NO LIE COMES FROM THE TRUTH.* He is speaking about the Gospel. We know the truth of the Gospel, so truth is in us. This is what needs to come out at all times.

It is important for Christians to always be truthful. If we know the truth, we should speak it. If we lie, we create many problems:

> We must remember our lies so the truth does not come out by mistake.
> We might implicate others in our lies.
> If someone knows the truth, we will be exposed in our lies, thus we are exposed as liars.
> If we are found out, we lose the trust of others.
> One lie can start us on a future of lies. One lie leads to another. Habitual liars started with just one lie. [7]

Lying sears our conscience. We get used to it. **1 TIMOTHY 4:2,** *SUCH TEACHINGS COME THROUGH HYPOCRITICAL LIARS, WHOSE CONSCIENCES HAVE BEEN SEARED AS WITH A HOT IRON.*

We are not only lying to someone, we are lying to God as well as ourselves. We give Satan a foothold in our lives. It is all he needs. He will keep reminding us of what liars we are, thus what sinners we are.

We can also lie when we say we love God yet hate our brother. **1 JOHN 4:20,** *IF ANYONE SAYS, "I LOVE GOD," YET HATES HIS BROTHER, HE IS A LIAR. FOR ANYONE WHO DOES NOT LOVE HIS BROTHER, WHOM HE HAS SEEN, CANNOT LOVE GOD, WHOM HE HAS NOT SEEN.* We are to love our brothers as we love the Lord. Who are our brothers? Fellow Christians.

Another liar is the person who denies that Jesus is the Christ. **1 JOHN 2:22A,** *WHO IS THE LIAR? IT IS THE MAN WHO DENIES THAT JESUS IS THE CHRIST.* In today's world, this would include a multitude of people. Many see Jesus as a good man, a great teacher, a prophet, but they do not see Him as the Christ, the Son of God. [8]

Another way to lie is by omission. Either we don't tell the whole truth or we just don't speak up at all. Children are great at this, so we cannot be child-like when it comes to truth. It can be very frustrating when someone says, "you never asked me exactly that question," when in reality they kind of went around what you wanted to know. This is an area that is very frustrating to the police. We are to tell the truth, the whole truth, and nothing but the truth. We are to speak as if we are under oath all the time. **ROMANS 3:23,** *FOR ALL HAVE SINNED AND FALL SHORT OF THE GLORY OF GOD.*

We also lie to ourselves in many ways. We can say "I have no sin in my life." This would be a lie. **1 JOHN 1:8,** *IF WE CLAIM TO BE WITHOUT SIN, WE DECEIVE OURSELVES AND THE TRUTH IS NOT IN US.* We look at others and the sin in their lives and think to ourselves "thank goodness we are not like that person." But we are. We all sin and fall short of the glory of God.

We don't want to sin, but we do. Even Paul says this. He does what he doesn't want to do and doesn't do what he wants to do. (See **ROMANS 7:15–20.**) We are lying to ourselves when we see ourselves as perfect. We are to continue growing in the Lord until he comes again. Then we will be made perfect; but not on earth in our lifetime.

The way we live our lives in sin can also be lies. **1 JOHN 1:6** explains it this way, *IF WE CLAIM TO HAVE FELLOWSHIP WITH HIM YET WALK IN DARKNESS, WE LIE AND DO NOT LIVE BY THE TRUTH.* The life we live is our testimony. It is not only what we say, but what we do. Are we holding back part of our lives from the Lord that is sinful because we like it and think it makes no difference? Is there anything more frustrating than a hypocrite—one who says one thing then does another? Do not be this person. Try telling our children to do what we say and not what we do. It won't work. They will see the real truth in the way we live. [9]

Do you know the commands of the Lord? Do you keep them? **1 JOHN 2:4** explains it this way, *THE MAN WHO SAYS, "I KNOW HIM," BUT DOES NOT DO WHAT HE COMMANDS IS A LIAR, AND THE TRUTH IS NOT IN HIM.* We are to study the Bible so we know what the Lord expects from us. We are to commit ourselves to following these commands. We are to listen to the Holy Spirit as He speaks to us in our daily walk so we know what we are supposed to do and not supposed to do.

We can be untruthful to the Lord in the way we handle our money. We make a vow to the Lord to give so much, and then we fall back on that vow. **ECCLESIASTES 5:5** tells us, *IT IS BETTER NOT TO VOW THAN TO MAKE A VOW AND NOT FULFILL IT.* We say, Lord, all I have is yours, then dishonor Him by not giving to Him to help build

His church. Or we make a pledge to give so much and then never fulfill it. This is lying to the Lord. A vow to the Lord is not to be taken lightly. **[10]**

Also, to take credit for money given to the Lord that we did not give or what we promised is a lie. Remember the story of Ananias and Sapphira? It was their right to do what they wanted with the money of the property they sold, but then they lied about giving all of it to the Lord when in reality they kept some back. As Peter said in **ACTS 5:4B,** *YOU HAVE NOT LIED TO MEN BUT TO GOD.* Their lying cost them their lives.

Lying is so easy, we don't even realize we are doing it in our daily lives.

"I will pray for you."
Then we don't.
"I will be in touch."
Then we aren't.
"Lord, it is a new year and I will read my Bible daily."
Then we don't.
"Lord, if you make this happen, I will do such and such."
Then we don't.
"Lord, if you get me out of this mess, I will never do this again."
When He does, we don't.
"I will treat all with respect and love."
Then we don't.
"I will be nicer to my spouse."
Then we aren't.
"Lord, help me spend more time with my family."
Then we make excuses.
"I will follow the words of the hymns I sing on Sunday."
Then we don't. **[11]**

This is a difficult subject because lying creeps into our lives. But we are commanded not to lie to each other, and we are also commanded to tell each other the truth. It is key to Christians to be able to trust each other. What we hear from our Christian brothers must be true. Let the Holy Spirit speak and guide us in truthfulness. Let Him guide us to be more Christ-like. Remember, it is key to not lie to each other by the ways we live our lives.
[12], [13], [14]

QUESTIONS ON DO NOT LIE

1. Why would Jesus say this so often?

2. Do you agree or disagree? Why or why not?

3. Some people do not see a problem with a politician lying, do you?

4. Why do we not hold some people to telling the truth?

5. Is truthfulness a key to your marriage?

6. Do you know someone like this? Do you spend much time with them? What are your feelings about them?

7. What other problems come from lying?

8. Who would this be today?

9. How important is the way you live your life when it comes to lying?

10. What other vows to you are sacred?

11. Why is it so important not to lie to yourself?

12. Do you always tell the truth? If not, why not?

13. Can people trust you? Why would you say so?

14. Why is it so important to tell the truth as a Christian?

CHAPTER TWENTY-FIVE

BITING AND DEVOURING

GALATIANS 5:15, *IF YOU KEEP ON BITING AND DEVOURING EACH OTHER, WATCH OUT OR YOU WILL BE DESTROYED BY EACH OTHER.* [1]

A strong warning from Paul, but what does he really mean and why would he have to tell Christians not to do these things?

What does it mean to "bite" each other? When I think of biting, I think of a couple of different things. Mosquitoes—they bite, and they can irritate the dickens out of you. It seems when you are outside in the summer, no matter what you do, you will get bit. You try to get away and they turn up no matter where you go. The bite doesn't really hurt too much because the bites are small. The bites irritate you for a few days, but the bite itself can bring on complications. Many diseases are carried by mosquitoes. The diseases can kill. The little bites can become life threatening.

Another pest that comes to mind is the fire ant. If you live in the South, you know about their bites. First you will feel one bite and when you look down, you are covered in ants and all of them are biting you. The bites keep itching and then get infected. Nothing good comes from a fire ant bite.

Thinking about other things that bite, I think of snakes. Their bites can be venomous. Their bite can kill you. Dogs bite and they can inflict great pain on people. But what is Paul talking about when he says we are to keep from biting each other? [2]

Are people like a mosquito or a fire ant? Are we really like a dog or a snake? Sometimes we can be like these pests. What do we do when insects try to bite us? We swat at them. We want them to get away from us. Same for snakes and dogs. How does this relate to people? How does this relate to my Christian brothers?

When a person bites us, what are they doing? They are saying things that irritate us. They sometimes seem like they are nitpicking. They say things like:

Who does he think he is?
Why does he think he is in charge?
Does she know what she really looks like?
Let me tell you what that person is really like.
They should not be the one to be in that position.
They are the pastor's pets.
They are not who you think they are.

We see this as backbiting. They are friends to our face but bite us from behind. Not much hurts worse than when a friend says something behind our back. A friend we trust. A friend we think will defend us from others. [3]

What happens when friends bite us? We have the tendency to bite back, and sometimes we want to bite them harder than they bit us. Usually we hit back with stinging words so we can hit them where it hurts. If this escalates, others from the congregation will get involved and take sides. Think of this as a pack of animals attacking what they see as the weaker animal. Their goal is to devour that animal until nothing is left. They are destroyed. This may sound strong, but it does happen within the body, much to our embarrassment and sometimes ruin. Continual biting degenerates into devouring.

Jesus had to deal with his disciples wanting to devour the Samaritans. They felt that Jesus was not welcomed by them so in **LUKE 9:54B–56,** James and John ask Jesus, *"LORD, DO YOU WANT US TO CALL FIRE DOWN FROM HEAVEN TO DESTROY THEM?" BUT JESUS TURNED AND REBUKED THEM, AND THEY WENT TO ANOTHER VILLAGE.* Jesus saw no need to do damage to the Samaritans even though they rejected Him.

We, as Christians, must be careful we do not have this same attitude. This attitude of intolerance needs to be kept out of our lives. Attitudes like this cannot be in the church or in the lives of believers. Intolerance leads to biting and devouring.   [4]

Biting usually comes from gossip, which is terrible within the church. If we hear gossip within the body, we need to do our best to stomp it out. Do not pass it on. If someone wants to talk to us about what someone did to them, suggest they go to that person and talk things over. This way they will get to the heart of the matter instead of hearsay. If it is a real problem, get the two parties to go to the church pastor and work things out. There have been occasions where someone starts biting another in my presence and I have suggested that they go straight to the other person. Almost always they will leave my presence and do nothing; they would rather gossip than fix the problem. **PROVERBS 26:20,** *WITHOUT WOOD A FIRE GOES OUT; WITHOUT GOSSIP A QUARREL DIES DOWN.* If gossip is not repeated, then the biting will stop. James speaks to what the tongue can do to others when he says in **JAMES 3:5,** *LIKEWISE THE TONGUE IS A SMALL PART OF THE BODY, BUT IT MAKES GREAT BOASTS. CONSIDER WHAT A GREAT FOREST IS SET ON FIRE BY A SMALL SPARK.* The tongue can be used in such a way that it is very biting. It can hurt others and will entice a response that will set things on fire. The tongue can destroy.   [5]

Do not be a part of biting or devouring to destroy other brothers within the body. We are taught to encourage our brothers, to build them up, not tear them down. We are to forgive, not get even. We are to live in unity and harmony, not intolerance. We are not to return wrong for wrong. **GALATIANS 5:14** is the verse that leads into not biting and devouring one another. It says *THE ENTIRE LAW IS SUMMED UP IN A SINGLE COMMAND: "LOVE YOUR NEIGHBOR AS YOURSELF."* We are not to be part of hurting one another with our words and deeds, instead we are to love one another. The hurtful attitude we sometimes have and show to one another must grieve the Lord as He watches our actions. Instead we are to love one another.   [6]

QUESTIONS ON BITING AND DEVOURING

1.   Do Christians today bite and devour to destroy one another? Explain.

2.   What is meant when we are told not to bite each other?

3.   What do you do when someone "bites" you? How do you feel?

4.   Do you ever have this attitude?

5.   Why do we do this?

6.   How would you say **GALATIANS 5:14–15** applies to today's churches?

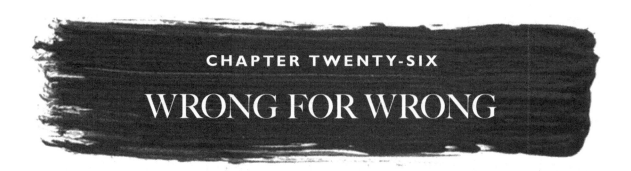

CHAPTER TWENTY-SIX

WRONG FOR WRONG

1 THESSALONIANS 5:15, *MAKE SURE THAT NOBODY PAYS BACK WRONG FOR WRONG, BUT ALWAYS TRY TO BE KIND TO EACH OTHER AND TO EVERYONE ELSE.*

1 PETER 3:9A, *DO NOT REPAY EVIL WITH EVIL.*

Are these two commands the same? Is evil equated with doing wrong to someone? I checked with my pastor, Dr. Jim Smith, to see if the words have a different meaning in the original Greek. He said that essentially they mean exactly the same. Thus, if we wrong someone, it is the same as doing evil to them. When looking up both words in the dictionary, they both say: *morally bad.* [1]

What does it mean to treat someone wrongly? Do we know when we have done this? Were our intentions good or were they vengeful? Were they done to get even with someone who we felt had wronged us? Have we ever felt a desire to get even when we or a loved one was treated unfairly without proper justice? What is so wrong with getting even when everyone does it?

What brings about this feeling of being wronged? [2]

It is just not fair how that person has treated me.
I do not deserve what they have done to me.
They treat others better than me.
Why should they get away with those actions?
Why doesn't the Lord take action? I guess it is up to me.

Who hasn't had some of the above feelings? The big difference is some of us decide to act on these feelings. We want to retaliate. We want to get even. We want pay-backs. We want revenge. The key word here is "WE." We are putting ourselves into the position of acting as if we are God. We are not leaving justice up to the Father but instead taking it upon ourselves to dispense justice. When we respond and do a wrong for a wrong, it is our sinful nature rearing its ugly face in our actions. "They can't treat me or my friends that way and get away with it." [3]

I will relate a personal "wrong for a wrong" that I am not proud of. As a teen and as a man, I played on lots of softball teams. Some teams were for businesses, some were for my friends, one was the local police and fire department, but I always played on one team a year representing my church. One year on a church team an opposing player from another church ran over our elderly shortstop breaking his collarbone. That was wrong as I saw it. The following year I hit a routine single but saw that person covering second base. I continued running and basically did my best to run him over. Making an out wasn't important, getting revenge was. Immediately I felt awful. I knew what I had done was wrong. Since that experience I have been determined not to try to pay back a perceived wrong for a wrong. [4]

As Christians, we are not to have actions such as this. We are not to seek revenge. **ROMANS 12:19, *DO NOT TAKE REVENGE, MY FRIENDS, BUT LEAVE ROOM FOR GOD'S WRATH, FOR IT IS WRITTEN: "IT IS MINE TO AVENGE; I WILL REPAY," SAYS THE LORD.***

What is wrong when we seek to avenge? We are taking the actions that belong to God. It is as if we do not trust that God will take care of the wrongs done to others, including ourselves. We are showing our lack of faith in God. **ROMANS 2:6, *GOD "WILL GIVE TO EACH PERSON ACCORDING TO WHAT HE HAS DONE."*** We have this promise. God will not overlook what wrongs people do here on earth. He will repay with wrath and anger. The problem we have with this promise is the waiting for it to happen.

We want results now. We want the person punished immediately after we see a wrong. "Do not pass GO, GO immediately to jail" is our feeling.

Our example of how to handle being wronged, comes from our Lord. **1 PETER 2:21–23,** *TO THIS YOU WERE CALLED, BECAUSE CHRIST SUFFERED FOR YOU, LEAVING YOU AN EXAMPLE, THAT YOU SHOULD FOLLOW IN HIS STEPS. "HE COMMITTED NO SIN, AND NO DECEIT WAS FOUND IN HIS MOUTH." WHEN THEY HURLED THEIR INSULTS AT HIM, HE DID NOT RETALIATE; WHEN HE SUFFERED, HE MADE NO THREATS. INSTEAD, HE ENTRUSTED HIMSELF TO HIM WHO JUDGES JUSTLY.*

Jesus could have easily retaliated, but He did not. No wrong was found in Him. He left it to His Father to judge the ones who wronged Him. The song, "Ten Thousand Angels," written by Ray Overholt, says this, *"He could have called ten thousand angels to destroy the world…but He died alone, for you and me."* Even though He had the power, He did not use it. He relied on the Father for justice.

1 CORINTHIANS 6:7–8 says *THE VERY FACT THAT YOU HAVE LAWSUITS AMONG YOU MEANS YOU HAVE BEEN COMPLETELY DEFEATED ALREADY. WHY NOT RATHER BE WRONGED? WHY NOT RATHER BE CHEATED? INSTEAD, YOU YOURSELVES CHEAT AND DO WRONG, AND YOU DO THIS TO YOUR BROTHERS.* [5]

What is the lesson Paul is telling the Corinthian brothers? It is better to be wronged and cheated than trying to get even. Sometimes we must give up our personal "rights" to be a good Christian brother. Again, leave the wrong with the Lord. Paul also points out that the suing brother is not completely innocent. Something about "living in glass houses" comes to mind. [6]

COLOSSIANS 3:25 gives us the reminder *ANYONE WHO DOES WRONG WILL BE REPAID FOR HIS WRONG, AND THERE IS NO FAVORITISM.* Our God is fair and just. No one will be spared from the Lord bringing justice. The "fix" is not in. People will not be able to hide from the Lord's judgment. He does not show favoritism. All the people who think they got away with something are in for a surprise. This judge cannot and will not be "paid off." [7]

In the Old Testament, **PROVERBS 10:12** says *HATRED STIRS UP DISSENSION, BUT LOVE COVERS OVER ALL WRONGS.* And in the New Testament in **1 CORINTHIANS 13:5,** Paul's great chapter on love, he says *IT IS NOT RUDE, IT IS NOT SELF-SEEKING, IT IS NOT EASILY ANGERED, IT KEEPS NO RECORD OF WRONGS.* This verse is key in both marriages and in personal relationships with our Christian brothers. We cannot go back and keep revisiting perceived wrongs. Either we must let it drop or the marriage or friendship will never last and will be ruined. [8]

But if someone is wrong, we do have the right to talk to him about what is going on in his life. Our best example of this is when Paul is speaking to Peter in **GALATIANS 2:11.** Paul tells us, *WHEN PETER CAME TO ANTIOCH, I OPPOSED HIM TO HIS FACE, BECAUSE HE WAS CLEARLY IN THE WRONG.* Paul sees Peter as a "hypocrite" Christian. Acting one way in front of one group and differently with another group. Note what Paul did—he went to Peter directly and confronted him about his actions. He did not gossip, talk behind his back or try to get even, instead he sat down with Peter and let him know personally that he was wrong. Peter's actions were influencing others to follow him in his actions, and they were also wrong. Paul wanted to right a wrong before it influenced new Christians on how to live the Christian life.

When it comes to repaying evil for evil it just seems like it is worse than wrong for wrong. But when we wrong others intentionally, we are repaying it with evil. We know what we are doing, and we do it anyhow.

Peter's advice is when someone does evil to us, we are not to repay evil back to them. Paul gives the same advice in **ROMANS 12:17,** *DO NOT REPAY ANYONE EVIL FOR EVIL. BE CAREFUL TO DO WHAT IS RIGHT IN THE EYES OF EVERYBODY.* Why would both of these Christian leaders give the same advice? They did not always agree, but on this principle they did. The Holy Spirit within us wants no part of evil. It cannot be a part of a Christian's life.

ROMANS 12:9, *LOVE MUST BE SINCERE. HATE WHAT IS EVIL; CLING TO WHAT IS GOOD.* We, as Christians are to grow and mature and train ourselves so we can distinguish good from evil. If we know the difference between good and evil, we should be able to avoid evil. **HEBREWS 5:14,** *BUT SOLID FOOD IS FOR THE MATURE, WHO BY CONSTANT USE HAVE TRAINED THEMSELVES TO DISTINGUISH GOOD FROM EVIL.*

Later in **ROMANS 12:21,** Paul says ***DO NOT BE OVERCOME BY EVIL, BUT OVERCOME EVIL WITH GOOD.*** Not only are we to have no part of evil or repaying evil for evil, we are to give back good for evil. How hard is that? We, in our own strength cannot do this, but the Holy Spirit will help us live the Christian life. Why do this? To show the other person that the Lord controls our lives. We want others to see the Lord in action and what better way to show it. By doing this, Paul gives us the reason in the preceding verses. **VERSES 19–20,** ***DO NOT TAKE REVENGE, MY FRIENDS, BUT LEAVE ROOM FOR GOD'S WRATH, FOR IT IS WRITTEN: "IT IS MINE TO AVENGE; I WILL REPAY," SAYS THE LORD. ON THE CONTRARY: "IF YOUR ENEMY IS HUNGRY, FEED HIM; IF HE IS THIRSTY, GIVE HIM SOMETHING TO DRINK. IN DOING THIS, YOU WILL HEAP BURNING COALS ON HIS HEAD."*** By repaying good for evil, it might just inspire a feeling of repentance from the offending person. **[9]**

3 JOHN 11, ***DEAR FRIEND, DO NOT IMITATE WHAT IS EVIL BUT WHAT IS GOOD. ANYONE WHO DOES WHAT IS GOOD IS FROM GOD. ANYONE WHO DOES WHAT IS EVIL HAS NOT SEEN GOD.*** Strong words, but true. For us today, we need to follow Christ's example. Let the Lord handle any perceived wrongs someone has done to us. Do not take matters into our own hands. **[10]**

When we accepted Christ, we were called to follow Christ's example. We are to be a better person for our own sake and to be a witness in this evil world.

QUESTIONS ON WRONG FOR WRONG

1. What is the difference, in your opinion, between wrong for wrong and evil for evil?

2. What is your feeling when someone "wrongs you"? What is your response?

3. Do you agree? What do you really want to do? Why is that?

4. What should have been my actions?

5. Is it wrong for Christians to sue one another?

6. Do you agree?

7. Is showing no favoritism important? Why?

8. Why is it important that love keeps no track of wrongs?

9. Do you agree with this type of retaliation? Can you do what the verse is telling you?

10. Can you do this?

CHAPTER TWENTY-SEVEN

INSULT

1 PETER 3:8–9, *FINALLY, ALL OF YOU, LIVE IN HARMONY WITH ONE ANOTHER; BE SYMPATHETIC, LOVE AS BROTHERS, BE COMPASSIONATE AND HUMBLE. DO NOT REPAY EVIL WITH EVIL OR INSULT WITH INSULT, BUT WITH BLESSING, BECAUSE TO THIS YOU WERE CALLED SO THAT YOU MAY INHERIT A BLESSING.*

Webster's definition of insult: *to speak or act in a way that hurts the feelings or pride of a person that rouses his anger. An insulting remark or action.*

We, as Christians are not to insult our brothers. But notice what Peter emphasizes here. He puts the emphasis on our response to an insult. He is saying if someone insults you, do not respond with an insult back at them. Why would this be so important? Solomon in **PROVERBS 12:16** says *A FOOL SHOWS HIS ANNOYANCE AT ONCE, BUT A PRUDENT MAN OVERLOOKS AN INSULT.* The lesson from this proverb is when we are insulted, we are to overlook it. How easy is that? Not easy at all. When someone insults us, our tendency is to fire back. Repaying an insult for an insult. This is not what the Lord wants. [1]

Why are we not to do this? This brings about escalation of feelings. Trading insults just antagonizes both parties. This is a way to start a fire that will not go out. Bad feelings will creep into other people. This is just a beginning of something that can divide a church. All of a sudden people are picking sides and the fire begins.

Insults to each other is a poor example within and outside the church. If outsiders come to the church, they will sense tension. In most cases it will keep them from returning. They will recognize that the love of one another is not within the church. If ignoring the insult from a brother will stop the insults, be prudent and accept the insult and go forward. If it doesn't stop, then go to the person and try to figure out the problem. It might be prudent to take a third party to keep tempers at bay, then listen to each other and straighten things out so you both can move forward. Do not dwell on what was said and done, put it behind you. Yes, it might hurt, but be the bigger person. Someone must be the adult.

Sometimes we are not insulted directly. **PSALM 69:9B** is an example. *AND THE INSULTS OF THOSE WHO INSULT YOU FALL ON ME.* People who insult our God, are actually insulting us as well. We must not insult the person back, but if someone insults our God, we do have the right and responsibility to express our displeasure. Christians can be easy targets and people know we are taught not to fight back. Yes, that is true, but we are not to be weak. We need to stand up and stand strong in the protection of our God and of our faith.

We are given lots of examples of how to handle people insulting us. Christ is our example in most of these. Jesus says in **LUKE 6:22,** *"BLESSED ARE YOU WHEN MEN HATE YOU, WHEN THEY EXCLUDE YOU AND INSULT YOU AND REJECT YOUR NAME AS EVIL, BECAUSE OF THE SON OF MAN."* Jesus is telling his followers that we should expect to be hated, rejected and insulted because we follow Him. But because we withstand their insults, we will be blessed.

Then later Peter expounds on this in **1 PETER 4:14,** *IF YOU ARE INSULTED BECAUSE OF THE NAME OF CHRIST, YOU ARE BLESSED, FOR THE SPIRIT OF GLORY AND OF GOD RESTS ON YOU.* Peter also tells us we will be blessed because we follow the Lord and have the Holy Spirit within us. [2]

In **JOHN 15:18–19,** Jesus knew that non-Christians would hate us. *"IF THE WORLD HATES YOU, KEEP IN MIND THAT IT HATED ME FIRST. IF YOU BELONG TO THE WORLD, IT WOULD LOVE YOU AS ITS OWN. AS IT IS, YOU DO NOT BELONG TO THE WORLD, BUT I HAVE CHOSEN YOU OUT OF THE WORLD.*

THAT IS WHY THE WORLD HATES YOU." Since we are tied to Christ, if people hate Him, they will hate us. If He is insulted, so are we. If we are insulted, so is He. We are tied together by the Holy Spirit.

When Jesus healed a blind man in **JOHN 9:1–12,** the Pharisees (the most religious of the Jews), brought the blind man into their presence to be questioned. Speaking to the blind man in **VERSES 28–29,** *THEN THEY HURLED INSULTS AT HIM AND SAID, "YOU ARE THIS FELLOW'S DISCIPLE! WE ARE DISCIPLES OF MOSES! WE KNOW THAT GOD SPOKE TO MOSES, BUT AS FOR THIS FELLOW, WE DON'T EVEN KNOW WHERE HE COMES FROM."* The healed blind man was insulted because of Jesus. He did not trade insult for insult. He later meets up with Jesus and tells him in **VERSE 38,** *"LORD, I BELIEVE," AND HE WORSHIPED HIM.*   [3]

We have a couple of examples of how Jesus handled insults while He was on the cross. **MARK 15:29–32,** *THOSE WHO PASSED BY HURLED INSULTS AT HIM, SHAKING THEIR HEADS AND SAYING, "SO! YOU WHO ARE GOING TO DESTROY THE TEMPLE AND BUILD IT IN THREE DAYS, COME DOWN FROM THE CROSS AND SAVE YOURSELF!" IN THE SAME WAY THE CHIEF PRIESTS AND THE TEACHERS OF THE LAW MOCKED HIM AMONG THEMSELVES. "HE SAVED OTHERS," THEY SAID, "BUT HE CAN'T SAVE HIMSELF! LET THIS CHRIST, THIS KING OF ISRAEL, COME DOWN NOW FROM THE CROSS, THAT WE MAY SEE AND BELIEVE." THOSE CRUCIFIED WITH HIM ALSO HEAPED INSULTS ON HIM.*   [4]

Peter also tells of how Jesus was treated while on the cross and dying. **1 PETER 2:23,** *WHEN THEY HURLED THEIR INSULTS AT HIM, HE DID NOT RETALIATE; WHEN HE SUFFERED, HE MADE NO THREATS. INSTEAD, HE ENTRUSTED HIMSELF TO HIM WHO JUDGES JUSTLY.* Notice Jesus did not trade insults with them. He simply leaned on His Father who will be the ultimate judge. This is our example of how to handle insults. Leave it up to God to judge. We are not to retaliate.   [5]

Why would all those people hurl insults at Jesus when He was on the cross? It is easy to insult people when they are at their lowest. People like to kick a man when he is down. We have a tendency to jump on the bandwagon and try to hurt a person even more than he is already hurting. In today's news, if a person makes a mistake and apologizes, that is not enough. People want to insult everything about him, even if it is not true.

Jesus' example to us? **LUKE 23:34, *JESUS SAID, "FATHER, FORGIVE THEM, FOR THEY DO NOT KNOW WHAT THEY ARE DOING."*** Not all insults come to us by words. Many times, people insult brothers and they don't even realize it. Insults come in many forms. When others do not include some people in their group, it is an insult and can leave lasting scars. Sometimes Christians are not invited because of course everyone knows, "Christians are no fun." We can also be insulted by fellow Christians when they simply ignore Christian friends. Or when they want nothing to do with them. **[6]**

Insults from our Christian brothers can come from facial expressions or when they make fun of fellow Christians. Sometimes they won't even speak to their brothers. Do Christians actually do any of these things to one another? I am sorry to say, "yes, they do." **[7]**

What is key is how we handle these insults. Always go back and look at Christ's example.

Paul also talks about people who insult him. **2 CORINTHIANS 12:10, *THAT IS WHY, FOR CHRIST'S SAKE, I DELIGHT IN WEAKNESSES, IN INSULTS, IN HARDSHIPS, IN PERSECUTIONS, IN DIFFICULTIES. FOR WHEN I AM WEAK, THEN I AM STRONG.***

What Paul is saying, is that during tough times when he is insulted and persecuted, he knows the presence of the Lord is with him to make him strong. He himself is weak, but as the Lord is with him, he is strong. **[8]**

Again, this should be an example to us. During difficult times, we must learn to lean on the Lord. We must be very careful how we handle insults. If handled incorrectly, there can be many consequences within the body. Remember **PROVERBS 15:1, *A GENTLE ANSWER TURNS AWAY WRATH, BUT A HARSH WORD STIRS UP ANGER.*** Do not be a part of insulting your brothers, love your brothers in Christ. **1 PETER 3:9** says when we do not insult others when we are insulted, we ***INHERIT A BLESSING.*** **[9]**

QUESTIONS ON INSULT

1. Have you ever been insulted by another Christian? How did you respond?

2. Does this still happen today?

3. Why did the Pharisees insult the man who was healed from blindness?

4. Why would people insult Jesus when He was on the cross?

5. What example does Jesus give to us when this happens? Can you be Christ-like when insulted?

6. Do you have any childhood or adult-age memories of this happening to you?

7. Have you ever insulted another Christian brother? In what way? Did you make things right?

8. Have you found this to be true?

9. What do you do when this happens to you?

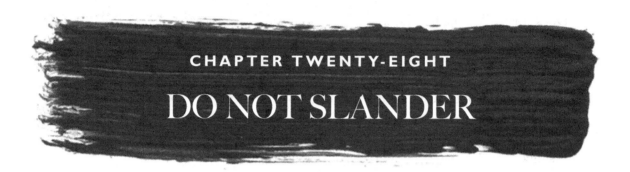

CHAPTER TWENTY-EIGHT

DO NOT SLANDER

JAMES 4:11A, *BROTHERS, DO NOT SLANDER ONE ANOTHER.*

Webster defines slander as: *a false and malicious statement injurious to another's reputation.*

Why would James have to tell Christians not to slander one another? Wouldn't this be a given? Christians would not do this would they? I am sure it is no different now than it was when James put pen to paper. [1]

Why would anyone slander someone else? Here are a few reasons.

1. To make themselves look better or important. We see this all the time in politics. One person runs against the other and tells a lie about his opponent just to make himself look better. Politicians have found out if they tell a lie long enough and loud enough, people will believe it. A couple come to mind:

    President Obama is not an American citizen. Totally false; but because it was said for so long, many still believe it.

    President G. W. Bush is dumb. He could never have achieved a degree. Yet if you check Wikipedia, he ranks in the top twenty Presidents with his I.Q. score.

Keep telling a lie and slandering a person, even if it is not true, and people will believe. That holds true when one Christian slanders another. Sometimes the more outrageous it sounds, the more people will believe it.

2. People perceive a wrong, so they make up something to get even and slander the other person, whether the wrong really happened at all. If we feel someone slandered us, we should immediately go to the person and find out what they really said or did. We are not to retaliate. Do not get into a position of trading slander for slander.

3. People want to humiliate someone else, so they make up malicious statements just to put the person in a poor light to others. The slanderer is seeking to gain an advantage over the other person.

4. Some people just want to hurt other people. It can be for a multitude of reasons. That person gets all the attention. That person is always the one getting ahead. That person makes more money than they do. So, they slander the others to bring them down to their level, at least in their minds.

5. Jealousy. I always looked at the word *jealousy* as "just-lousy" because this is the way it makes us feel or makes us act. People see other people as rivals, so they slander them to get them out of their lives. If two men have feelings for the same woman, one of these men might slander the other just to try get him out of the picture. It could be anything to make the first man look better in the woman's eyes.

6. Just plain hatred. If one person hates another, slander can happen. They want to injure the other person, as much and as often as possible. They will show no remorse, just vengeance.

7. Discord. One brother gets into an argument with another brother and slanders him to stir up trouble.

8. Envy. This is a frustration because someone has something the other wants—a possession, a person, a job, an honor, a position, someone's trust. If it is envy about a position, the envious person will slander the other person to try to take that position away so he can have it for himself. They want to eliminate the competition by slandering someone else.

9. Dissensions and factions. When one group is against another. One group slanders the other, just to bring them down, to hurt them in the eyes of others. They are trying to put them in a bad light. We see this in the political arena way too much today. One candidate does not agree with his competition and will try to slander that person so that the voters will not see him in a good light. They might say things like he is racist, he is homophobic, she is a liar, or he is going to take away Social Security. These slander words are used today way too often; selfish ambition showing its ugly head. People do not run on issues today but on a campaign of putting the other person in a bad light by slander, smearing the person. After the election, it is usually found that all the slander was nothing but lies, but by that time it is too late. We see this in the music world, in Hollywood, in sports; words being used to tear down the reputation of another. Dissensions and factions can also happen within the local church body. If one person disagrees with another on a subject, slander can happen.   [2]

None of these areas belong in a Christian's life. Matter of fact, five of the above items come from **GALATIANS 5:19–21. *THE ACTS OF THE SINFUL NATURE ARE OBVIOUS: SEXUAL IMMORALITY, IMPURITY AND DEBAUCHERY; IDOLATRY AND WITCHCRAFT; HATRED, DISCORD, JEALOUSY, FITS OF RAGE, SELFISH AMBITION, DISSENSIONS, FACTIONS AND ENVY; DRUNKENNESS, ORGIES, AND THE LIKE. I WARN YOU, AS I DID BEFORE, THAT THOSE WHO LIVE LIKE THIS WILL NOT INHERIT THE KINGDOM OF GOD.*** These items are in the list of a sinful nature which we as Christians should not have in our lives as we model Christ.

Instead of these sinful items, we are to have the fruit of the Spirit growing within our lives. We find the list in **GALATIANS 5: 22–23A, *BUT THE FRUIT OF THE SPIRIT IS LOVE, JOY, PEACE, PATIENCE, KINDNESS, GOODNESS, FAITHFULNESS, GENTLENESS AND SELF-CONTROL.*** If we slander someone, it does not bring about peace to us or to others, it shows no love or joy. It's just plain mean spirited. We show no kindness or goodness to the people we slander. We are not faithful or loving to our Christian brothers or self-controlled. We strive to hurt our brothers in Christ. None of the areas of slander come from the fruit of the Spirit, they all come from our sinful nature.

If we have love in our hearts, this keeps out hatred. If we have joy, we have no need to make ourselves look better than others. If we have peace in our hearts, we cannot have envy or jealousy. If we have patience, we will not have discord. If we have kindness, we will not seek revenge or be trying to get even. If we have goodness, we will not try to hurt others. If we have faithfulness to our brothers, we will not try to humiliate others. If we have gentleness, we will show no ill will. If we are self-controlled, we will not have dissensions and factions. [3]

We are to be such good Christians that Peter says in **1 PETER 3:16, *KEEPING A CLEAR CONSCIENCE, SO THAT THOSE WHO SPEAK MALICIOUSLY AGAINST YOUR GOOD BEHAVIOR IN CHRIST MAY BE ASHAMED OF THEIR SLANDER.*** If we live a Christ-led life, living by the Spirit's guidance, we will have no reason for anyone, Christian or non-Christian, to slander us on the way we live our lives. We will be above reproach because we live a Christ-led life. When I think of someone like this, Billy Graham comes to mind. He was always above reproach.

If we are slandered, we need to follow the directions found in **1 CORINTHIANS 4:13A, *WHEN WE ARE SLANDERED, WE ANSWER KINDLY.*** We are not to repay slander for slander. We are directed not to slander Christians, but we are also directed to not slander anyone. In **TITUS 3:2A** we are told ***TO SLANDER NO ONE.*** In the previous verse, it is talking about ***RULERS AND AUTHORITIES.*** These leaders probably are slandered more than any others. People making up lies about the person in charge. Have you ever noticed when a person says he is running for a certain office, in just a short time someone will come forth to slander him? We are not to be a part of this. We should be praying for our leaders whether we agree with them or not, not to join in the slander.

TITUS 2:3A says ***LIKEWISE, TEACH THE OLDER WOMEN TO BE REVERENT IN THE WAY THEY LIVE, NOT TO BE SLANDERERS.*** What we need to take away from this is the key word, *teach*. The way we talk about others is teachable. We can teach our children not to slander others. We need to teach by word and also by our actions. We also see in this verse that we are never too old to be taught how to live our lives in a Christ-like manner. Slander cannot be a part of our lives. It can be and is very hurtful.

When I think about slander, it seems like gossip goes right along with it. By keeping both of these areas out of our lives, we will be better Christians. In **1 CORINTHIANS 6:9–10** Paul lists some of the sins of the wicked that will not allow them to inherit heaven. ***DO YOU NOT KNOW THAT THE WICKED WILL NOT INHERIT THE KINGDOM OF GOD? DO NOT BE DECEIVED: NEITHER THE SEXUALLY IMMORAL NOR IDOLATERS NOR ADULTERERS NOR MALE PROSTITUTES***

NOR HOMOSEXUAL OFFENDERS NOR THIEVES NOR THE GREEDY NOR DRUNKARDS NOR SLANDERERS NOR SWINDLERS WILL INHERIT THE KINGDOM OF GOD. We, as Christians, speak out against many of the sins mentioned in this verse. We are bold in speaking about homosexuality, yet when it comes to slander, we can be a part of it and not think anything of it. We may be agreeing with someone that might be slandering a senator or even the President. But it falls in the same category as someone being sexually immoral. God does not rank sins. Sin is sin. This is why it is important not to slander and to teach others the same. [4]

We need to check out our speech and see if there is any slander in our lives. If so, replace it with the fruit of the Spirit, which will drive it away.

QUESTIONS ON DO NOT SLANDER

1. Does this still happen today?

2. Have you evidence of this list in your church? How can it be eradicated?

3. What would you add to this list?

4. If you heard someone slander another, what would you do?

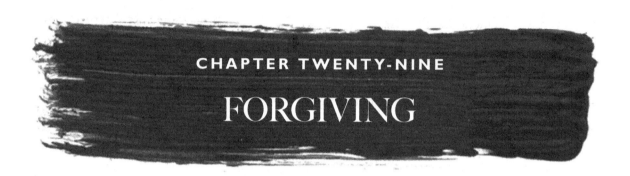

CHAPTER TWENTY-NINE

FORGIVING

EPHESIANS 4:32, *BE KIND AND COMPASSIONATE TO ONE ANOTHER, FORGIVING EACH OTHER, JUST AS IN CHRIST GOD FORGAVE YOU.*

Forgiveness within the body of believers is a problem today just as it must have been when Paul wrote the letter to the Ephesians. Why do Christians have such a hard time with forgiveness? When we don't forgive our brothers within the church, it can and does create many problems, some so serious that the church might even split from this problem. Note in the above verse Paul says we are to forgive as Christ forgave. What does that mean? How did Jesus forgive each of us personally? Solely because of His mercy. Solely because of His love for us. It was nothing we did or deserved; it was a gift given with no "catches." His forgiveness is there for the receiving. All we have to do is ask!

The Bible is very explicit concerning forgiveness and forgiving one another. It points out the correct way to forgive.

Paul, in **2 CORINTHIANS 2:5–11,** expounds on how to handle a person's forgiveness when he has sinned within the church. Paul is saying once we have reprimanded the person, forgive and then comfort him. If not, the person may be overwhelmed by excessive sorrow. Then we must reaffirm our love for him. The church must forgive the person and quit beating him up. This is like kicking a man when he is down. The key is to forgive and forget. If our spouses ask forgiveness and we give it to them, but we keep bringing it up, have we really forgiven them? The next key is to show the person love. If we don't handle this properly, Satan can find his way into the church. [1]

Once forgiveness is asked for and the person is repentant, give the person forgiveness and then move on. Do not keep throwing his past actions at him and never ever gossip about what the sin was. Gossip is a sin unto itself. Do not feel like we need to get "a pound of flesh" from the repentant person. Instead we are to reaffirm our love for the person. Jesus, in **LUKE 17:3B,** tells us how to handle a sinful brother. *"IF YOUR BROTHER SINS, REBUKE HIM, AND IF HE REPENTS, FORGIVE HIM."* How simple is that?

When the disciples asked Jesus to teach them to pray, He said this in **LUKE 11:4A,** *"FORGIVE US OUR SINS, FOR WE ALSO FORGIVE EVERYONE WHO SINS AGAINST US."* Some places say "debts," but the meaning is the same. If we feel someone has wronged us, we are to forgive that person even before they come to us and ask forgiveness. We are to be proactive in forgiving others. We are to be the better person even if they never come to us.

Many years ago, I had a friend that, in my opinion, "wronged" me. After weeks of being resentful I turned it over to the Lord. I forgave the person. He probably never even noticed my actions, but I did. The person never came to me and he probably never felt he had wronged anyone. Who is the one affected here? The one who does not forgive. [2]

Jesus tells us in **MARK 11:25** how important forgiveness is in a Christian life. He says, *"AND WHEN YOU STAND PRAYING, IF YOU HOLD ANYTHING AGAINST ANYONE, FORGIVE HIM, SO THAT YOUR FATHER IN HEAVEN MAY FORGIVE YOU YOUR SINS."* If the Holy Spirit speaks to us during prayer time, or anytime, listen, then act on His conviction. Why? If we are unforgiving to others, why would the Lord feel like He has to forgive us and answer our prayers? God's forgiveness toward us is tied to how we forgive others. Another example is given in **LUKE 6:37B,** *"FORGIVE, AND YOU WILL BE FORGIVEN."* We want and expect forgiveness from the Lord. Jesus and His Father will forgive us just like we forgive others. The burden of forgiveness is on us. We are not to hold a grudge, we are to forgive others, unconditionally. [3]

Our best example of what this means is the parable of the "unmerciful servant." In **MATTHEW 18:23–34,** Jesus tells the story of a servant who had been forgiven of much debt by his master, so much debt that the servant could never have paid it all. Yet when someone came to the servant and asked for forgiveness for a very small amount, the servant could not, and would not forgive the debt. The story ends with the master having the servant put into jail and tortured until he repays the entire debt. Jesus goes on to tell the disciples in **VERSE 35,** *"THIS IS HOW MY HEAVENLY FATHER WILL TREAT EACH OF YOU UNLESS YOU FORGIVE YOUR BROTHER FROM YOUR HEART."* **[4]**

In the preceding verses, just before Jesus tells this parable of the unforgiving debtor, and right after Jesus teaches forgiveness to the disciples, Peter asks Jesus this question in **MATTHEW 18:21,** *"LORD, HOW MANY TIMES SHALL I FORGIVE MY BROTHER WHEN HE SINS AGAINST ME? UP TO SEVEN TIMES?"* The Rabbis' taught that you must forgive a brother at least three times based on Old Testament scripture, **AMOS 1:3** and **JOB 33:29–30.** Thus, Peter felt he was doing a good thing by offering to forgive a brother up to seven times. **MATTHEW 18:22,** *JESUS ANSWERED, "I TELL YOU, NOT SEVEN TIMES, BUT SEVENTY-SEVEN TIMES."* What Jesus was teaching was forgiving every time a brother asks for forgiveness; just give it. Do not keep count. This holds true for all of us today. But can we really forgive someone that much? Would we not forgive our spouse or our child multiple times if asked? Thank the Lord I have a forgiving wife since it seems I am always asking her for forgiveness. Many times it is for the same thing, I am sorry to say. **[5]**

Our example is the Lord in this case. How many times have I gone to Him and asked forgiveness for a sin? Many times the same sin. Many times it is over and over. Do I deserve to be forgiven? Absolutely not! But thank goodness, He forgives anyway.

If someone comes to us and asks for forgiveness, we have the responsibility to forgive them. If we do not give them forgiveness, then the burden of unforgiveness is on our heads. My wife and I had a couple that were very good friends and they felt they were wronged within the church body. Maybe rightfully so. The offending party came to them and asked for forgiveness, but he was not received with the spirit of forgiveness. He was rejected. The offended parties did not forgive him. The person asking forgiveness was upset with them and felt he had done the right thing, which he had by following the Bible's requirement. Since the offended parties never gave forgiveness, it has never been resolved and still festers within the body after many years. This is not how it should be or has to be.

When we realize we have offended a brother, we must go to them and ask for forgiveness. If we are not sure, it is better to go to them anyway, just in case. The person we go to must receive the request as an act of forgiveness and forgive the person wholeheartedly and unconditionally. There are times we do not get the apology we expect, or when we expect it. We must learn to let it go and give it to the Lord so our actions and reactions do not affect the church body. [6]

COLOSSIANS 3:13, *BEAR WITH EACH OTHER AND FORGIVE WHATEVER GRIEVANCES YOU MAY HAVE AGAINST ONE ANOTHER. FORGIVE AS THE LORD FORGAVE YOU.* How does the Lord forgive us? [7]

1. He forgives us when we do not deserve forgiveness.

2. He forgets our sins. **PSALM 103:12,** *AS FAR AS THE EAST IS FROM THE WEST, SO FAR HAS HE REMOVED OUR TRANSGRESSIONS FROM US.*

Our best examples:

1. God sent His Son to die so we would be able to have forgiveness from sins.

2. God's Son showed forgiveness even while on the cross. **LUKE 23:34,** *JESUS SAID, "FATHER, FORGIVE THEM, FOR THEY DO NOT KNOW WHAT THEY ARE DOING."*

These are the examples we are to live by. Forgive our brother even when he does not deserve it. Forgive his sin and cast it from our minds. These are easy things to say, but hard to live by.

I read a book on marital relations that said if you want a happy marriage, "never dig up old bones." In other words, don't keep bringing back old issues that are in the past. It serves no purpose to rehash old faults. We cannot keep dredging up past issues if we want our marriages to grow or our relationships with friends to move forward. [8]

We are to show forgiveness in the worst of times, even when we feel someone is "crucifying" us. We need to have a tender heart to the Lord so we can find this type of forgiveness in our hearts. Christ says we are to forgive, so we need to obey. My friend who does divorce counseling says forgiveness is the bottom line in healing. Forgiveness may happen but forgetting is the hard part.

Dwelling on hurts can have a devastating effect on people. The hurt never seems to go away. We must strive for the type of forgiveness our Lord has shown us. [9]

QUESTIONS ON FORGIVING

1. After reading **2 CORINTHIANS 2:5–11,** explain how Satan's schemes relate to forgiveness.

2. Has this ever happened to you?

3. Is our forgiveness really tied to us forgiving others?

4. What is your take on this parable?

5. If we keep forgiving a person, won't this encourage more bad behavior? Doesn't there have to be some limit? What about something like drunk driving?

6. Have you seen the lack of forgiveness in your church? Why do some people have such a hard time with forgiveness, either asking for or giving forgiveness?

7. What is your answer?

8. Is this a problem in your marriage? Is this a problem in some of your relationships? How can we get by this issue?

9. Is forgiving a brother a problem for you? Why is that so?

CHAPTER THIRTY

STRENGTHEN

ACTS 15:32, *JUDAS AND SILAS, WHO THEMSELVES WERE PROPHETS, SAID MUCH TO ENCOURAGE AND STRENGTHEN THE BROTHERS.* [1]

This is our example to strengthen others in their service to the Lord.

But how were the followers of Christ strengthened? How are we strengthened? Where does all this strength come from? Who is doing all this strengthening? [2]

COLOSSIANS 1:11A tells us we are strengthened with the power of God. *BEING STRENGTHENED WITH ALL POWER ACCORDING TO HIS GLORIOUS MIGHT SO THAT YOU MAY HAVE GREAT ENDURANCE AND PATIENCE.* As we are told in **EPHESIANS 1:19–20,** this is the same strength that raised Jesus from the dead. *AND HIS INCOMPARABLY GREAT POWER FOR US WHO BELIEVE. THAT POWER IS LIKE THE WORKING OF HIS MIGHTY STRENGTH, WHICH HE EXERTED IN CHRIST WHEN HE RAISED HIM FROM THE DEAD AND SEATED HIM AT HIS RIGHT HAND IN THE HEAVENLY REALMS.* We have the hand of God giving us strength. It is our Father who gives us the power to help strengthen others.

We also receive strength and power through the Holy Spirit. **EPHESIANS 3:16,** *I PRAY THAT OUT OF HIS GLORIOUS RICHES HE MAY STRENGTHEN YOU WITH POWER THROUGH HIS SPIRIT IN YOUR INNER BEING.* We have the Holy Spirit in us because we became Christians. He strengthens us in our time of need.

Jesus gives us strength. He empowers. When we think of receiving power from the Lord the following verse comes to mind: **PHILIPPIANS 4:13,** *I CAN DO EVERYTHING THROUGH HIM WHO GIVES ME STRENGTH.* This is a favorite verse for many Christians, but does it really mean everything? Some have it all wrong. Why? It is not strength for what I want to do, but strength to do what God wants me to do. If God wants me to do it (whatever that might be), I can lean on Him for the power to do it. No matter what it is, even if it seems impossible, God will give me the strength and resources to do His will, if I allow Him to be in control. [3]

Do I believe and trust Him when He asks me to:

> Tithe?
> Witness to my neighbor?
> Give of my time?
> Break a sinful habit?
> Help someone in a bad relationship?
> Hold a position in the church?
> Write a book? [4]

I either believe He gives me strength, or I don't. He tells me He will give me the strength; thus, I am to rely on Him. I am to trust in the Lord. I am to step out on faith. Can I do this? I must! If I believe my strength comes from Him, I must trust Him.

COLOSSIANS 2:7, by being ***ROOTED AND BUILT UP IN HIM,*** we are ***STRENGTHENED IN THE FAITH.*** [5]

How are we rooted?

> By studying the Bible
> By living a Christian life
> By striving to be more Christ-like daily
> By being sensitive to the Holy Spirit who is at work in our lives [6]

1 THESSALONIANS 3:13A, *MAY HE STRENGTHEN YOUR HEARTS SO THAT YOU WILL BE BLAMELESS AND HOLY IN THE PRESENCE OF OUR GOD AND FATHER.* Why do we need this strength? So, in our daily lives we will not falter and will serve the Lord in the way He is expecting of us. **MARK 12:30,** *LOVE THE LORD YOUR GOD WITH ALL YOUR HEART AND WITH ALL YOUR SOUL AND WITH ALL YOUR MIND AND WITH ALL YOUR STRENGTH.* [7]

We also need to be strengthened so we will live our lives for Christ, both in our actions and words, and in the way we live day to day.

If this is how we are strengthened, through the Holy Trinity (Father, Son, and Holy Spirit), then how are we to be involved in strengthening others? We are told to strengthen others in various ways. **1 CORINTHIANS 14:26B,** *WHEN YOU COME TOGETHER, EVERYONE HAS A HYMN, OR A WORD OF INSTRUCTION, A REVELATION, A TONGUE OR AN INTERPRETATION. ALL OF THESE MUST BE DONE FOR THE STRENGTHENING OF THE CHURCH.* Notice it says, "all of these must be done." [7]

By worshiping together
  There is strength in numbers.
  We will draw strength from one another.
A hymn
  We raise our voices together in song and praise.
  Multiple voices strengthens all participants.
A revelation
  What God has pointed out to us in our lives.
  Giving our testimony to others on how God is working in our lives.
An interpretation
  A scripture we have read is now clear to us, and we want to share with the body.

When the verse speaks of coming together it could mean during:

Sunday school class
Worship service
Small groups
A prayer group
A men or women's group

Or any other times together when you are discussing things of the Lord. **[8]**

By being together we gain strength for the rest of the week. We see our fellow believers as they struggle and as they have overcome adversity through the strength the Lord has given them. We share the gospel and what it has meant to us in a new way. We sing unto the Lord with voices raised in praise. All of these things strengthen us. Yes, there is strength in numbers, so do not neglect being with your brothers and sisters in Christ. Sometimes we strengthen them and at times they strengthen us. Yes, we get power through the Trinity, but we are also to give strength and receive strength from one another.

We can encourage others and give them strength when we tell them of our struggles and our victories.

Peter was told to strengthen his brothers after he had denied the Lord. (See **LUKE 22:32**.) I am sure Peter praised the Lord for his forgiveness and the Lord's continual love for him. This would have given strength to others who had sinned in the same way.

Find ways to give strength to others. As we gain strength, pass it on. **[9]**

QUESTIONS ON STRENGTHEN

1. We are told to strengthen one another. What does this mean to you? How would you go about doing it?

2. What can someone do to help strengthen you?

3. How do you interpret **PHILIPPIANS 4:13?**

4. Add your thoughts to this list.

5. What strengthens your faith?

6. Where did your roots come from?

7. Put this verse into your own words.

8. What is the purpose of gaining all this strength?

9. What gives you strength to serve the Lord?

CHAPTER THIRTY-ONE

RESTORE

GALATIANS 6:1, *BROTHERS, IF SOMEONE IS CAUGHT IN A SIN, YOU WHO ARE SPIRITUAL SHOULD RESTORE HIM GENTLY. BUT WATCH YOURSELF, OR YOU ALSO MAY BE TEMPTED.* [1]

We can take the following from this verse:

> A Christian brother can sin.
> Paul is speaking about catching someone in a sin.
> The person is to be restored.
> They are to be restored gently.
> This restoration is to be done by a spiritual person.
> The restorer must be careful less he be tempted.

Before a Christian is confronted about a sin it is very important to consider why others are to go to him. It is for one main reason, restoration. So, the person can get back into the good graces of the Lord and to help the person resume his Christian life and grow from this lapse.

Paul is talking about a brother, a fellow Christian that has sinned. This is a person who has been leading a Christian life.

What does it mean to be caught in a sin? Did you personally see the sin, or did you hear gossip? Be very careful of hearsay. The Old Testament says there must be more than one witness before a person is labeled guilty. **DEUTERONOMY 19:15,** *ONE WITNESS IS NOT ENOUGH TO CONVICT A MAN ACCUSED OF ANY CRIME OR OFFENSE HE MAY HAVE COMMITTED. A MATTER MUST BE ESTABLISHED BY THE TESTIMONY OF TWO OR THREE WITNESSES.* Some people like to make things up and like to start gossip, so don't believe just one person.

Was it really a sin or was it a sin in someone else's opinion, like yours? There are many areas of life that are not touched upon in the Bible. We must be careful calling them sins when they are not labeled as such in the Bible. For example, some would call dancing a sin and might confront someone who dances. Yet we have references in the Bible about dancing that was giving praise to the Lord. David is an obvious example. The point being, before we confront someone make sure it is not just our opinion with no Biblical backing. If it is not Biblical, then it probably is only our opinion.

Are we confronting someone about a sin that we ourselves have or are committing? Make sure we are free from sin before we confront another, otherwise we are nothing more than hypocrites. Jesus gives us an example of what we are to do if someone sins. **MATTHEW 7:3–5,** *"WHY DO YOU LOOK AT THE SPECK OF SAWDUST IN YOUR BROTHER'S EYE AND PAY NO ATTENTION TO THE PLANK IN YOUR OWN EYE? HOW CAN YOU SAY TO YOUR BROTHER, 'LET ME TAKE THE SPECK OUT OF YOUR EYE,' WHEN ALL THE TIME THERE IS A PLANK IN YOUR OWN EYE? YOU HYPOCRITE, FIRST TAKE THE PLANK OUT OF YOUR OWN EYE, AND THEN YOU WILL SEE CLEARLY TO REMOVE THE SPECK FROM YOUR BROTHER'S EYE."* [2]

Do we have an ulterior motive? Are we judging? Remember **MATTHEW 7:1–2** says if we judge we will be judged by our own standards.

Was it a sin committed intentionally or was it something they kind of fell into? My pastor, Dr. Jim Smith, explained it this way: a more literal interpretation of **GALATIANS 6:1** would read, *FELLOW CHRISTIANS, EVEN IF A HUMAN HAS BEEN SURPRISED BY A CERTAIN SIN.* Surprised, to be taken unawares, an unexpected event. Some sins are not blatant sins but an error on our part. It is like potholes. They are there and sometimes we are not looking out for them and are caught unawares, surprised. There are potholes of sin on our way to heaven. David looked out of his window and saw Bathsheba taking a bath—an unintentional sin. What he did from there was intentional. This explanation helped me understand this verse in a different light. We fall into the surprise of a temptation. We get asked a question and to protect ourselves we lie even before we think of what we are doing, or we let our anger get the best of ourselves.   [3]

My wife had a friend that had to move away from all of her friends to a place where she knew no one. A female neighbor befriended her. They got very close since my wife's friend and husband were going through a very difficult time in their marriage. The lady was propositioned by this new friend to get into a lesbian relationship. She spent hours talking over the situation with my wife. She had not seen the proposition coming and was thus caught unaware. With my wife's counseling she was able to get away from the temptation.

Paul speaks to this by saying in **ROMANS 7:15,** *I DO NOT UNDERSTAND WHAT I DO. FOR WHAT I WANT TO DO, I DO NOT DO, BUT WHAT I HATE I DO.* Then in **VERSE 18B,** *FOR I HAVE THE DESIRE TO DO WHAT IS GOOD, BUT I CANNOT CARRY IT OUT.* There are moments in all our lives that we look back on and say, "If only I could do all that over again."   [4]

Paul goes on to tell us that the person who is to be involved is a "spiritual person." Aren't all Christians spiritual? Well yes, but some Christians have raised themselves or have been raised by the Lord to a higher plane. Surely, we recognize that some in our midst are what could be termed a "stronger, more spiritual" Christian. The person or persons who are trying to restore the person must be living their lives close to the Lord. They have the mind of the Lord. Their lives must be full of the Fruit of the Spirit. The person must have a servant's heart and be one who is serving his fellow brothers in Christ. The one in sin must be able to have respect for the person who is confronting them.   [5]

Remember back in **GALATIANS 6:1,** Paul points out that person needs to be restored "gently." The key is going to someone with love in our heart. We love our brother and want to help him in his Christian life. There can be no anger or "righteous indignation" in our heart. I had a friend that was confronted about his sin. It was not handled at all well because the people who went to him went with a whole lot of anger in their hearts. All they did was drive the person away, thus he was not restored. Do not confront a person with the attitude of "I'll straighten him out." It is not a time for gloating or feeling triumph over the person's failings. Do not be like the time of the Inquisition, when it became a time for people with ulterior motives to punish others. [6]

Paul, within the verse, gives a warning. We are to watch ourselves least we be tempted. Why such a warning? We could fall into a worse sin and need restored. All of us are tempted at some point. [7]

Before we go to a brother make sure we are in the will of the Holy Spirit. Are we the right person to be involved in another's restoration? If so, are we going with humility? Do we have the right attitude? Are we full of love for the person? Do we want to restore the person or drive him away? Restore others as we would want to be restored. Have we prayed over what we are to do? To go to another will be one of the hardest things we have ever done. Have you talked things over with your pastor? You never know, the pastor may be counseling the person about the same issue.

Not everyone will be restored. Some will continue to sin. One friend I talked to about being in an adulterous situation said to me "the Lord will just have to understand my needs." Sorry, but God does not understand or tolerate sin. Sin will harden a person's heart and the heart that is hardened does not respond well to confrontation.

I also know of two instances where pastors were caught up in temptations. Others went to them, with love in their hearts, and both were restored. This is a case where their mistakes only made them stronger. They learned the lesson that they must trust the Lord and lean on Him for guidance, not themselves. [8]

If a person is restored, do not shun him or you will drive him away and he will lose the influence of Christian brothers. Bring him back into the fold with love. Do not gossip about what the person was doing as this is a sin unto itself. Gossip is not done to build up people but rather to tear them down.

Remember, the key to restoration is *love*. [9]

QUESTIONS ON RESTORE

1. Explain "restore him."

2. What strikes you from **MATTHEW 7:3–5?** Have you ever been guilty of this action?

3. What are your comments on the literal translation?

4. Ever thought this? What changes would you have made in your life? Why?

5. What does it mean "you who are spiritual"?

6. Why try to restore someone instead of getting them out of the church?

7. Why the warning about possibly being tempted?

8. Has your church had to confront someone about sin? How was it handled? What were the results?

9. What's love got to do with this whole area of restoration?

CHAPTER THIRTY-TWO

HARMONY

1 PETER 3:8A, *FINALLY, ALL OF YOU, LIVE IN HARMONY WITH ONE ANOTHER.*

Then again in **ROMANS 12:16A,** *LIVE IN HARMONY WITH ONE ANOTHER.* But note the rest of the verse goes on to say *DO NOT BE PROUD, BUT BE WILLING TO ASSOCIATE WITH PEOPLE OF LOW POSITION. DO NOT BE CONCEITED.*

What does it mean to live in harmony with one another? [1]

In the dictionary the first three definitions of harmony all relate to music.

1. The combination of musical notes to form chords
2. The study or chords and chord progressive
3. A pleasant chord or progression of chords

The last definition relates to people in harmony; *agreement, concord, we were in perfect harmony with each other.* To understand how to be in harmony with one another, the use of the musical definition is key to our understanding.

Have we ever heard music that was not in harmony? Music that did not harmonize but was in discord? It sounds terrible. We want to get away from it or cover up our ears. Why? Because it is not pleasing to be around.

My grandson started playing the saxophone for the first time in the sixth grade. The band was practicing for their first performance at Christmas. The night of the performance they played two numbers. The next up was the seventh-grade band and they played two numbers, one being the same as the sixth grade. Then the eighth and ninth grade bands played two numbers, again one number the same as the first two bands. Finally, the high school band played their numbers including the same song.

The music director said the reason for playing the same song gave the audience the chance to see the progression of the kids from four months of practice to six years of practice. The harmonizing effect was definitely noticeable. It takes time for a group to work together to bring harmony. It is the same for us within the church body. It takes practice. It takes patience. It takes desire. It takes being together. It takes working together. It takes repetition. It takes forgiveness when one person messes up. But the outcome is worth the effort.

I had the privilege of attending a seminar where a full orchestra was brought in to show how everything within an orchestra works together to bring the best sound, perfect harmony. Then we were to adapt this to business principles. The conductor pointed out the section leaders and said it was up to them to make sure their sound was in harmony within their section. Then they were to be in harmony with the other sections and then in harmony with the conductor. All the musicians were experts at what they played but they then relied on the conductor to lead them in perfect harmony. They all knew the music, but their timing must be perfect for the end effect to be in perfect harmony.

At the end of the seminar a few of us had the privilege of standing immediately behind the conductor to hear a selected piece of classical music. Being so close in proximity of the instruments was unbelievable. Each musician was using his talent to reach the goal of a beautiful sound, yet together they humbled themselves to make everything work with the correct timing and equal volume. [2]

This is exactly what the Lord wants for us as Christians within *His* church. Perfect harmony within the church, making beautiful music because we are following the Lord and the Holy Spirit's direction, not our own.

To be in harmony in the body of Christ, we can take a lesson from a symphonic orchestra.

Everybody needs to be on the same page of the same song, the plan.
  Does everybody have the same plan in mind?
  Is everybody liked minded?
Everybody plays different instruments.
  Everyone has a different part, but they are still in harmony.
  Not everyone can play a flute or a violin or else total harmony is not reached.
  Each is using his talent (gift) of a different nature, but still in harmony.
  A church, just like an orchestra, must have harmonious diversity.
There can be only one conductor or director, but many various section leaders.
  All must watch the conductor to keep everything together.
  All must stay with the conductor to stay in harmony.
Everyone must play in the same tempo.
  Some want to go fast, others slow but it is up to the conductor to keep everyone together.
Everyone must play with the same volume.
  Some want to play loud, others soft, but it is up to the conductor.
There are rules to follow.
You can't bring a kazoo.   [3]

If the conductor can direct all of this, the result is beautiful harmony.

If an orchestra is not in harmony, people will not attend the performance. This is the same for a church that is not in harmony, or if certain people of the church are not in harmony. Visitors recognize when a church is not getting along and will avoid that church.

But how can this be accomplished?   [4]

Paul gives us some of the answer in **ROMANS 12:16** when he tells us not to be proud, not to be conceited. This is when we have high opinions of ourselves. When we have these high opinions of ourselves, it gives us the opportunity to look down on others since we see ourselves above them. To be proud of an accomplishment is one thing, but to look down on others is wrong. The verse continues to say we are to be willing to associate with people of low position. This can mean different things. Compare versions from the parallel Bibles.

Be with people that are poor in monetary things.
  Share your money and/or property.
Be with people that are humble.
  They will help keep you humble.
Do not seek out the company of people of eminence.
  We are to seek out people of all backgrounds.
Do not try to get into the good graces of important people.
  Enjoy the company of everyday people.

The company we keep is important. If we are always with conceited people, we can become the same as them. Are we like a person in the orchestra that plays the kettle drums? They may never hear the piccolo, so to them it might not be as important in their minds. Yet without all the instruments, the orchestra does not have total harmony.

If an owner of a big company never talks to any employee "beneath him," does it affect the harmony of the company? The same can be said for a principal of a school that will not speak to the teachers since he sees them below him. Again, no harmony. **[5]**

How would this apply to the church? Paul points out that some people with less visible gifts must not be overlooked, since they might even be more important than the person with the visible gift. It says in **1 CORINTHIANS 12:22, *ON THE CONTRARY, THOSE PARTS OF THE BODY THAT SEEM TO BE WEAKER ARE INDISPENSABLE.*** When we recognize the importance of others, it can definitely make harmony easier to accomplish. As we treat others as our equals, we should want to get along with them at church, work, school or home.

We should learn a lesson from the Pharisees. They saw themselves above all others since they knew and followed all the laws, traditions, rules and regulations. They would not bring themselves down like Jesus to be seen with tax collectors and sinners. It would be beneath them. In **MATTHEW 23:5–7** Jesus says *"EVERYTHING THEY DO IS DONE FOR MEN TO SEE: THEY MAKE THEIR PHYLACTERIES WIDE AND THE TASSELS ON THEIR GARMENTS LONG; THEY LOVE THE PLACE OF HONOR AT BANQUETS AND THE MOST IMPORTANT SEATS IN THE SYNAGOGUES; THEY LOVE TO BE GREETED IN THE MARKETPLACES AND TO HAVE MEN CALL THEM 'RABBI'."*

LUKE 18:9–11 gives us another insight into the Pharisees lives. *TO SOME WHO WERE CONFIDENT OF THEIR OWN RIGHTEOUSNESS AND LOOKED DOWN ON EVERYBODY ELSE, JESUS TOLD THIS PARABLE: "TWO MEN WENT UP TO THE TEMPLE TO PRAY, ONE A PHARISEE AND THE OTHER A TAX COLLECTOR. THE PHARISEE STOOD UP AND PRAYED ABOUT HIMSELF: 'GOD, I THANK YOU THAT I AM NOT LIKE OTHER MEN—ROBBERS, EVILDOERS, ADULTERERS—OR EVEN LIKE THIS TAX COLLECTOR'."* How did this attitude affect harmony within the Jewish nation? It destroyed it. We cannot be in harmony with someone without respect for that person. We cannot be in harmony with someone to whom we feel superior.

We must be vigilant so we do not become self-righteous and thus keep harmony from the body. We, as mature Christians, must be in harmony with newly saved brothers. We are to see all brothers as our equal. Paul says in his letter, **PHILIPPIANS 2:2,** *THEN MAKE MY JOY COMPLETE BY BEING LIKE-MINDED, HAVING THE SAME LOVE, BEING ONE IN SPIRIT AND PURPOSE.* If every church had the same love and was one in the Spirit and purpose, we would have no trouble with harmony. Being one in the spirit is very important to a church and to individuals. **[6]**

Jesus keys in on this in His prayer to the Father in **JOHN 17:11,** *"I WILL REMAIN IN THE WORLD NO LONGER, BUT THEY ARE STILL IN THE WORLD, AND I AM COMING TO YOU. HOLY FATHER, PROTECT THEM BY THE POWER OF YOUR NAME—THE NAME YOU GAVE ME—SO THAT THEY MAY BE ONE AS WE ARE ONE."* **[7]**

He goes on to say in **VERSES 22–23A,** *"I HAVE GIVEN THEM THE GLORY THAT YOU GAVE ME, THAT THEY MAY BE ONE AS WE ARE ONE: I IN THEM AND YOU IN ME."*

Jesus is in perfect harmony with God the Father. He is our example on how to be in harmony with one another.

As an individual within the church body, we must make an effort to live in harmony with one another. It does not happen overnight; it can take a while but the end result is what is expected from all of us. Get to know all our brothers and sisters in Christ no matter what their social standing or how new they are to the church. Being in harmony takes practice.

It takes work. It can bring frustration, but it is worth it. Ask any choir director or any quartet. **[8]**

If we are not proud but humble within the body and others are the same, there will be harmony. **[9], [10]**

QUESTIONS ON HARMONY

1. What is your answer?

2. What does the illustration about the orchestra say to you?

3. What else can you add to this list on harmony?

4. How does a church look and act when it is harmony?

5. Have you ever worked in an environment like this? What was it like?

6. What does it mean to be like-minded or "in one Spirit"? Do we all have to think alike? (Hint: see the last word of the verse.)

7. Put **JOHN 17:11, 22–23** in your own words.

8. What keeps a church in harmony?

9. What is your part in harmony within your church body?

10. What can you do in the future to encourage harmony within the body of your church?

CHAPTER THIRTY-THREE

PEACE

MARK 9:50B, Jesus tells us to *"HAVE SALT IN YOURSELVES, AND BE AT PEACE WITH EACH OTHER."*   [1]

Webster's defines peace as *the absence of hostility. A state of harmony. Freedom from disquieting feelings. Thoughts of serenity.*

To put this into context, go back to **MARK 9:38.** Here John is speaking for himself as well as the other disciples. They saw a man driving out demons in the name of Jesus, but they told him to stop since he was not one of the "in group." This shows a very selfish attitude. They were only going to allow someone from their own circle to receive the accolades for the miracles performed. It was more important that the man cease what he was doing, rather than the removal of a demon from the possessed man. Doesn't this sound like us today creating drama or overreacting? Their objective seemed to be more about themselves than winning others. They did not have God in mind, just themselves.

Look at Jesus' reaction. **VERSES 39–41,** *"DO NOT STOP HIM," JESUS SAID. "NO ONE WHO DOES A MIRACLE IN MY NAME CAN IN THE NEXT MOMENT SAY ANYTHING BAD ABOUT ME, FOR WHOEVER IS NOT AGAINST US IS FOR US. I TELL YOU THE TRUTH, ANYONE WHO GIVES YOU A CUP OF WATER IN MY NAME BECAUSE YOU BELONG TO CHRIST WILL CERTAINLY NOT LOSE HIS*

REWARD. Jesus is saying don't keep a person who is not in our group from doing good. Be at peace with him. Keep our minds and attitudes on the Lord.

Peace is talked about many times in the New Testament, almost always in conjunction with the Lord. The peace we have with the Lord comes about because of our reconciliation. **ROMANS 5:1,** *THEREFORE, SINCE WE HAVE BEEN JUSTIFIED THROUGH FAITH, WE HAVE PEACE WITH GOD THROUGH OUR LORD JESUS CHRIST.* This happens when we give our hearts to the Lord. We are then reconciled with God. This is the peace of being "right with God."

Paul tells us in **PHILIPPIANS 4:7,** *AND THE PEACE OF GOD, WHICH TRANSCENDS ALL UNDERSTANDING, WILL GUARD YOUR HEARTS AND YOUR MINDS IN CHRIST JESUS.* This is the type of peace that does not come from the definition in Webster's dictionary. Why does it transcend our understanding? It goes beyond the range of human experience or beliefs. It surpasses our understanding. Why can't we totally comprehend the peace of God? Only God can give it, man cannot. If we have this peace with God in us, we have no conflict with him. We have a Father–son relationship. God looks on us and sees the blood of Jesus Christ covering our sins and He is at peace with us.

Paul says this peace will guard our hearts and minds. How does this work?

> We pray about anxiety.
> > We receive the peace of God, knowing He is in charge.
> Jesus is guarding our hearts.
> > He is like a soldier on duty 24/7, always watching out for us. Over our inner life. Our minds. Our lives seem out of control at times, but the Lord's peace reminds us He is in control.

Jesus explains in **JOHN 14:27,** *"PEACE I LEAVE WITH YOU; MY PEACE I GIVE YOU. I DO NOT GIVE TO YOU AS THE WORLD GIVES. DO NOT LET YOUR HEARTS BE TROUBLED AND DO NOT BE AFRAID."* Once we accept the Lord, Jesus brings us a peace, so we have confidence that He is with us always and during times of trouble. This is the type of peace He is talking about.

Then in **JOHN 16:33** He continues, *"I HAVE TOLD YOU THESE THINGS, SO THAT IN ME YOU MAY HAVE PEACE. IN THIS WORLD YOU WILL HAVE TROUBLE.*

BUT TAKE HEART! I HAVE OVERCOME THE WORLD." The key phrase here is "in me." We cannot get this type of peace on our own, no matter what we do or what we say. This can only come when we are living in tune with the Lord and the Holy Spirit who will guide us. We can rely on the Lord to bring peace to us as individuals.

How does peace like this from the Lord come about? The peace I have with the Lord comes about when I am reconciled. I am restored in my relationship with God. It comes when I put my trust in the Lord versus what I can do with my puny abilities. It comes through prayer, talking to God about my concerns, my requests, my petitions, and my thanksgiving. Peace comes upon me, I am no longer at odds with God, I am not out of kilter. I am at peace.[2]

When I accept the Lord as my Savior, the Holy Spirit, who has been wooing me, comes in me to stay and brings peace. The Spirit of the Lord is in me, the Spirit of peace.

ROMANS 8:5–6 tells us when we live in accordance with the Spirit and have our minds set on doing what the Spirit desires, our minds will be controlled by the Spirit, the Spirit of life and peace. Peace is just part of the fruit that the Holy Spirit brings into our lives when we let Him have control. There is a warning as well, we are not to become conceited, provoking and envying each other. (See **GALATIANS 5:22–26**.)

In **MARK 9:42,** Jesus says *"AND IF ANYONE CAUSES ONE OF THESE LITTLE ONES WHO BELIEVE IN ME TO SIN, IT WOULD BE BETTER FOR HIM TO BE THROWN INTO THE SEA WITH A LARGE MILLSTONE TIED AROUND HIS NECK."*

He is talking about the children who were there, but He could also be referring to "newborn Christians." How easy it is for us to take to task the "new Christian" who does not do everything right according to what we believe is correct by our standards. Is this being at peace with each other, or is it creating tension with our brothers? When we are told to be at peace with each other it is not just for a day, it is an enduring peace. [3]

This peace takes an effort. In **ROMANS 14:19,** Paul says *LET US THEREFORE MAKE EVERY EFFORT TO DO WHAT LEADS TO PEACE AND TO MUTUAL EDIFICATION.* [4]

Satan does not want us to have this peace. As Christians we are in a battle with Satan, we are to fight against him, not "each other."

Now that we are at peace with the Lord, how do we have peace with our Christian brothers? We as Christians are called to peace. It is to rule in our hearts since we are one body—the body of Christ, the church. (See **COLOSSIANS 3:15**.) As Paul says in **1 THESSALONIANS 5:13B,** *LIVE IN PEACE WITH EACH OTHER.*

What keeps us from having this peace with one another? We are usually not at peace with God or ourselves which shows up in many actions:

Stubbornness
Resentful hearts
Lack of forgiveness
Lack of humility
Lack of respect for our brothers
Lack of willingness to serve our brothers
Grumbling about each other
Not living in harmony or unity with our brothers
Not accepting our brothers
Not loving our brothers as we have been commanded

To have peace with God is to love Him with all our heart and to please Him by walking in His ways.

To put Him first in our lives
To have nothing between the Lord and ourselves.
To live a Christ-like life every day

Is it any different to be at peace with our fellow Christian brothers? We are to have nothing between our brothers and ourselves. In our daily life we are to look out for our brothers. This would include:

Showing love to our brothers
Being concerned for their lives
Encouraging them
Praying for our brothers in Christ
Being in unity and harmony with them
Having fellowship together

Building them up through instruction and teaching

Going to them if we have issues

This list could go on and on. [5]

MARK 9:33–35 tells us this story, *THEY CAME TO CAPERNAUM. WHEN HE WAS IN THE HOUSE, HE ASKED THEM, "WHAT WERE YOU ARGUING ABOUT ON THE ROAD?" BUT THEY KEPT QUIET BECAUSE ON THE WAY THEY HAD ARGUED ABOUT WHO WAS THE GREATEST. SITTING DOWN, JESUS CALLED THE TWELVE AND SAID, "IF ANYONE WANTS TO BE FIRST, HE MUST BE THE VERY LAST, AND THE SERVANT OF ALL."* Peace with our brothers comes from putting them first, but the key to it all is to love our brothers just as Christ has loved us.

These are the keys to peace with "one another."

Repeating **PHILIPPIANS 4:7,** *AND THE PEACE OF GOD, WHICH TRANSCENDS ALL UNDERSTANDING, WILL GUARD YOUR HEARTS AND YOUR MINDS IN CHRIST JESUS.*

This peace we have with the Lord should allow us to extend our love to our brothers, which brings about peace with one another. If we are not at peace with a brother, go to him and reconcile. Do not allow discord in the body. [6]

QUESTIONS ON PEACE

1.   What does peace with one another look and feel like?

2.   Give your best description of the peace of God.

3.   As a Christian we are to be at peace with God. Do you feel at peace with God? If not, why not?

4.   Why does it take an effort to be at peace with one another?

5.   What would you add to the list?

6.   Are you at peace with all of your brothers and sisters in Christ? If not, what do you intend to do about it?

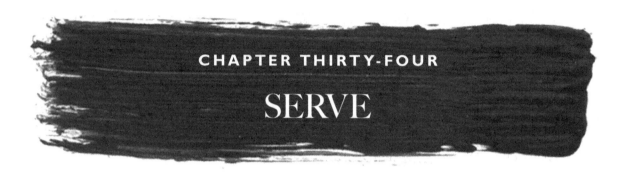

CHAPTER THIRTY-FOUR

SERVE

GALATIANS 5:13, *YOU, MY BROTHERS, WERE CALLED TO BE FREE. BUT DO NOT USE YOUR FREEDOM TO INDULGE THE SINFUL NATURE; RATHER, SERVE ONE ANOTHER IN LOVE.*

We, as Christians, are given many different directions in the Bible on how we are to serve.

First, we are to serve God. Jesus said to Satan when He was tempted: **MATTHEW 4:10,** *JESUS SAID TO HIM, "AWAY FROM ME, SATAN! FOR IT IS WRITTEN: 'WORSHIP THE LORD YOUR GOD, AND SERVE HIM ONLY.'"* There is only one God, God our Father and creator of all. This is who all Christians are to serve without hesitation.

Second, we are to serve Jesus. Jesus says in **JOHN 12:26,** *"WHOEVER SERVES ME MUST FOLLOW ME; AND WHERE I AM, MY SERVANT ALSO WILL BE. MY FATHER WILL HONOR THE ONE WHO SERVES ME."*

COLOSSIANS 3:24B, *IT IS THE LORD CHRIST YOU ARE SERVING.* If it is the Lord we are serving, we are to do it to the best of our ability. We are not to give the Lord second best. But what does this really mean? How can we bring this into a practical part of our lives?

The best example I can personally give is what I came to see in my own life. As a young man, I loved to participate in sports. I was there for every practice, on time for every game, and always gave my all. It meant a lot to me. Then I started looking at the way I served the Lord. Was I willing to give of my time, my energy and devotion to the service to the Lord in the same way? Sorry to say the answer was "no." I realized there were changes I had to make in my life. Did I have to give up my love for sports? No, but it was necessary for me to change priorities. The Lord had to come first, not second or third. I am to honor the Lord with my service because of my love for the Lord.

The Lord is our example on how to serve. In **PHILIPPIANS 2:5–7A** it tells us *YOUR ATTITUDE SHOULD BE THE SAME AS THAT OF CHRIST JESUS: WHO, BEING IN VERY NATURE GOD, DID NOT CONSIDER EQUALITY WITH GOD SOMETHING TO BE GRASPED, BUT MADE HIMSELF NOTHING, TAKING THE VERY NATURE OF A SERVANT.*

What examples did Jesus give us?

> He cared about the people.
> He taught them to serve by his examples, such as when He washed the feet of the disciples.
> He was obedient to the Father even unto death. (See **HEBREWS 9:14.**)
> He humbled Himself by becoming a man and obedient to death. (See **PHILIPPIANS 2:8.**)
> He gave Himself up for our sins. He was the true servant. **MATTHEW 20:28A,** *JUST AS THE SON OF MAN DID NOT COME TO BE SERVED, BUT TO SERVE.* [1]
> He was His Father's servant even though He was the Son of God.
> He loved the Master, His Father. [2]

Third, Paul tells about being a servant to the gospel in **COLOSSIANS 1:23B** when he said, *THIS IS THE GOSPEL THAT YOU HEARD AND THAT HAS BEEN PROCLAIMED TO EVERY CREATURE UNDER HEAVEN, AND OF WHICH I, PAUL, HAVE BECOME A SERVANT.* Paul is a servant to the gospel, the good news, and he shows it by devoting all his time and energy in spreading the gospel. He is willing to go anywhere, stand in front of anyone, and proclaim the good news of Jesus Christ with no excuse for his love for the gospel. He is the ultimate servant! [3]

Fourth, we are to serve the body without quarreling. **2 TIMOTHY 2:24A,** *AND THE LORD'S SERVANT MUST NOT QUARREL.* The body is our fellow Christians. When we become Christians, we all become a part of this body, the church. We are to get along. **[4]**

Fifth, we have been given gifts to be used to serve one another, and we are to do it with love in our hearts and in our actions. In **1 PETER 4:10A,** Peter gave this message to the church: *EACH ONE SHOULD USE WHATEVER GIFT HE HAS RECEIVED TO SERVE OTHERS.* What Peter is pointing out is that gifts are not for our own benefit, but they are to be used for the betterment of the body, the church of the Lord. **[5]**

Our church leaders have gifts and they are for building up the church. **EPHESIANS 4:12,** speaking about apostles, prophets, evangelists, pastors, and teachers says their gifts were given *TO PREPARE GOD'S PEOPLE FOR WORKS OF SERVICE, SO THAT THE BODY OF CHRIST MAY BE BUILT UP.* The gifts we have been given are for a distinct purpose. To prepare all of us to serve in whatever capacity we can. They are not for our glory, our ego, or our own self-satisfaction. To be used properly, they must be used to serve the Lord.

Some have the gift of serving, but we are all called to serve. We can and must serve even if we do not have the gift. We are all called to have the heart of a servant.

Some in the body are called to serve in a non-leadership role. To serve in the background. Why would this be so? We are like bees. Not everyone can be the queen. There must be worker bees to get things accomplished. The key to our gifts is to use them to the best of our abilities in service of the Lord on a continual basis. **1 PETER 4:11B** tells us when we serve, we *SHOULD DO IT WITH THE STRENGTH GOD PROVIDES, SO THAT IN ALL THINGS GOD MAY BE PRAISED THROUGH JESUS CHRIST.* So how can we do this? **PHILIPPIANS 4:13,** *I CAN DO EVERYTHING THROUGH HIM WHO GIVES ME STRENGTH.* Rely on the Lord to give us direction and strength to serve the Master. Then give it our all by using the gifts we have been given.

Jesus gave us an example of what is expected of a servant in **MATTHEW 24:36–51. [6]**

The keys are:

It is unknown when the Master might return.

Don't be caught up in just doing life's day to day work.
We are to keep watch.
As a servant it is good to be doing what is expected of us.
Don't be caught up in life just because the Lord has not yet come back.
He is returning.   [7]

We are to continue serving until the Lord comes or until we are called home. This is to be done on a daily basis. It is expected by our Master.

We know we are to serve one another, but what does that mean?   [8]

Service in the church can entail many things; some in the forefront, but most in the background:

Ushering
Greeting
Helping in the nursery
Mowing grass
Singing in choir
Visiting
Listening to someone
Helping someone move
Folding the bulletin
Helping in the church library
Keeping up with the flower beds
Being a prayer warrior
Helping at church dinners
Volunteering where needed   [9]

Just doing anything that assists or supports someone else is being a servant. It is not about us; it is about the other person. It is up to each of us to take the initiative when we see where we can be servants. The focus is not on us, we are to focus first on the Lord, then on others.

LUKE 17:10, Jesus says, *"SO YOU ALSO, WHEN YOU HAVE DONE EVERYTHING YOU WERE TOLD TO DO, SHOULD SAY, 'WE ARE UNWORTHY SERVANTS; WE HAVE ONLY DONE OUR DUTY.'"*   [10]

What is this verse telling us?

> Serving is expected of us.
> It is our duty until we are called home.
> Serving one another is not something we ever retire from doing.
> Serving is its own reward. Don't expect anything else.

When we serve, we are only doing our duty. Nothing more or less, but we need to do more than just our duty, we need to go above and beyond.

When we are God's servants, we serve because that is who we are. We serve just like we breathe. It should be automatic. It is an attitude of service. As the Lord's servant, we are to look for ways to serve. The church can always use more servants.

What would the church be like if we were to take this area of servanthood to heart? What would we be like if we took this area of servanthood to heart? **[11]**

QUESTIONS ON SERVE

1. Look at **MATTHEW 20:27–28** and then explain "slave."

2. Relate some other areas you remember of Jesus' servanthood. Whom did He serve?

3. Explain Paul's servanthood.

4. Explain serving the body. What is the body? Why is it important not to quarrel?

5. **1 PETER 4:10–14,** why did we each receive a gift? What is its purpose?

6. Put **MATTHEW 24:36–51** into your own words.

7. What areas have you been given stewardship over? What do you think you need to be doing until the Lord returns?

8. What does it really mean to serve one another?

9. Add to this list.

10. Explain **LUKE 17:10** in your own words. Relate it to your Christian life.

11. Tell of a person you see as a good servant and why you think so.

CHAPTER THIRTY-FIVE

WAIT FOR

1 CORINTHIANS 11:33, *SO THEN, MY BROTHERS, WHEN YOU COME TOGETHER TO EAT, WAIT FOR EACH OTHER.*

Paul uses the words *SO THEN,* so then we need to go back to **1 CORINTHIANS 11:17–22, 34** and see why he uses these words. Paul was giving direction to the new Christians as they met and ate together. After the meal they would celebrate the sacrament of Communion. Having Communion together celebrates the bond it brings to all Christians by remembering the Lord who gave His life for all, rich or poor, slave or free, Jew or Gentile. Paul was frustrated with the way they handled the meals, but also how it related to the Communion that followed. The habit of the church at that time was to get together on Sunday evening for a meal (we would term it a potluck supper) followed by Communion. The problem was that the rich would bring in much more food than the poor, because they could afford to. But then the rich would go first and eat most of the food, thus the poor would get little to eat. The attitude and actions of the rich brought about resentment from the poor. Paul felt that this did not belong within the church body. By their actions, they were taking away the solidarity the sacrament of Communion was supposed to bring. It is hard to bring about bonding if some are not being sensitive to the feelings and or needs of others. [1], [2]

1 CORINTHIANS 11:18, Paul speaks of *DIVISIONS AMONG YOU.* Later in **VERSE 21,** he brings out that one of the divisions is some are going ahead of others without waiting. By doing this he says *ONE REMAINS HUNGRY, ANOTHER GETS DRUNK.* He then goes on to ask in **VERSE 22,** *DON'T YOU HAVE HOMES TO EAT AND DRINK IN?* By doing this they look as if they *DESPISE THE CHURCH OF GOD.* He goes on and asks if their actions *HUMILIATE THOSE WHO HAVE NOTHING?* The rich humiliate the poor by taking most of the food and drink.

He goes on to offer ways to eliminate these problems. **VERSE 34,** *IF ANYONE IS HUNGRY, HE SHOULD EAT AT HOME, SO THAT WHEN YOU MEET TOGETHER IT MAY NOT RESULT IN JUDGMENT.* He sets up rules for the dinner part of their get together. He does not want some pushing their way to the front of the line and then eating all the food. How would we like it if people would do this today at a church carry-in dinner? Not so much! Is there anything more frustrating than a line crasher, someone who feels he is better than the rest of the people? This can come about in a store, a bank, in traffic; someone bullies himself ahead to the inconvenience of others. How would we feel? What if this was your Christian brother? Can we see why Paul addresses the problem? We are to be servants to one another just as Christ was a servant. He is our example. [3]

Notice in **VERSE 34,** Paul mentions that their actions can *RESULT IN JUDGMENT.* Where is this coming from? **VERSE 27** says *THEREFORE, WHOEVER EATS THE BREAD OR DRINKS THE CUP OF THE LORD IN AN UNWORTHY MANNER WILL BE GUILTY OF SINNING AGAINST THE BODY AND BLOOD OF THE LORD.* Then he points out in **VERSE 30,** *THAT IS WHY MANY AMONG YOU ARE WEAK AND SICK, AND A NUMBER OF YOU HAVE FALLEN ASLEEP.*

By their actions they are bringing judgment upon themselves. This lesson is not just for the Corinthians, it is for all of us today. We must take the sacrament of Holy Communion seriously. At the time of Communion, are we right with God? Are we at odds with a brother? Are we in step with the Lord in our daily lives? If not, we should not take Communion. We just read the consequences. [4]

We are to take the issue of treating all peoples alike just as serious; no matter their income, color or race or what other differences we see. There are to be no divisions within the body. God sees us as all the same. **GALATIANS 3:26–28** says it best, *YOU ARE ALL*

SONS OF GOD THROUGH FAITH IN CHRIST JESUS, FOR ALL OF YOU WHO WERE BAPTIZED INTO CHRIST HAVE CLOTHED YOURSELVES WITH CHRIST. THERE IS NEITHER JEW NOR GREEK, SLAVE NOR FREE, MALE NOR FEMALE, FOR YOU ARE ALL ONE IN CHRIST JESUS. Make sure we live our lives this way. [5]

QUESTIONS ON WAIT FOR

1. How would you explain Communion to a fellow Christian or to a non-Christian?

2. Is the Communion sacrament sacred to you? Explain.

3. How would this apply today?

4. Why is Paul making such a big a fuss about the way they take Communion?

5. How would you apply this verse to your life today and how you live it?

CHAPTER THIRTY-SIX

WARN THOSE WHO ARE IDLE

1 THESSALONIANS 5:14A, *AND WE URGE YOU, BROTHERS, WARN THOSE WHO ARE IDLE.*

Who is Paul talking about? He could be talking about Christians who are not doing any work in the church. Do we have any people that do no work for the Lord in our church? At least in our opinion? It could be a Christian that won't get involved or they are just shy. Or it could just be a lazy Christian, at least in our own opinion. It seems they are doing nothing. [1]

Be very careful here. When I got married, I was a gung-ho Christian, involved in everything within the church body. I was a Sunday school teacher, the Sunday school director, a church board member, player and coach on the church softball team, a youth leader along with my wife, church choir member along with my wife, plus on other committees. I grew frustrated with other Christians that seemed to be doing nothing within the church body. I was passing judgment on them. To me it seemed like they deserved it. [2]

One weekend when my pastor was out of town, he called me and asked if I would make a hospital visit since there was no deacon available and the patient's wife had asked that someone from the church visit with her husband. Hospital visitation was definitely not my calling, but I could not say no. To put it bluntly, while I was on my way there, I was frustrated with all the other people in the church who, in my mind, were all sitting at home with their families doing nothing. At least that was my opinion. When I arrived at the hospital, an elderly gentleman from our church was in with the patient. The patient's wife came out to thank me for coming. She went on to tell me what a godsend the elderly person was. How many times he came to visit, how he continually witnessed to her husband and through this witnessing her husband had accepted the Lord as his Savior. She and her husband both agreed they could not have done without him. He was not in any official capacity, he just visited out of the love of his heart.

My ego went to zilch, I was totally ashamed of myself and ashamed of what the Lord was thinking of me. This experience taught me a humbling lesson. Who am I to judge the work of others? Many workers are never seen, they work in the background. They just do what the Lord leads them to do, not expecting any praise from man. So be very careful of thinking of people as idle, we never know what all they might be doing in the church behind the scenes.   [3]

Yes, we are all called to use the gifts we have been given for the church. Each gift is given to make the body complete, but it's not up to us to judge what people are doing for the Lord. Even God works as we are told in **ROMANS 8:28,** *AND WE KNOW THAT IN ALL THINGS GOD WORKS FOR THE GOOD OF THOSE WHO LOVE HIM, WHO HAVE BEEN CALLED ACCORDING TO HIS PURPOSE.* Jesus asks for more workers in **MATTHEW 9:37–38,** *THEN HE SAID TO HIS DISCIPLES, "THE HARVEST IS PLENTIFUL BUT THE WORKERS ARE FEW. ASK THE LORD OF THE HARVEST, THEREFORE, TO SEND OUT WORKERS INTO HIS HARVEST FIELD."* These workers are all the Christian followers of Jesus. You and me. We are given gifts for a reason. **EPHESIANS 4:11–12** tells us the reason. *IT WAS HE* (the Holy Spirit) *WHO GAVE SOME TO BE APOSTLES, SOME TO BE PROPHETS, SOME TO BE EVANGELISTS, AND SOME TO BE PASTORS AND TEACHERS, TO PREPARE GOD'S PEOPLE FOR WORKS OF SERVICE, SO THAT THE BODY OF CHRIST MAY BE BUILT UP.* **VERSE 16** goes on to say *FROM HIM THE WHOLE BODY, JOINED AND HELD TOGETHER BY EVERY SUPPORTING LIGAMENT, GROWS AND BUILDS ITSELF UP IN LOVE, AS EACH PART DOES ITS WORK.* Doing work for the Lord is just an outgrowth of each of us becoming a Christian. As James tells us in **JAMES 2:18,** *BUT SOMEONE WILL SAY, "YOU HAVE FAITH; I HAVE DEEDS." SHOW ME YOUR FAITH WITHOUT DEEDS, AND I WILL SHOW YOU MY FAITH BY WHAT I DO.* He goes on in **VERSE 24,** when he is speaking of Abraham.

YOU SEE THAT A PERSON IS JUSTIFIED BY WHAT HE DOES AND NOT BY FAITH ALONE. James is saying works and faith go hand in hand. No, we are not saved by works, but works needs to be a part of our faith. It takes both. **[4]**

So, is this what Paul is telling the Thessalonians? Warn those who are idle in the church, meaning those who are doing no work? It could be this, but he can also be telling the brothers to warn those who are not doing any work outside the church. This is probably what Paul is talking about. Some in the church body had decided that since the Lord was coming back soon, they did not have to work to earn a living. The other Christians would and should help them out, after all isn't that what Christians do? Well, yes, and no. If a Christian brother is in trouble and cannot work, it is up to us as fellow Christians to help that person in his time of need. But if a person decides not to work, do we as his fellow Christians have the same responsibility? **[5]**

2 THESSALONIANS 3:6–7, *IN THE NAME OF THE LORD JESUS CHRIST, WE COMMAND YOU, BROTHERS, TO KEEP AWAY FROM EVERY BROTHER WHO IS IDLE AND DOES NOT LIVE ACCORDING TO THE TEACHING YOU RECEIVED FROM US. FOR YOU YOURSELVES KNOW HOW YOU OUGHT TO FOLLOW OUR EXAMPLE. WE WERE NOT IDLE WHEN WE WERE WITH YOU.* Paul goes on to say they (Paul, Silas and Timothy) did not eat their food without paying for it. They did not rely on them to feed and to take care of them. They worked day and night to support their own needs. Why? He said he did this to be a model for the people to follow. In **VERSE 10** he says *FOR EVEN WHEN WE WERE WITH YOU, WE GAVE YOU THIS RULE: "IF A MAN WILL NOT WORK, HE SHALL NOT EAT."* These are strong words, but notice it is the man's choice, "if he *will not* work." The person had made a choice to not work, so Paul is saying since this is the decision he has made, give him no help. Strong words from Paul but he is saying the non-worker is to receive no food since it is his choice not to earn any money. One place says these people are loafers. **[6], [7]**

What is the matter with idle church workers? Laziness breeds laziness. Paul recognizes that if some people are working and others are not doing anything, it won't be long until others decide not to work. Have you ever had a person working for you that was a good worker and then hired a goof off to work with him? What happens? The lazy worker's habits rub off on the excellent worker, and before long you have two lazy people. This is one reason to avoid idle Christians.

Another reason to avoid the idle is because they can cause problems within the church body. **2 THESSALONIANS 3:11–13,** *WE HEAR THAT SOME AMONG YOU ARE IDLE. THEY ARE NOT BUSY; THEY ARE BUSYBODIES. SUCH PEOPLE WE COMMAND AND URGE IN THE LORD JESUS CHRIST TO SETTLE DOWN AND EARN THE BREAD THEY EAT. AND AS FOR YOU, BROTHERS, NEVER TIRE OF DOING WHAT IS RIGHT.* Since they are not busy working, they have time on their hands, they now have become busybodies. What comes to mind when someone is called a busybody? Someone that meddles in other people's affairs. People with time on their hands seem to know what everyone else should be doing, and if they don't know what others are doing, they want to know. They will tell us what to do, when they won't do it themselves. They will be glad to tell us what we are doing wrong. Know anyone like this?   [8]

Idlers also become gossips. **1 TIMOTHY 5:13,** Paul is talking about idle, young widows when he says *BESIDES, THEY GET INTO THE HABIT OF BEING IDLE AND GOING ABOUT FROM HOUSE TO HOUSE. AND NOT ONLY DO THEY BECOME IDLERS, BUT ALSO GOSSIPS AND BUSYBODIES, SAYING THINGS THEY OUGHT NOT TO.* Is there anything worse in the church than someone who gossips? Someone who passes along juicy tidbits. Some of which might be true, but other gossip that might just be that, gossip. Paul knows if someone is busy, they do not have time to talk to others and gossip. They do not have the time to pass on things that do not need to be passed around. The problem with gossip is most of it is made up and not even true in the first place.   [9]

The wisest man, Solomon, wrote many proverbs about gossips. **PROVERBS 16:28,** *A PERVERSE MAN STIRS UP DISSENSION, AND A GOSSIP SEPARATES CLOSE FRIENDS.* How many times has gossip torn up a friendship? Too many times. There are many more proverbs about gossiping. (See **PROVERBS 11:13, 20:19, 26:20** and **26:22**.)   [10]

Paul goes on to say in **2 THESSALONIANS 3:14–15,** *IF ANYONE DOES NOT OBEY OUR INSTRUCTION IN THIS LETTER, TAKE SPECIAL NOTE OF HIM. DO NOT ASSOCIATE WITH HIM, IN ORDER THAT HE MAY FEEL ASHAMED. YET DO NOT REGARD HIM AS AN ENEMY, BUT WARN HIM AS A BROTHER.*

Our fellow Christians are not the enemy, Satan is our enemy. But at the same time, we need to stay away from those who disobey the Christian guidelines that have been laid out for us in the New Testament. If people do not want to work, we are to warn them of the consequences of their decision. If they come to us with gossip, turn them aside. Do not get caught up in their gossip. If they are idle, go to them and find out why they are not working. If they want to work, do all we can to help them find work. If it is by their choice, we have no reason to support them. In today's society, this is very relevant to the body. **[11]**

HEBREWS 6:10–12, *GOD IS NOT UNJUST; HE WILL NOT FORGET YOUR WORK AND THE LOVE YOU HAVE SHOWN HIM AS YOU HAVE HELPED HIS PEOPLE AND CONTINUE TO HELP THEM. WE WANT EACH OF YOU TO SHOW THIS SAME DILIGENCE TO THE VERY END, IN ORDER TO MAKE YOUR HOPE SURE. WE DO NOT WANT YOU TO BECOME LAZY, BUT TO IMITATE THOSE WHO THROUGH FAITH AND PATIENCE INHERIT WHAT HAS BEEN PROMISED.*

Keep working until the Lord comes and warn the idle to do the Lord's work. **[12]**

QUESTIONS ON WARN THOSE WHO ARE IDLE

1. What are your true feelings to idle Christians, ones who seem to do no work within the body?

2. Have you ever felt this way?

3. Have you ever been surprised by someone's work within the body and you knew nothing about it?

4. Explain faith versus works using **JAMES 2:14–26.**

5. What are your true feelings about Christians that don't work outside the home?

6. In **2 THESSALONIANS 3:6–7,** why does Paul say we are to stay away from those who are idle? Why did Paul use himself as an example?

7. How does this apply to today's society?

8. Have you seen this within the church body?

9. Do you agree with **1 TIMOTHY 5:13** that those who are idle can become busybodies?

10. Look up and review the parables listed in **PROVERBS.**

11. Using **2 THESSALONIANS 3:14–15,** why should we not associate with the people Paul is talking about? Is he being too harsh?

12. What can you do to help either type of idler?

CHAPTER THIRTY-SEVEN

HONOR

ROMANS 12:10B, *HONOR ONE ANOTHER ABOVE YOURSELVES.*

Webster's definition: *great respect, high public regard* [1]

When the word honor comes up, it is easy to think about the term *your honor.* Judges receive this respect by what they have accomplished; it is a title they have earned. People are given this title for the position they hold. The same is true in this command. We are to give this title to fellow Christians. Not that we go around calling fellow Christians *your honor,* but this should be in our mind. We are to treat them with the honor they received since becoming Christians. We are all part of the family of God thus we should treat each other as God's chosen sons and daughters.

We are to hold our Christian brothers in high regard, particularly in public. We are also to treat them with great respect. What would our churches be like if we did this? Surely they would be different from what they are today. How would the world view the church if we were to honor one another the way we are commanded? [2]

It is not that we are not to disagree; Paul and Peter disagreed. (See **GALATIANS 2.**) But they respected each other for what the Lord had done for them in the past and was doing in their individual lives at that time. The Lord had blessed each of them and they had brought converts to the Lord, both Jews and Gentiles. [3]

Honor is not just how we talk to people; it is our actions. We are told in **EXODUS 20:12A** to **_HONOR YOUR FATHER AND YOUR MOTHER,_** and we might do this in the way we speak to them, but we can dishonor them in the way we live our lives. How are we to honor our fathers and mothers?

> By treating them with the honor they deserve
> By keeping in contact with them
> By looking out for their best interests
> By doing for them what they cannot do for themselves
> By telling them _thank you_ for what they have done for us
> By letting them know we love them
> By living our lives in such a way that it would bring honor to them versus dishonor [4]

These are some of the ways we are to honor our mothers and fathers. Take this list and use it on how to honor fellow Christians.

Jesus said this in regard to himself to his fellow Jews in **MATTHEW 15:7–8, _"YOU HYPOCRITES! ISAIAH WAS RIGHT WHEN HE PROPHESIED ABOUT YOU: 'THESE PEOPLE HONOR ME WITH THEIR LIPS, BUT THEIR HEARTS ARE FAR FROM ME.'"_** We can be the same way with our Christian friends. We treat them all right to their face, but behind their backs we gossip about them. We talk bad about them. We try to hurt them and bring them down to our level. This is not what Paul is telling the Roman Christians to do to each other in his command to honor one another. (See **ROMANS 12:10**.) [5]

We love to be honored. This is just our nature, who doesn't? Jesus saw this in the Jewish leaders. **MATTHEW 23:6–7, _"THEY LOVE THE PLACE OF HONOR AT BANQUETS AND THE MOST IMPORTANT SEATS IN THE SYNAGOGUES; THEY LOVE TO BE GREETED IN THE MARKETPLACES AND TO HAVE MEN CALL THEM 'RABBI'."_** Self-promotion is huge today, be it sports figures, politicians, musical artists, actors and actresses, business leaders, world leaders, or just famous for being famous. (See reality TV.) They all do everything and anything to promote themselves to try to bring themselves honor. We should not allow ourselves to get caught up in it. This is not how Christians are to act.

Jesus later goes on to tell the story about a wedding feast in **LUKE 14:7–11.** The key verse is **LUKE 14:11.** He says, *"FOR EVERYONE WHO EXALTS HIMSELF WILL BE HUMBLED, AND HE WHO HUMBLES HIMSELF WILL BE EXALTED."* [6]

As we read these teachings, notice it is okay to let someone honor us, but it is not up to us to honor ourselves.

Jesus is our example. He honored others above Himself. The prime example was when He washed the feet of the apostles as told in **JOHN 13:1–17.** This was the ultimate in being humble. **JOHN 13:3,** *JESUS KNEW THAT THE FATHER HAD PUT ALL THINGS UNDER HIS POWER, AND THAT HE HAD COME FROM GOD AND WAS RETURNING TO GOD. JOHN 13:14–15, "NOW THAT I, YOUR LORD AND TEACHER, HAVE WASHED YOUR FEET, YOU ALSO SHOULD WASH ONE ANOTHER'S FEET. I HAVE SET YOU AN EXAMPLE THAT YOU SHOULD DO AS I HAVE DONE FOR YOU."*

What did He do? He humbled Himself and took the action of a slave to give honor to His disciples. He taught them to do the same, to honor each other over themselves. He ends the lesson by telling in **JOHN 13:16–17,** *"I TELL YOU THE TRUTH, NO SERVANT IS GREATER THAN HIS MASTER, NOR IS A MESSENGER GREATER THAN THE ONE WHO SENT HIM. NOW THAT YOU KNOW THESE THINGS, YOU WILL BE BLESSED IF YOU DO THEM."* We are the messengers that our Master has sent. We are not greater than Him. We are to humble ourselves and give honor to one another. Blessings will follow if we humble ourselves.

We are also to honor God with our body. Paul tells the Thessalonian church in **1 THESSALONIANS 4:3–4,** *IT IS GOD'S WILL THAT YOU SHOULD BE SANCTIFIED (set apart): THAT YOU SHOULD AVOID SEXUAL IMMORALITY; THAT EACH OF YOU SHOULD LEARN TO CONTROL HIS OWN BODY IN A WAY THAT IS HOLY AND HONORABLE.* What does this mean? Immoral sexual acts include:

Adultery
Pornography
Homosexuality
Sex outside marriage

Is this all *honoring your body* means? No, it has a deeper meaning than that.

We were given our bodies and lives by God.
We are not to abuse our bodies.
We are not to hate our bodies.
We are to take care of our bodies.
We are to use our bodies and lives for the Lord.

This is key to our Christian lives. We are told in **EPHESIANS 5:29–30,** that we are to feed and care for our bodies for we are members of His body. Yes, this does include keeping our bodies in shape by watching our diet and exercising. We are to turn over our worries and concerns to keep from undo stress. Personally, I also feel we are not to take extreme risks that could end our lives just for the *thrill* of danger. Our lives belong to the Lord, not to us. The Lord has great plans for each of us. Do not be careless with our lives.

In **1 CORINTHIANS 6:19–20** Paul says *DO YOU NOT KNOW THAT YOUR BODY IS A TEMPLE OF THE HOLY SPIRIT, WHO IS IN YOU, WHOM YOU HAVE RECEIVED FROM GOD? YOU ARE NOT YOUR OWN; YOU WERE BOUGHT AT A PRICE. THEREFORE HONOR GOD WITH YOUR BODY.*

Why is our body not our own?
We were bought at a price.
The price was the death of Jesus.
His blood was spilled.
The Holy Spirit dwells in us.
He has given us eternal life with Him.
We are to honor God with our bodies.
Our bodies are to be used to reflect the Lord to others. [7]

One of the key areas about honoring one another is found in **1 CORINTHIANS 12:21–27.** Paul talks about the *body parts*. The body parts are the people of the church. Just as we are to honor God with our bodies, we are to honor the body of Christ, the church.

Some of the key points from this passage are:

> We need each other.
> The parts that seem the weakest are indispensable.
> The parts we see as less honorable are treated with special honor.
> Parts that are not presentable are treated with special modesty.
> God had combined the parts to work together.
> He has given greater honor to the parts that lack it.
> All parts are to have equal concern for each other.
> If one part suffers, we all suffer.
> If one part is honored, we all rejoice.
> We are shaped for His use.
> We are one body, but diverse.
> Same Lord, same Spirit, same mission.

These verses are talking about the gifts the Holy Spirit has given each part, each person, our fellow Christians. Within the body, each gift, each person, is needed for the church to function the way the Lord planned for it to work. Even though some people have weaker gifts, they are just as necessary as the ones with the greater gift. Paul tells us in **1 CORINTHIANS 12:21–22, *THE EYE CANNOT SAY TO THE HAND, "I DON'T NEED YOU!" AND THE HEAD CANNOT SAY TO THE FEET, "I DON'T NEED YOU!" ON THE CONTRARY, THOSE PARTS OF THE BODY THAT SEEM TO BE WEAKER ARE INDISPENSABLE.*** Whom is Paul talking about? Maybe the person who has the gift of helps, mercy or serving. All are people that we do not see using their gifts. Christians that work in the background are doing the Lord's service, and they deserve special honor. The people with the greater gifts, preaching or teaching, receive their honor just from being in the forefront.

We are told to honor fellow Christians within the church body. Particularly the ones with the weaker gifts. How do we do this? We need to somehow find a way. Some suggestions might be:

> A yearly prayer time for all people in service for the church
> A yearly awards banquet
> A weekly list of different workers asking the congregation for prayer
> A weekly section in the church bulletin for a *get to know you* for a different worker [8]

Ways need to be found to honor those in service within the body. Some for the work they do and others for the words they say.

To gain honor, high regard and respect; live a life that is Christ-like. People will see the difference in you and others and will honor your life. You might not always know it, but it will be true none the less. **[9]**

Be the example in your church showing honor to all, and others will follow in your footsteps. Blessings will follow. **[10]**

QUESTIONS ON HONOR

1. What is your definition of honor?

2. Why is honor so important between Christians?

3. Is it possible to disagree with fellow Christians and still honor them? How would you go about it?

4. In what ways do you honor your father and mother?

5. What keeps you from honoring fellow Christians?

6. How can you relate the parable in **LUKE 14** to your life today?

7. How do you think people honor or dishonor their bodies today?

8. What suggestions do you have?

9. Do you think people today see Christians as honorable? Why or why not?

10. How do you personally honor the people in the body of believers? The different body parts?

CHAPTER THIRTY-EIGHT
CONFESS YOUR SINS

JAMES 5:16, *THEREFORE CONFESS YOUR SINS TO EACH OTHER AND PRAY FOR EACH OTHER SO THAT YOU MAY BE HEALED. THE PRAYER OF A RIGHTEOUS MAN IS POWERFUL AND EFFECTIVE.*

Surely James cannot be asking Christians to go around and confess their sins to each other, can he? This is exactly what he is saying, but quoting an old TV show, Lost In Space, *"DANGER, WILL ROBINSON!"* [1]

Why do this? The verse tells us that the ***PRAYER OF A RIGHTEOUS MAN IS POWERFUL AND EFFECTIVE.*** When we sin, we must go to the Lord and confess our sins, then He will forgive us. But when I sin against someone, and I go to the Lord, that does not let the person know I realize I have sinned against them. I need to go to them and confess my sin to them and seek their forgiveness. There have been times in my life I have gone to someone and asked forgiveness and they did not realize what I had done. It is better to go and ask for forgiveness than to let the sin go. If in our mind we have sinned, we need to go to the person.

There are other times when we sin, and it is not against one person but maybe the whole body of believers. Then it is best to go the body and ask for forgiveness. Other times if we are fighting a sin and not winning, this is the time to go to one person and let them know our battle and ask for prayer.

I had a very close Christian friend that came to me and said he wanted me to pray for him as he was dealing with a specific sin and the temptation of that sin. He told me straight out what the sin was. I confessed to him that I have had and still had a problem with the same sin. For years we prayed for each other for strength to overcome. In this case I was able to deal openly and frankly with a stubborn sin. It was actually a release to be able to talk about it openly.   [2]

Why do this? The person we go to, we see as a righteous person, one that we trust and see as the right person to pray for us. This person's prayer is seen as powerful and effective. This is the person we want to pray for us.

Yes, we are to confess our sins to one another, but we must be very careful when we do this. Make sure:

- We can trust the person. We must be totally confident in and know that person's character. They have a great potential to do us harm.
- Never tell a gossip. If this is the type of person that passes things on, do not go to them. If this person is a gossip carrier, run away. This should go without being said but sometimes people error.

Partner with a person that will pray for you. The whole purpose of going to others is for their help in praying for us. We need their prayers to be a petition to the Lord on our behalf. At the same time, if we commit to pray for others, do not let them down. If we cannot continually pray for the person, do not agree to do so. Honor the commitment.

We must make sure we confess our sin to the Lord first. This absolutely must have priority.

Talk to a strong, mature Christian instead of a new Christian. Someone that will try to help us work through problems. Talking to a new Christian might throw stumbling blocks in front of them. If a new Christian sees us as a strong, mature Christian, and we go to them and confess a sin, they might have a hard time getting past our sin to even pray for us. It might set them back in their new Christian experience.

When asking someone for prayer to defeat a sin, is it a sin we are committed to getting out of our life? There must be a commitment that we want the sin gone, no games. If we want others to pray for us, we must be serious about the matter.

If others come to us, never, ever betray their confidence. Personally, when someone tells me something in confidence, I rarely tell my spouse. Is it because I can't trust her? No, just the opposite, but if the story gets out, I'll know it did not come from her. It is a protection for my wife.

Confession is best done one on one. Do not go to the body unless we are directed to do so by the Holy Spirit. We stand a strong chance of alienating the whole group when we tell them all at once. Only confess to the body of believers when it is a sin against all of them. [3]

One of the keys to confessing our sin is knowing with confidence that the Lord forgives us our sins when we confess our sins to Him. With the Lord they are then forgotten, unlike what we do to others. We might forgive, but it seems as if we can never forget.

The first time something like this comes up in the New Testament is with John the Baptist. **MATTHEW 3:5–6, *PEOPLE WENT OUT TO HIM FROM JERUSALEM AND ALL JUDEA AND THE WHOLE REGION OF JORDAN. CONFESSING THEIR SINS, THEY WERE BAPTIZED BY HIM IN THE JORDAN RIVER.*** The people went to him and were declaring openly their sins. Once they had confessed their sins, John baptized them. Were they telling only John or the whole crowd? This is unknown. But from the message of John, the people knew they needed to repent from their sins. Were they telling John each sin, or were they simply saying, "I am a sinner unclean, forgive me Lord"? Not many people have the nerve to stand in front of a group and tell everyone their personal sins. I know I don't. It is exceedingly uncomfortable.

We must confess our sins to the Lord. By doing this, it will help us grow as Christians. We should be able to tell friends that we have a problem with a sin in our lives so we can then request prayer. We might even say we have an unspoken request. The key is we need corporate prayer for our lives to be more Christ-like. My pastor, Dr. Jim Smith, said "it takes a church to raise a Christian."

Christians do sin. Again, all Christians sin. It is what we do after we sin that is important. **1 JOHN 1:8–10, *IF WE CLAIM TO BE WITHOUT SIN, WE DECEIVE OURSELVES AND THE TRUTH IS NOT IN US. IF WE CONFESS OUR SINS, HE IS FAITHFUL AND JUST AND WILL FORGIVE US OUR SINS AND PURIFY US FROM ALL UNRIGHTEOUSNESS. IF WE CLAIM WE HAVE NOT SINNED, WE MAKE HIM OUT TO BE A LIAR AND HIS WORD HAS NO PLACE IN OUR LIVES.***

We are human; even after our conversion we sin. We need to confess our sins when we recognize them as sins. Since the Lord forgets our sin after we confess them, we do not need to keep going back to the Lord and confessing them again and again. Sometimes people beat themselves up and cannot get past a sin they have committed. **PSALM 103:12,** ***AS FAR AS THE EAST IS FROM THE WEST, SO FAR HAS HE REMOVED OUR TRANSGRESSIONS FROM US.*** We confess, He forgives, He forgets. We do not have to keep confessing the same sin unless we keep committing the same sin. **[4]**

The power of Alcoholics Anonymous is their use of first names only, and by not knowing each other, there is a freedom to confessing without recrimination. Their identity is safe. When someone confesses to a sin, it makes it easier for others to say, "me too." Christians must do the same thing. No recrimination, just forgiveness and prayer.

Yes, confessing our sins to each other and asking for prayer can be very powerful, but again I urge much caution. **[5]**

QUESTIONS ON CONFESS YOUR SINS

1. Does this make you nervous? Have you ever tried this? What were the results?

2. How would you personally handle this? Do you recommend this?

3. Do you agree?

4. Is this a problem for you? Why?

5. Have you ever had poor consequences come from this? Why would this have worked in the time of James and not today?

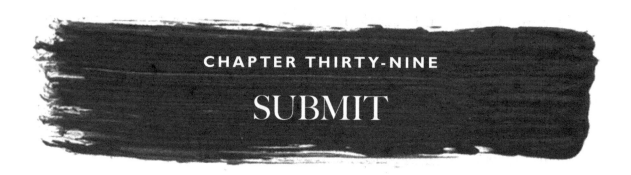

CHAPTER THIRTY-NINE

SUBMIT

EPHESIANS 5:21, *SUBMIT TO ONE ANOTHER OUT OF REVERENCE FOR CHRIST.*

No, this is not about husbands and wives. Paul does write about wives and husbands and their responsibilities immediately after this verse. This is about how we, as Christian brothers, are to submit to one another in our lives together. [1]

Other areas in the Bible tell us to submit to God. **JAMES 4:7A** says *SUBMIT YOURSELVES, THEN, TO GOD. RESIST THE DEVIL.* Notice in the same sentence, James talks about submitting to God, he brings up resisting the devil. Why would he do this? Our pride gets in the way of submission. The devil gets a foothold in our lives when we don't submit ourselves to the Lord. We must fight the tendency of our pride that doesn't allow ourselves to submit to God, much less submitting to one another.

ROMANS 13:1A states *EVERYONE MUST SUBMIT HIMSELF TO THE GOVERNING AUTHORITIES.* Paul goes into detail in the following **VERSES 1B–7** explaining why this is important in the lives of Christians. The reason? God has established governing authorities.

But in **EPHESIANS 5:21,** he is speaking about submission of Christian to Christian. How does this work? If we all submit to each other, we will get nothing done. Within the local church, someone must be the leader. To submit means we yield to the authority of another. We are to submit to the person who is in charge of a particular area. Why must we submit to this person? To get things done and to make that leader's responsibility within the body a joy to him. **HEBREWS 13:17,** *OBEY YOUR LEADERS AND SUBMIT TO THEIR AUTHORITY. THEY KEEP WATCH OVER YOU AS MEN WHO MUST GIVE AN ACCOUNT. OBEY THEM SO THAT THEIR WORK WILL BE A JOY, NOT A BURDEN, FOR THAT WOULD BE OF NO ADVANTAGE TO YOU.* [2]

As a leader, there is nothing worse than trying to get things done and have others trying to lead by doing things their way. It is so frustrating when someone else is trying to lead from behind the scenes, trying to undermine the leader, constantly stirring up trouble just to get his own way. Most times, if we have two leaders we will not get anything done. Have we ever seen a football team trying to use two quarterbacks equally? How did that work out? It did not. Have you ever worked in a position where you had two bosses and had to follow both of their directions? How did that work out? It absolutely did not. Someone has to be in control and the other people must submit. This is how it is to work within the local church. [3]

We are to work with our leaders as one. My Ohio pastor, Dr. Jim Smith, says the word submission comes from the meaning of being "yoked together." Animals yoked together must work together equally or nothing will get accomplished. If one animal wants to go right and the other left, all we have is a standstill. If one pulls harder than the other, the stronger will get tired first and give up. But if the weaker does nothing, holds his ground, nothing will happen. We see this in the political arena as Republicans and Democrats, yoked together in Congress, want their own way. What gets accomplished? Nothing, except the frustration of both parties and frustrated constituents. But if both parties, or animals, are yoked together and pull using the same amount of force, going in the same direction, it is a treat to see what they can accomplish. The same holds true for Christian brothers working together.

My pastor also said the word *submission* can be broken down this way: sub-under. Thus, submission means *under the mission of.* Thus, what is the mission of the church? What is the mission of the area that we lead? If we don't know what the mission is, then how can we pull together? The leader must define the mission and then keep everyone heading in the right direction at the same speed. If everyone knows what is to be accomplished, it makes it easier to submit. Everyone then knows what is expected of them. If we, as subordinates, know what we are trying to do, things will get done, otherwise it will be every man for himself.

Working smoothly together within the church is like watching a basketball team that has no stars. The stars have submitted themselves to the mission—winning! Just because a team has great stars does not mean they will win it all. In most cases they don't because it is hard for stars to submit for the best of the team.   [4]

It can bring dire consequences to a church when they have others trying to lead when they are not in the leadership capacity. This is what is going on in **3 JOHN 9–10,** *I WROTE TO THE CHURCH, BUT DIOTREPHES, WHO LOVES TO BE FIRST, WILL HAVE NOTHING TO DO WITH US. SO IF I COME, I WILL CALL ATTENTION TO WHAT HE IS DOING, GOSSIPING MALICIOUSLY ABOUT US. NOT SATISFIED WITH THAT, HE REFUSES TO WELCOME THE BROTHERS. HE ALSO STOPS THOSE WHO WANT TO DO SO AND PUTS THEM OUT OF THE CHURCH.* This was happening then, and it can happen today. It cannot make the Lord happy when things like this happen within His church. Do not allow someone within the body to take over when they have not been authorized to do so. This can, and does, demoralize a church.

Paul in his letter to the church in Thessalonica says in **1 THESSALONIANS 5:12,** *NOW WE ASK YOU, BROTHERS, TO RESPECT THOSE WHO WORK HARD AMONG YOU, WHO ARE OVER YOU IN THE LORD AND WHO ADMONISH YOU.* Everyone knows that respect is earned, not demanded, but as for the people in leadership in the local congregation, remember they were put there by others that respected them and saw in them a capacity to do a good job. They should be humble and work to the best of their ability. We are to respect the decision and thus respect them. To show disrespect to church leadership is just wrong. The Lord has them in a position of leadership, and it is not up to us to challenge the decision. We might disagree with the leader, but there are ways to do it respectfully. We are not to be hurtful to others' feelings and not take cheap shots at ones in authority. Leaders are working hard, to the best of their ability to please the church and thus to please the Lord.

We must make sure of our reasons behind the urge to challenge a person in leadership. Are we challenging them just so we can be first? Is it just for our ego? We are to be humble and it takes humbleness to be able to submit to others in authority. If we have an issue with a leader, we need to pray daily for him. It is hard to disrespect someone we are praying for on a daily basis. If someone seems to be struggling in his or her leadership capacity, offer help, but do not try to take over. Reading on in **1 THESSALONIANS 5:13,** Paul says this about leaders, ***HOLD THEM IN THE HIGHEST REGARD IN LOVE BECAUSE OF THEIR WORK. LIVE IN PEACE WITH EACH OTHER.***

If we are put into a leadership capacity, it is important to know the individuals within the group in such a way that will enable us to get the best out of each one. Know the ones that are inclined to give us trouble, the ones that have the tendency to want to take over, or the ones who just want to complain. If we can identify group members like this, try to use them in such a way that will appeal to their ego. But remember the mission and what we are trying to accomplish.

A leader is to love his Christian workers within the group. Keep them in his prayers, show them love, and in all things use the love of the Lord. Showing love helps to defuse tension and pride within the group. Love conquers all.

To accomplish any mission, everyone must do the job or task that is assigned to them. This is true in sports, in a work environment, in the military or within the church. If one part fails, then the mission is lost.

As Christian brothers, are we able to submit to a higher authority? Have we set aside our ego and pride to accomplish the mission given us? Are we the thorns in the side to ones in leadership? We need to take a good look at ourselves and ask the Holy Spirit to speak to us and give us guidance. Always stay humble. Submit to one another so we can pull evenly, for the good of the church to grow and the good of the Lord. Can we do this?   **[5]**

QUESTIONS ON SUBMIT

1.   Is this a hard verse for you? Why?

2.   **HEBREWS 13:17** says to submit to authority. If they are poor leaders, do we still have to submit to them?

3.   Have you ever seen this happen? What were the consequences?

4.   Ever seen a sports team like this? What were your observations?

5.   What must be done by you to enable you to submit to one another?

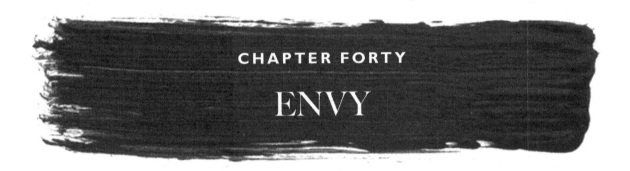

CHAPTER FORTY

ENVY

GALATIANS 5:26, *LET US NOT BECOME CONCEITED, PROVOKING AND ENVYING EACH OTHER.*

Webster's definition of envy: *a feeling of discontent aroused by someone else's possessions of things one would like to have for one's self.*

Possessions of another person would be the main reason for envy, but it goes much deeper than that. We can be and are envious of many other things besides possessions. **[1]**

This area of envy showed its ugly head early in the Bible. Satan is the beginning of envy in the Bible. **ISAIAH 14:13–14,** *YOU SAID IN YOUR HEART, "I WILL ASCEND TO HEAVEN; I WILL RAISE MY THRONE ABOVE THE STARS OF GOD; I WILL SIT ENTHRONED ON THE MOUNT OF ASSEMBLY, ON THE UTMOST HEIGHTS OF THE SACRED MOUNTAIN. I WILL ASCEND ABOVE THE TOPS OF THE CLOUDS; I WILL MAKE MYSELF LIKE THE MOST HIGH."* Satan was also described in **EZEKIEL 28:12B, "YOU WERE THE MODEL OF PERFECTION, FULL OF WISDOM AND PERFECT IN BEAUTY."** Satan may have been a model of perfection, but he envied God. He wanted to be like God or even above Him. Envy brought his fall. It was not a single possession that God had, Satan wanted it all. **[2]**

Adam and Eve got kicked out of the Garden of Eden because they wanted to be like God. In **GENESIS 3:3–6** Eve says, *"BUT GOD DID SAY, 'YOU MUST NOT EAT FRUIT FROM THE TREE THAT IS IN THE MIDDLE OF THE GARDEN, AND YOU MUST NOT TOUCH IT, OR YOU WILL DIE.'" "YOU WILL NOT SURELY DIE," THE SERPENT SAID TO THE WOMAN. "FOR GOD KNOWS THAT WHEN YOU EAT OF IT YOUR EYES WILL BE OPENED, AND YOU WILL BE LIKE GOD, KNOWING GOOD AND EVIL." WHEN THE WOMAN SAW THAT THE FRUIT OF THE TREE WAS GOOD FOR FOOD AND PLEASING TO THE EYE, AND ALSO DESIRABLE FOR GAINING WISDOM, SHE TOOK SOME AND ATE IT. SHE ALSO GAVE SOME TO HER HUSBAND, WHO WAS WITH HER, AND HE ATE IT.* Why did Adam and Eve eat the forbidden fruit? Because they wanted to be like God. They wanted His powers. They envied the Lord and Satan played upon that envy. They sinned due to envy.

The death of Abel was the result of envy. Cain resented Abel because Abel's sacrifices were accepted by God and Cain's were not. Cain hated him and his envious attitude brought about the murder of Abel. Cain did not want Abel's possessions, he wanted the love and respect that God was giving to Abel. (See **GENESIS 4:3–12**.)

Jacob's sons envied the love that Jacob showed Joseph. This envy brought about hatred and the selling of Joseph. The brothers hated Joseph because of the love their father showed to Joseph. (See **GENESIS 37:3–4**.)

PSALM 106:16 tells of the Jews being envious of Moses and Aaron. *IN THE CAMP THEY GREW ENVIOUS OF MOSES AND OF AARON, WHO WAS CONSECRATED TO THE LORD.* Moses and Aaron were hated because of God's love for them and the leadership that the Lord gave to them.

David was envious of Uriah the Hittite because of his wife, Bathsheba. The result was treachery, murder, and finally the death of David's newborn son. (See **2 SAMUEL 11**.)

But the ultimate act of envy is when the chief priests and the Sanhedrin brought Jesus to Pilate. **MATTHEW 27:18,** *FOR HE KNEW IT WAS OUT OF ENVY THAT THEY HAD HANDED JESUS OVER TO HIM.* Why would these religious leaders be envious of the Lord? Large groups of people were following Jesus and He was taking away some of their followers. He was a threat to their power and influence. They saw themselves as the guardians and experts on the law versus this untrained, uneducated upstart. Due to envy, they were ready to kill Jesus.

As we can see, within the Bible there are many occasions of envy and the lengths people would go to resolve their envy.

We also can see that possessions are not the only reason people are envious. People are envious for other reasons.

A special relationship another sibling has with a parent.
  A brother who is closer to mom or dad.
The loving relationship some people have with their spouse.
  And our marriage is faltering.
Someone seems so blessed by the Lord.
  And we, a better Christian in our mind, do not get blessed.
Another Christian brother's relationship with the Lord seems so good.
  And ours never seems that good.
A friend is in good health and never does anything to help his health.
  Our health is poor even though we take care of ourselves.
A Christian receives many honors.
  We do more and we are never honored.
Some people are always in leadership.
  We never get asked.   [3]

A list like this could go on and on. Are we envious people? Do we find ourselves talking about what other people have? It is hard to be happy if we are dissatisfied. What comes out of being envious? Resentment and bitterness. We resent what others have and we don't. Envy is a selfish sin. It is all about us and our selfish desires. The more we resent what others have, the more we become bitter. We can even be bitter with the Lord. He is not blessing us like He blesses others. We don't understand we are to use what we have been given for the work of the Lord. The Lord has a plan for all of us, an individual plan that will use what we have been given. He equips us so we can do the task He has given us. We are all created differently. We all have different gifts and talents and if we are envious of others it implies that God does not know what He is doing, that He is failing us. **PSALM 139:13–16,** *FOR YOU CREATED MY INMOST BEING; YOU KNIT ME TOGETHER IN MY MOTHER'S WOMB. I PRAISE YOU BECAUSE I AM FEARFULLY AND WONDERFULLY*

MADE; YOUR WORKS ARE WONDERFUL, I KNOW THAT FULL WELL. MY FRAME WAS NOT HIDDEN FROM YOU WHEN I WAS MADE IN THE SECRET PLACE. WHEN I WAS WOVEN TOGETHER IN THE DEPTHS OF THE EARTH, YOUR EYES SAW MY UNFORMED BODY. ALL THE DAYS ORDAINED FOR ME WERE WRITTEN IN YOUR BOOK BEFORE ONE OF THEM CAME TO BE.

Our frustration with envy can come from many areas, but how can we work through it?

> My friends seem so successful.
> Learn to celebrate what they have accomplished.
> Why do some people have it all and we don't?
> Nobody has it all. We never know what is going on in their lives.
> We want to compare ourselves to others.
> Comparing our lives to others is nothing but a losing proposition.
> We don't like people who have it all.
> If we start praying for them, our attitudes can and will change.
> If we only could have what others have, we would be happy.
> Things do not make us happy.
> Our friends seem in great physical shape.
> Are we working on it or do we just expect it to happen?
> My friends are envious people.
> Avoid them. [4]

We can lose friends because we are full of envy. We are never happy for them when they have achieved success. The way we look at it is if we don't have, they should not either. We are taught to be happy when our brothers are happy and to be sad when they are sad.

Envy can come about because we are not growing in the Lord. If we set our minds on the Lord, we will be less likely to have envy in our hearts. It is a growing process. In **1 PETER 2:1–3** Peter tells us we are to rid ourselves of many sins, including envy. **VERSES 2–3, *LIKE NEWBORN BABIES, CRAVE PURE SPIRITUAL MILK, SO THAT BY IT YOU MAY GROW UP IN YOUR SALVATION, NOW THAT YOU HAVE TASTED THAT THE LORD IS GOOD.*** How do we rid ourselves of envy? The answer is given to us in **1 CORINTHIANS 13:4.** *LOVE IS PATIENT, LOVE IS KIND. IT DOES NOT ENVY, IT DOES NOT BOAST, IT IS NOT PROUD.* We must replace envy with love. When we love one another, we have no room for envy.

GALATIANS 5:19–21 lists acts of the sinful nature of which envy is one. We are to replace them with what follows in **VERSES 22–23,** the fruit of the Spirit. Then **VERSE 24** says *THOSE WHO BELONG TO CHRIST JESUS HAVE CRUCIFIED THE SINFUL NATURE WITH ITS PASSIONS AND DESIRES.* We are to rid ourselves of sin and replace it with what the Lord wants in our hearts, not our sinful desires.

JAMES 3:16, *FOR WHERE YOU HAVE ENVY AND SELFISH AMBITION, THERE YOU FIND DISORDER AND EVERY EVIL PRACTICE.* James is saying that envy can lead to other sins. If we look back at the start of the lesson, we find many sins come from envy. Christianity is not to be a competition between Christians. The Lord wants unity and harmony within the body, we are to be one.   [5]

How can we overcome envy within our lives? Give thanks for what the Lord has given to us. Pray for our Christian friends. Let the Holy Spirit work in our lives to rid envy. This is a sin that can start small but can take over our lives and make us bitter. Replace envy with love.   [6]

Jesus, in **MARK 7:20–23,** lists sins that can make us unclean, with envy being one of them. **VERSE 23** says *"ALL THESE EVILS COME FROM INSIDE AND MAKE A MAN 'UNCLEAN.'"* It is from the inside, our carnal, sinful nature. This is where envy lurks. Be very careful not to envy, it can eat us up.   [7], [8]

I recently reheard a story about a missionary in Africa who was taking a ship home after over twenty years of service. On that same trip, President Teddy Roosevelt was returning from a short hunting exposition. When the ship landed, and the President stepped onto land the crowd roared with applause. The missionary said to the Lord, "This is unfair, I have spent over twenty years in service to you Lord and no one even knows I am here. Yet the President returns home after a short trip and he is given adulation by all." Then he thought, this world is not my home. My home is in heaven.

Our rewards are awaiting us in heaven so do not be guilty of envy here on earth.

QUESTIONS ON ENVY

1. How would you describe envy? What other words come to mind? How are jealousy, covertness and envy alike or different?

2. Do you see the cause of Satan's fall being envy? If not envy, then what?

3. Add to this list.

4. Have you ever been around someone that is full of envy? Did you like it? What bothered you about it?

5. Why would envy bring about discord? Has envy ever affected your church?

6. What other ways can we get rid of envy in our lives?

7. In **MARK 7:20–23,** does it surprise you that envy, when listed as a sin, is right up there with murder?

8. What brings out envy in you? Where is most of your envy directed? Why?

CHAPTER FORTY-ONE

HUMILITY

1 PETER 5:5B-6, *ALL OF YOU, CLOTHE YOURSELVES WITH HUMILITY TOWARD ONE ANOTHER, BECAUSE, "GOD OPPOSES THE PROUD BUT GIVES GRACE TO THE HUMBLE." HUMBLE YOURSELVES, THEREFORE, UNDER GOD'S MIGHTY HAND, THAT HE MAY LIFT YOU UP IN DUE TIME.*

Webster's definition of humility: *a humble condition or attitude of the mind.*

Webster's definition of humble: *having or showing a modest estimate of one's own importance, not proud.* [1]

Notice what humility is not. It is not being a "Casper Milktoast" or a person with low self-esteem. It is not someone that others can run over. It is not a person that goes around saying, "Woe is me, I can't do anything right." Or someone saying, "I cannot do that, I am not good enough or smart enough." [2]

According to Charles Spurgeon, *"humility is to make a right estimate of one's self."* We are to see our abilities, talents and gifts that the Lord has bestowed on us, and then use them to serve the Lord. If you have the ability to make money, use it to serve the Lord, not to hurt others. If you have the ability to organize and administrate others, put yourself into position to use that ability and do not be ashamed to use what the Lord has given you. To deny the ability to do something special is to deny where that ability came from. That ability came from God. Give praise and glory to the Lord, not to your own self. **[3]**

One of the best quotes I have heard on humility comes from Fred Smith, *"humility is not denying the power you have, but admitting that the power comes through you not from you."* You have been given certain skills. Where did they come from? They came from the Lord although we can fine tune those skills by hard work. A professional golfer did not start out hitting 300-yard drives straight down the fairway. It took lots of work. If we are teachers, we did not start out as great teachers. We had the ability, but we had to work at it. If we came in with the attitude, I can't do that, we would probably be right because we never gave it a chance. The first time I was asked to teach a class, I felt that the person who asked me to teach was out of their mind. But they saw something in me to get me started. Now I feel I am doing exactly what the Lord had in mind for me. Now if someone tells me I just taught a good class, I have learned to accept credit where credit is due. My lessons today are so much better because I have accepted the responsibility of study and preparation. Then when I bring the lessons to others it is up to the Lord to bless the class. My goal in the class is to bring the best prepared, in depth lesson I can bring, so the class can understand the scriptures better and want to know more. Not for my glory but for the Lord. **[4]**

It is not wrong to feel proud of what you are doing, but realize if you depend on the Lord, He will help you be even better. It is not up to me to put myself first but to put others first. If we focus on praising others, humility will come to us easier. Our life of learning humility will work better if we do not act like we are better than others. True humility is not putting yourself down. Many people have issues about self that they cannot get past, but we do need to think not only of ourselves. **[5]**

Be careful when others praise you. People can get caught up in applause and fame. Who doesn't like it when someone praises them? When we accept praise from others in the wrong way, it can make us think we did it all on our own. **JOHN 5:43–44, *"I HAVE COME IN MY FATHER'S NAME AND YOU DO NOT ACCEPT ME; BUT IF SOMEONE ELSE COMES IN HIS OWN NAME, YOU WILL ACCEPT HIM. HOW CAN YOU BELIEVE IF YOU ACCEPT PRAISE FROM ONE ANOTHER, YET MAKE NO EFFORT TO OBTAIN THE PRAISE THAT COMES FROM THE ONLY GOD?"*** We are not to focus on people's praise versus the praise we receive from the Lord. It is okay to accept praise from our Christian brothers for a job well done, but when we do good deeds for each other, we are doing for the Lord, not for man or ourselves. If we are doing work in the church just to see our name in the bulletin or to hear it from the pulpit, to be the people in the forefront, then we are doing it for the wrong reason. We need to check our hearts and make sure we are doing the work for the Lord and for the body for the right reasons. **[6]**

Paul in **PHILIPPIANS 2:3–4** says *DO NOTHING OUT OF SELFISH AMBITION OR VAIN CONCEIT, BUT IN HUMILITY CONSIDER OTHERS BETTER THAN YOURSELVES. EACH OF YOU SHOULD LOOK NOT ONLY TO YOUR OWN INTERESTS, BUT ALSO TO THE INTEREST OF OTHERS.* Being humble to one another falls right in line with "honoring" one another and "consider others better." Paul goes on to say in **VERSE 8,** when he speaks about Jesus, *AND BEING FOUND IN APPEARANCE AS A MAN, HE HUMBLED HIMSELF AND BECAME OBEDIENT TO DEATH—EVEN DEATH ON A CROSS!* This is our example. Jesus left heaven and became a man and then died for us. As the Son of God, He put away His power to give us grace, thus freedom from deaths hold over us. This is the ultimate lesson in showing humility to others. **[7]**

Jesus is the true example of being humble, not proud. **1 CORINTHIANS 13:4,** *LOVE IS PATIENT, LOVE IS KIND. IT DOES NOT ENVY, IT DOES NOT BOAST, IT IS NOT PROUD.* **[8]**

Satan is just the opposite. **ISAIAH 14:14** says of Satan *I WILL ASCEND ABOVE THE TOPS OF THE CLOUDS; I WILL MAKE MYSELF LIKE THE MOST HIGH.* **EZEKIEL 28:17** goes on to say of Satan *YOUR HEART BECAME PROUD ON ACCOUNT OF YOUR BEAUTY, AND YOU CORRUPTED YOUR WISDOM BECAUSE OF YOUR SPLENDOR.* True humility is putting away our pride and then doing whatever we can to serve the Lord. It is being Christ-like in all we do. It is showing our love to our fellow Christian brothers by keeping our pride in check.

JAMES 3:13 says *WHO IS WISE AND UNDERSTANDING AMONG YOU? LET HIM SHOW IT BY HIS GOOD LIFE, BY DEEDS DONE IN HUMILITY THAT COMES FROM WISDOM.* When we serve others, we are to do it with love in our hearts and our mind and put our pride behind us.

Jesus gives us the parable of the Pharisee and tax collector in **LUKE 18:9-14.** He brings up how the Pharisee went to the temple to pray and how *"THE PHARISEE STOOD UP AND PRAYED ABOUT HIMSELF: 'GOD, I THANK YOU THAT I AM NOT LIKE*

OTHER MEN—ROBBERS, EVILDOERS, ADULTERERS—OR EVEN LIKE THIS TAX COLLECTOR. I FAST TWICE A WEEK AND GIVE A TENTH OF ALL I GET.' BUT THE TAX COLLECTOR STOOD AT A DISTANCE. HE WOULD NOT EVEN LOOK UP TO HEAVEN, BUT BEAT HIS BREAST AND SAID, 'GOD, HAVE MERCY ON ME, A SINNER.' I TELL YOU THAT THIS MAN, RATHER THAN THE OTHER, WENT HOME JUSTIFIED BEFORE GOD. FOR EVERYONE WHO EXALTS HIMSELF WILL BE HUMBLED, AND HE WHO HUMBLES HIMSELF WILL BE EXALTED." Who is the one who sounds humble? Not the Pharisee who had pride in his own righteousness. We, as Christians must be careful we don't have the same attitude. The Pharisee was touting his works, while the tax collector was asking for mercy from the Lord. The Pharisee felt his righteousness was above all others because of what he did whereas the tax collector was humble before God. One is worshipping falsely, while the other is penitent. One is proud of the way he worships, while the other is humble. As a Christian we are not to be proud of the way we serve the Lord, or we will be just like the Pharisees.   [9], [10]

On another occasion in **MATTHEW 18:1-4,** the disciples argue about who would be the greatest. *AT THAT TIME THE DISCIPLES CAME TO JESUS AND ASKED, "WHO IS THE GREATEST IN THE KINGDOM OF HEAVEN?" HE CALLED A LITTLE CHILD AND HAD HIM STAND AMONG THEM. AND HE SAID: "I TELL YOU THE TRUTH, UNLESS YOU CHANGE AND BECOME LIKE LITTLE CHILDREN, YOU WILL NEVER ENTER THE KINGDOM OF HEAVEN. THEREFORE, WHOEVER HUMBLES HIMSELF LIKE THIS CHILD IS THE GREATEST IN THE KINGDOM OF HEAVEN."*   [11]

Is Jesus saying to the disciples they need to be little children all over again? No, He is saying they must change their way of thinking. They must be of another mind. They were thinking which person would be on His right hand or His left hand. Who would be in charge of finances? Who would be the prince along with their king? Children do not seek honor, do not seek stature. They are not too proud to be with others beneath them; they are open to learning and trying to gain understanding. Pride and ambition are getting in the way of the disciples' humbleness to serve. We are all to be born again and as a child we are to seek the kingdom of heaven. Pride is what brought down the angels and it can bring us down as well.

Jesus gives us many examples of humility, now it is up to us to imitate Him. Use the gifts you have been given for the Lord for we are told in **ROMANS 12:6,** *WE HAVE*

DIFFERENT GIFTS, ACCORDING TO THE GRACE GIVEN US. IF A MAN'S GIFT IS PROPHESYING, LET HIM USE IT IN PROPORTION TO HIS FAITH.
Paul goes on to list other gifts. No matter what gift it is, it was given to each of us to use for the body, which is the church. Use it with humility but in praise to the Lord.

It is being humble that our love becomes real, devoted and ardent. Jesus is the ultimate example of humility. **[12]**

QUESTIONS ON HUMILITY

1. Put humility in your own words.

2. What else is humility not?

3. How do we go about making a "right estimate" of ourselves?

4. Discuss the Fred Smith quote.

5. Is this attitude wrong?

6. Why do people say, "pride comes before a fall?" How does this relate? How can we be humble, yet proud of our accomplishments?

7. Tell of times when Jesus showed humility? How can we use these models for ourselves?

8. Explain this verse.

9. In this parable from **LUKE 18,** why would the Pharisee act this way? Why do you think the Pharisee had to point out all the things he did?

10. Can you relate to either one? What is your attitude of the "lesser" Christian?

11. Explain in your own words.

12. Do we have to be humble at work? In our everyday living? How can we use humility in our marriage, at work and in our Christian life?

CHAPTER FORTY-TWO
LAY DOWN OUR LIVES

1 JOHN 3:16, *THIS IS HOW WE KNOW WHAT LOVE IS: JESUS CHRIST LAID DOWN HIS LIFE FOR US. AND WE OUGHT TO LAY DOWN OUR LIVES FOR OUR BROTHERS.* [1]

John is talking about a self-sacrificing love that most of us will never encounter. We will probably never be called to make a decision to give up our life for another Christian brother. But during biblical times, decisions like this had to be made by Christians. Christians were being persecuted and killed, other Christians were being tortured and asked to give up their fellow Christian brothers. If they did not give them up, they would be put to death. Within 40–50 years after Christ's death, all but one of the eleven original disciples had been killed for following Jesus and for preaching the Word. It is ironic that John, who wrote this verse, was not one of the ones who was called to sacrifice his life. But surely, he was ready to give his life for the Lord.

Thankfully in our lifetime in the United States, we have not had to make that choice. We know in foreign lands, such as the Middle East, Africa and the Far East, Christians have had to make decisions like this and are still making them today. Recently in the news, it was reported by CESNUR* that Christians were listed as the number one persecuted entity in the world. Over 90,000 Christians were killed in 2016. Our prayer should be, Lord give us the grace and courage, if it comes to us, to honor and protect our brothers and sisters in Christ, even if it costs us our lives.

The key to the verse is how much love we have for brothers and sisters in Christ. Do we have so much love for them that we would be willing to die for them?

Most of us would die for our spouse.
Most of us would die for our children.
Most of us would die for our country and for freedom.

But are we willing to die for a Christian friend?

Quoting the Asbury Bible Commentary: *Love is the willingness to surrender that which has value for our own life. To enrich the life of another.* John is talking about the love and the willingness to protect one another. Love is sharing or giving up what we value the most. It is the willingness to surrender our most prized possession to enrich the life of another. **[2]**

This type of love is what Jesus showed us as an example of what self-sacrificing love really is. Jesus says in **JOHN 15:12–13, "MY COMMAND IS THIS: LOVE EACH OTHER AS I HAVE LOVED YOU. GREATER LOVE HAS NO ONE THAN THIS, THAT HE LAY DOWN HIS LIFE FOR HIS FRIENDS."** Jesus did more than talk about His love for us; He demonstrated it by dying on a cross. His actions speak loudly of His love for us. He gave all He had to give, His life. We are called to have our actions speak loudly of our love for our fellow Christians. **[3]**

Paul writes of this kind of love in **1 THESSALONIANS 2:8, WE LOVED YOU SO MUCH THAT WE WERE DELIGHTED TO SHARE WITH YOU NOT ONLY THE GOSPEL OF GOD BUT OUR LIVES AS WELL, BECAUSE YOU HAD BECOME SO DEAR TO US.** Paul was ready to give up everything to serve the Lord so others may be saved. He ended up doing just this. He was present when other Christians gave their lives for the Lord and then it came to him to do the same.

Another way for Christians to lay down their lives for other Christians is to devote themselves entirely to the Lord. Mother Teresa and missionaries come to mind. They each made a decision to give up everything to follow what the Lord would have them do. Many of us have sung songs like *I surrender all, I surrender all, all for Jesus I surrender, I surrender all,* or *I will go where you want me to go, I will do what you want me to do,* but have not been called to do what the words say. Missionaries love the Lord and they love the unsaved so much that they will commit their lives to bringing people to the Lord.

There are certain areas in our lives that some are called to commit entirely to the Lord. A businessman from Lima, Ohio, followed the Lord's direction. He started by giving the Lord 10% of his business profits and he kept 90%. Before it was all said and done, he was giving the Lord 90% and he lived on the 10%. In this case he was directed to lay down his money for the Lord and for fellow Christians.

We see families of Christian workers that willingly give up their family as they leave for the mission field or to some other type of ministry.

We see people who give their talents to praise the Lord. Billy Graham, George Beverly Shea and Bill Gaither come to mind. These men have traveled all over the world to praise the Lord and to bring the gospel message in the way their talents allow them to do it. They have laid down their lives for the Lord. They also have laid down their time as they have been called to do.   [4]

Many Christians have been called to actually lay down their lives.   [5]

If we really love our brothers, sacrifices must be made. For some it is their life, for others it might be time or money. Whatever it is, we must be devoted enough to do what we are called to do. Are we?   [6]

*The Center for Studies on New Religions

QUESTIONS ON LAY DOWN OUR LIVES

1. Since during this time Christians were being persecuted, is this verse only for that time?

2. Do you agree with this concept on love?

3. Could you actually do this?

4. If you cannot make this commitment, what else are you withholding from your brothers?

5. Are you ready to give the Lord this type of commitment?

6. Are you?

SYMPATHY

1 PETER 3:8, *FINALLY, ALL OF YOU, LIVE IN HARMONY WITH ONE ANOTHER; BE SYMPATHETIC, LOVE AS BROTHERS, BE COMPASSIONATE AND HUMBLE.*

Webster defines sympathy as: *feeling pity, tenderness towards one suffering pain or grief or trouble, the ability to share another person's emotions.* [1]

Sympathy is an emotion. It is an attitude. Just like all emotions and attitudes, we can control them to a certain degree. Some people show no emotion at all, others wear it on their sleeves.

Peter, of all people, is telling us as Christian brothers that we are to have sympathy for our fellow Christians, not just "I think I feel your pain."

When we hear of someone's ill fortune, does it strike a chord in our hearts? Or do we just think "I am glad that did not happen to me"? If a friend dies, do we feel for the family or is it more a casual "he seemed so young"?

When we think of being sympathetic for someone, we usually connect it with a death in the family or the death of a close friend. Of course, we are to sympathize with our Christian brothers when they lose a loved one even though we can be joyful because they will be with the Lord. Some people just seem to recognize what someone is going through and can sympathize with them; others, not so much. But we all need to develop/acquire an attitude of sympathy.   [2]

ROMANS 12:15 tells us *REJOICE WITH THOSE WHO REJOICE; MOURN WITH THOSE WHO MOURN.* We are to show emotions in good times and bad.

Sympathy, and its derivative sympathetic or sympathized, is only used three times in the New Testament. **HEBREWS 4:15,** *FOR WE DO NOT HAVE A HIGH PRIEST WHO IS UNABLE TO SYMPATHIZE WITH OUR WEAKNESSES, BUT WE HAVE ONE WHO HAS BEEN TEMPTED IN EVERY WAY, JUST AS WE ARE—YET WAS WITHOUT SIN.*

> This high priest is Jesus.
> Jesus feels our weaknesses.
> He has dealt with the same issues Himself.
> When we hurt emotionally, He feels our pain. He sympathizes with us.

So, when we are dealing with painful issues, we can be assured Jesus is feeling the pain we are going through. He has pity on us, knowing what we are dealing with during each issue. We have an understanding, sympathetic Savior.

A great example of His sympathy is seen in **LUKE 7:12–16.** When Jesus was approaching a town, He saw the funeral procession with a widowed mother mourning her only son. **VERSE 13** says *WHEN THE LORD SAW HER, HIS HEART WENT OUT TO HER AND HE SAID, "DON'T CRY."* Jesus raised her son from the dead. This is sympathy and compassion in action.

Do not be afraid to show emotion. It is okay to grieve for loved ones. Jesus wept at the grave of Lazarus, **JOHN 11:35.** He showed that it is okay to show emotion.   [3]

Another verse is **HEBREWS 10:34,** *YOU SYMPATHIZED WITH THOSE IN PRISON AND JOYFULLY ACCEPTED THE CONFISCATION OF YOUR PROPERTY, BECAUSE YOU KNEW THAT YOU YOURSELVES HAD BETTER AND LASTING POSSESSIONS.* The Christians then sympathized with those who were going through terrible treatment by non-Christians. Fellow Christians were being thrown into jail. Their brothers and sisters in Christ felt their pain and suffering. They sympathized, yet they were joyful in the future their brothers were going to have.

In the United States we might actually see property lost because someone is a Christian. Or they might end up in jail when they stay true to their beliefs. No mistake about it, Christians are discriminated against here and in other countries.

We must keep our brothers and sisters in prayer when we see them going through persecution because of faith. Persecution happens in many ways today:

Lack of promotions
Arm-length friendships in business or with neighbors
Backbiting in the workplace or in the neighborhood
Unfounded rumors that hurt their position, even causing job loss
A pastor not invited to parties since he is so "Christian"
A pastor's wife being picked on by others because of her position   [4]

We are to follow the example of Jesus, the Hebrew high priest and the Christ. We are to have sympathy for our Christian brothers as they go through various trials and are dealing with discrimination because they follow the Lord.

What ways can we use to show sympathy?

Let our brothers know we feel their pain.
Reach out to others to express our sympathy.
It is not what we say, but the caring attitude when we say something.
Be a card writer. Receiving a sympathy card picks us up.
Send an email or a text. It is the thought that counts, not the way it is sent.
Be a good listener. It helps for people to express their grief without judgment.
Do anything to express sympathy. It is always welcomed.   [5]

Any of us can do any of these with a little effort, a little "want to." It is always appreciated just to know that others are reaching out to us during our struggles.

Jesus says in **MATTHEW 22:39B** to *"LOVE YOUR NEIGHBOR AS YOURSELF."* What better way to show love than to show our sympathy during tough times?   [6]

QUESTIONS ON SYMPATHY

1. Define sympathy in your own words.

2. Why is it so hard for some people to be sympathetic? Which are you?

3. Is it really okay to grieve? If so, why do we have such a hard time showing this emotion?

4. What other ways have you witnessed Christian persecution?

5. Are you incapable of expressing sympathy for your brothers in Christ? Can this emotion be learned?

6. What other areas of your daily life besides death create sympathy from you?

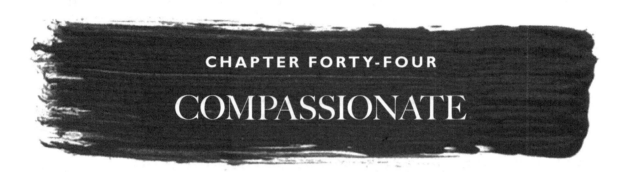

CHAPTER FORTY-FOUR

COMPASSIONATE

1 PETER 3:8, *FINALLY, ALL OF YOU, LIVE IN HARMONY WITH ONE ANOTHER; BE SYMPATHETIC, LOVE AS BROTHERS, BE COMPASSIONATE AND HUMBLE.*

Compassion is "I feel your pain and I want to help and or show you mercy." "I want to be involved."

Compassion is not only feeling others' pain, it is putting our love for them into action.

> We recognize the need of others, and act on that need.
> We take a role in helping them.
> We look for ways to help. We are pro-active. [1]

Our best example of compassion is Jesus.

MATTHEW 14:14, *WHEN JESUS LANDED AND SAW A LARGE CROWD, HE HAD COMPASSION ON THEM AND HEALED THEIR SICK.*

> He acted by helping them in a manner that was truly gracious.
> He did not say "maybe you should see a doctor."

He did not say "I hope you feel better" or "I'm sorry you are ill."
Instead He acted out of compassion. He healed them.

MATTHEW 20:29–34, Jesus had compassion on the two blind men, so He healed them.

MARK 1:40–42, Jesus had compassion on a man with leprosy and healed him.

MATTHEW 15:29–38, Jesus had been healing many people of many illnesses, then in **VERSE 32,** *JESUS CALLED HIS DISCIPLES TO HIM AND SAID, "I HAVE COMPASSION FOR THESE PEOPLE; THEY HAVE ALREADY BEEN WITH ME THREE DAYS AND HAVE NOTHING TO EAT. I DO NOT WANT TO SEND THEM AWAY HUNGRY, OR THEY MAY COLLAPSE ON THE WAY."*

Showing His compassion, and putting it into action, He fed the four thousand. He saw a need and the effect it was having on the people, and also the problem it might create in the future. He responded with an action that relieved the problem. He had the power to resolve their problems, and He used it. He did not turn His back on them.

Another area of people's lives that Jesus showed His compassion was teaching. **MARK 6:34,** *WHEN JESUS LANDED AND SAW A LARGE CROWD, HE HAD COMPASSION ON THEM, BECAUSE THEY WERE LIKE SHEEP WITHOUT A SHEPHERD. SO HE BEGAN TEACHING THEM MANY THINGS.* What do sheep without a shepherd do? They wander around, all going in different directions. They don't know where they are going or why they are going there. They have needs, but they don't know where to turn. This is speaking about us today just as much as it is speaking about the people then.

So, what can we draw from the Lord's examples? [2]

He figured out their most pressing needs and responded to those needs.

> Surely, they were all in need of a healer.
> Surely, they were all hungry.
> Surely, they all needed a teacher.

Yes, they did, but He met their most pressing needs. He also looked ahead at what might turn into a problem and headed that off as well. He saw the need, and He took action.

This is the way we are to have compassion for others. Try to figure out their most pressing needs and respond to those needs. It is not necessary to solve every problem they might have, just the most pressing.

What can we do now that not only solves a problem for a short while, but will affect long term problems? It might not be just helping with babysitting for an hour but looking to the future and searching out a way to solve the problem on a daily basis. They might need a ride somewhere. They might need listening ears; not just for one day, but for a while.

In **COLOSSIANS 3:12,** it says to *CLOTHE YOURSELVES WITH COMPASSION.* [3]

We are to have compassion at all times, night and day, no matter where we are, no matter who it is. Get involved.

I had a boss once who was an excellent example of getting involved. A group of us were standing around talking over a business problem:

Who to put in charge?
   One person or multiple people?
What needed to be done?
In what order should we do the project?
   Were there different ways to proceed?
When was the best time to start the project?
   Start now or wait awhile?
How bad was the problem?
   What's the overall cost and effect?

My boss, after listening for a while, finally said, "Are you going to talk about the problem, or are you going to do something?"

His point being, it is better to do something now than to try to make everything perfect by waiting.   [4]

If someone is hungry,
   they are not looking for a gourmet meal, just something to eat.
If someone needs clothes,
   they are not looking for the best clothes, just something appropriate.

If they feel lost,
>they do not want a GPS, just some direction and some help.

Get busy.

>Be active in compassion.
>Be inventive on what might help.
>We don't need to do everything ourselves.
>Realize we need to give others a chance to be involved.

The more people who get involved, the lighter the load, and thus more will receive a blessing for being compassionate and putting their compassion into action.

In **2 CORINTHIANS 1:3–5,** Paul says ***PRAISE BE TO THE GOD AND FATHER OF OUR LORD JESUS CHRIST, THE FATHER OF COMPASSION AND THE GOD OF ALL COMFORT, WHO COMFORTS US IN ALL OUR TROUBLES, SO THAT WE CAN COMFORT THOSE IN ANY TROUBLE WITH THE COMFORT WE OURSELVES HAVE RECEIVED FROM GOD. FOR JUST AS THE SUFFERINGS OF CHRIST FLOW OVER INTO OUR LIVES, SO ALSO THROUGH CHRIST OUR COMFORT OVERFLOWS.*** [5]

These verses tell us that God, the God of comfort, gives us comfort in our troubles, but He also expects us to comfort others.

>I want to be like my heavenly Father.
>Our Lord and our God is compassionate.
>He sent a Savior even though there was a huge cost.
>It cost Him His only Son. It wasn't just for that moment but for all times.

This is our example.

>Be active in compassion.
>Don't talk about it, do something. [6]

QUESTIONS ON COMPASSIONATE

1. Explain the difference between sympathy and compassion.

2. How would you answer this question?

3. What does it mean to "clothe yourself with compassion"?

4. Why do you not show compassion?

5. Why is it so important that God is compassionate and full of mercy?

6. Can you think of someone that is full of compassion? What are they like? What do they do that makes you notice them? What can we learn from them to help us be more compassionate?

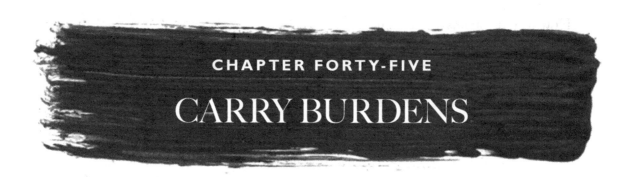

CHAPTER FORTY-FIVE

CARRY BURDENS

GALATIANS 6:2, *CARRY EACH OTHER'S BURDENS, AND IN THIS WAY YOU WILL FULFILL THE LAW OF CHRIST.*

A burden: *something carried, a heavy load that is difficult to support.*

We are to help our Christian brothers carry their burdens.   [1]

Why would I want to do that?

> I have burdens of my own.
> Don't we have individual responsibility of taking care of ourselves?
> Isn't this socialism?
> Doesn't the Bible teach I am to take care of my own load?   [2]

Yes, we are told to take care of our own loads in **GALATIANS 6:5,** *FOR EACH ONE SHOULD CARRY HIS OWN LOAD.*

> Well, which is it?
> Isn't this a contradiction?
> What am I to do?

Take a look at the meaning of these two directions.

> A load is something I can carry on my own.
> A burden needs the help of others.

We, as brothers to fellow Christians, are to help each other.

In **LUKE 11:46,** Jesus is talking to the experts in the law, the Pharisees and or the scribes and teachers of the law, when He tells them *"AND YOU EXPERTS IN THE LAW, WOE TO YOU, BECAUSE YOU LOAD PEOPLE DOWN WITH BURDENS THEY CAN HARDLY CARRY, AND YOU YOURSELVES WILL NOT LIFT ONE FINGER TO HELP THEM."*

Here Jesus is talking about the burden of the law, and all the rules they have added to the law. This would weigh heavy on the people. The burden was impossible to handle. Why? No one could keep all of the laws that the Pharisees had laid upon the people. There were multiple laws on how to wash their hands. It was overwhelming! Since the people felt they could not keep all the laws, they felt burdened down by man and God. How frustrating this must have been.

Christ has the answer to the burden of the law. He gives the answer in **MATTHEW 11:28–30,** *"COME TO ME, ALL YOU WHO ARE WEARY AND BURDENED, AND I WILL GIVE YOU REST. TAKE MY YOKE UPON YOU AND LEARN FROM ME, FOR I AM GENTLE AND HUMBLE IN HEART, AND YOU WILL FIND REST FOR YOUR SOULS. FOR MY YOKE IS EASY AND MY BURDEN IS LIGHT."*

Jesus is saying His offer of grace is so much lighter than the law.

> Let me help you with your salvation.
> Lean on my teachings.
> Lean on my mercy.
> Lean on my grace.
> Lean on me.

Paul tells the Galatians in **GALATIANS 5:1,** *IT IS FOR FREEDOM THAT CHRIST HAS SET US FREE. STAND FIRM, THEN, AND DO NOT LET YOURSELVES BE BURDENED AGAIN BY A YOKE OF SLAVERY.* This yoke of slavery is the yoke of the law. It was unbearable. But we are saved by grace, by the love of the Father who sent His Son to lift from us this yoke of the law through His death and resurrection. Christians no longer have that yoke on them. It was taken away by the Lord. [3]

By the Holy Spirit, giving us direction and showing us the way, we have the desire to follow the Lord and do what pleases Him. We strive to be like Him, not following laws to please Him. This is living under grace versus living under the law. [4]

John says in **1 JOHN 5:2–14** that our love for God is shown by how we love the children of God. We show it by loving God and carrying out His commands. **VERSES 3–4A, *THIS IS LOVE FOR GOD: TO OBEY HIS COMMANDS. AND HIS COMMANDS ARE NOT BURDENSOME, FOR EVERYONE BORN OF GOD OVERCOMES THE WORLD.***

When we love the Lord and turn to Him, the Holy Spirit enters us, and the Holy Spirit is the one who brings us the ability to truly love one another. The Holy Spirit is the enabler to help us to love and help our fellow Christians.

But this carrying of one another's burdens also means something else. What burdens are too heavy for one person to carry alone?

Sometimes it depends on the person.

> If we are sick with a cold, can we handle day-to-day issues?
>> It might be a struggle, but we can get along.
> What if we break a leg and cannot get out of bed?
>> There is a problem.
>> This is beyond our load-carrying ability.
>> Help is needed.
> If our mother or father is ill, can we handle that up to a point?
>> It might cause us some extra work.
>> Our load might get a little heavier, but it is still manageable.
> But if a parent dies do we feel overwhelmed?
>> This burden is too much.
>> We are really struggling with this burden.
>> We need friends to grieve with us, to hug us, and show love and comfort and care for us. Friends might cry with us or offer their sympathy. They might just take time and listen to us grieve.

All of these areas of sympathy and compassion help lighten the burdens we are carrying. They are helping us with our burdens. **[5]**

We as Christians are to be aware of one another's burdens. We need to jump in there when needed. We are not to be ambivalent or unaware or to act like it is not our problem. We need to be aware when someone is struggling, and then to be there to help them carry their burdens. **[6]**

Of course, some people need more help than others, but there are those who will never let us know when they are in a struggle. **[7]**

If we see someone struggling, we shouldn't wait to be asked for help; go into action. Show our love and care for them. Sometimes it is best to not offer our help, but just tell someone we are doing something for them. When someone's loved one passes away, don't ask permission to bring food over, just do it.

When people are unable to go to the grocery store, don't ask if they need help. Usually they will answer "no." They do not want to be a burden to others. But if we call and tell them we will be stopping by to pick up their grocery list, it comes across as different. My mother was exactly like this. She wanted to be totally independent, and she was until the last year or two of her life. She did not drive very well so I would offer to go to the store for her. Her answer was always "no." So I just started going to her house when I was going to the grocery and ask her for her list. Since I was already going, she would let me shop for her. It would be hard to say "no" under these circumstances.

If we have a loved one that is carrying the burden of a spouse having major medical issues, we need to figure out how we can carry some of the load.

Ask them out for lunch.
Run an errand for them.
Stay with the spouse to give them a break.
Just listen. (Letting them talk about their struggles can lighten the load.)

Sometimes we can be the burden to others. In **HEBREWS 13:17**, we are told *OBEY YOUR LEADERS AND SUBMIT TO THEIR AUTHORITY. THEY KEEP WATCH OVER YOU AS MEN WHO MUST GIVE AN ACCOUNT. OBEY THEM SO THAT*

THEIR WORK WILL BE A JOY, NOT A BURDEN, FOR THAT WOULD BE OF NO ADVANTAGE TO YOU.

There is joy in the work of the Lord. Why let our negative actions take away from the joy of the Lord's work by a pastor or another leader within the body? Be a help, not a hindrance. This verse tells me I can be burden to my church leaders.

How could this happen?

> By talking about them behind their back
> By my lack of support
> By continually saying I don't like some of the things a leader is doing
> By questioning what the leader is doing without going directly to him

We are not to be guilty of being a burden to our leaders. [8]

What do we take away from this area of carrying one another's burdens? Show our love by being active in helping our fellow Christians as they go through the day to day struggles of carrying heavy burdens. We are to show our love for the sake of the Lord.

Who benefits from helping someone carry their burden? Both parties—the one whose burden became lighter and the one who helped. For **ACTS 20:35** says *IN EVERYTHING I DID, I SHOWED YOU THAT BY THIS KIND OF HARD WORK WE MUST HELP THE WEAK, REMEMBERING THE WORDS THE LORD JESUS HIMSELF SAID: "IT IS MORE BLESSED TO GIVE THAN TO RECEIVE."*

We all need to be aware when someone is having a hard time carrying a burden. Be attentive to your brothers in Christ and lend a helping hand. [9]

QUESTIONS ON CARRY BURDENS

1. Why is this thought so repugnant?

2. Do you have patience and empathy for the downtrodden? Do people deserve your help?

3. Explain law versus grace.

4. Can you do this without the Holy Spirit at work in your life?

5. Have you ever needed help with a burden?

6. How did someone help you carry a burden?

7. Do you ask for help or do you expect people to be mind readers?

8. As a leader, have any of these happened to you? How did you feel?

9. How did you feel when someone has helped you with a burden? How did you feel when you helped someone with a burden?

CHAPTER FORTY-SIX
CONCERN

1 CORINTHIANS 12:25, *SO THAT THERE SHOULD BE NO DIVISION IN THE BODY, BUT THAT ITS PARTS SHOULD HAVE EQUAL CONCERN FOR EACH OTHER.*

Concern: *worry or anxiety* [1]

Jesus tells in **MATTHEW 6:25–26** not to worry about the following things:

Your life
What you will eat or drink
About your body
What you will wear

After reading these verses, we should realize that there is not much left to worry about, but we still do. [2]

Then in **MATTHEW 6:27,** He ends by saying *"WHO OF YOU BY WORRYING CAN ADD A SINGLE HOUR TO HIS LIFE?"* Worry can actually take away years from our lives. Stress to a person's life can definitely do some damage. How many people in the U.S. take blood pressure medicine or other medicine needed because of what stress and worry does to the body?

In **1 PETER 5:7,** Peter says *CAST ALL YOUR ANXIETY ON HIM BECAUSE HE CARES FOR YOU.*

Paul writes in **PHILIPPIANS 4:6,** *DO NOT BE ANXIOUS ABOUT ANYTHING, BUT IN EVERYTHING, BY PRAYER AND PETITION, WITH THANKSGIVING, PRESENT YOUR REQUESTS TO GOD.*

Seems to me like a contradiction in the Scriptures when we are told to have concern for each other. How can I have equal concern for the body of believers and not be anxious or worried? [3]

As a Christian, is there an appropriate amount of worry without crossing a line? How do I know where the line begins and where it ends? Is it really a legitimate concern or am I worrying over nothing? Am I to be like the song, *"Don't Worry, Be Happy"*? Seems kind of flippant doesn't it?

A dear friend recently lost both her husband and father. My wife and I have concern for her. We are concerned for her ability to cope with these huge losses in her life so close together.

Is she okay financially?
Is she staying strong spiritually?
Is her physical health remaining strong?
Is she eating right?
Is she getting enough rest?
Is her emotional health doing okay?
Will she be able to continue her job?
Does she have a good financial adviser?

Of course we express to her our feelings, but we can never be sure about all the issues she is dealing with when she is going through such an emotional time.

Is this concern okay with the Lord? Absolutely!...up to a point. [4]

We cannot allow it to get to a debilitating issue with our own health or with our own mental state. We must and will turn these concerns over to the Lord. He is the one in control. He is the one to speak to her and give her comfort through the Holy Spirit. Jesus sent the Great

Comforter to us when He went to be with the Father. He is the one to be involved in all the issues in her life. All my worry, anxiety and concern can do nothing but harm me.

Another friend is going through marital issues. Is it okay to be concerned? Absolutely!… up to a point.

What am I to do personally with the concerns I have for my friends? Just forget about them? No!   [5]

> I can talk to them and express concern, and let them know I am there for them, no matter what.
> I can suggest counseling.
> I can let them know my wife and I are praying for them.
> I can listen to both parties and not take sides, just be a listener.
> My wife and I can try to spend time with them either together or separately.

Then I am to turn it over to the Lord and let Him deal with their marriage and their emotions. I am to continue praying for them as long as the Spirit leads me. Remember, prayer is not *"the least we can do,"* it is vital.

A friend loses his job. Am I concerned? You better believe it. Should I have concern? Absolutely!…up to a point.

We should let him know we are praying for him and keep him in our prayers. When we tell someone we'll pray for them, it is important to follow through with our prayers.

What else can I do?

> Take food, if it is appropriate.
> Use any contacts I have to help him find work.
> Take him and his family to dinner.
> Invite him and his family over for the evening.
> Ask if he needs anything at this time, and then ask him the same thing in later weeks.
> Have a one on one lunch, then listen.
> Do anything I can to keep him involved.
> Let him know I understand what he is going through (if this has happened to you).

When people lose their job, it messes with their sense of self-worth. It is like they have let the family down. It can be a very emotional time, so be aware. Keep in touch. Our concern can, and at times must, have actions to go with worry.

PROVERBS 12:25 tells us *AN ANXIOUS HEART WEIGHS A MAN DOWN, BUT A KIND WORD CHEERS HIM UP.*

If I see a spiritual leader going through some tough times should I be concerned? Absolutely!... up to a point. What can I do?

> Give him encouragement.
> Express my feelings of love for him.
> Get him away for a break if I can.
> Be in constant prayer and let him know I am praying for him.
> Remind him of the love the Lord has for him.
> Shouldn't he know this? Yes, but we all need reminding at times of how much our Savior loves and cares for us. **[6]**

There is something extremely comforting knowing that someone is praying for me, particularly in times of stress. I must realize that at times I have a hard time praying for myself. There is nothing wrong with asking my friends to pray for me, just the opposite, it is the Lord's will. *(See Chapter 50.)*

Are concerns, anxiety and worry normal human emotions? Yes, they are. But we as Christians have the Lord to turn to in these times of trouble. We can and are to lean on Him. In **JOHN 14:1,** Jesus says *"DO NOT LET YOUR HEARTS BE TROUBLED. TRUST IN GOD; TRUST ALSO IN ME."* In all the circumstances above we should have concern. We are to have actions with these concerns. When we have concerns, we are not to rely on our own puny power to try and fix it all. We cannot fix it all. All we do from trying to fix everything is to mess it up. Learn to lean on the Lord. He has the power.

Paul experienced concern for the churches. **2 CORINTHIANS 11:28,** *BESIDES EVERYTHING ELSE, I FACE DAILY THE PRESSURE OF MY CONCERN FOR ALL THE CHURCHES.* What are his concerns? He goes on to say he is concerned for the weak and ones who are led into sin. I am sure pastors today feel the same concern. We as parents feel this same concern as well. Paul mentions in **2 CORINTHIANS 8:16** that he is thankful that Titus has the same concerns.

In **2 CORINTHIANS 7:7,** Paul acknowledges their deep concern for him. In **PHILIPPIANS 4:10,** Paul even rejoices that they have renewed their concern for him. Paul needed to know that others were concerned for him and his ministry.

Conclusion:

> We are to have concern for our fellow Christians.
> > We are all part of the body of Christ.
> We are to take actions with our concerns, whatever they might be.
> > God expects us to take action.
> We are to take our concerns to the Lord.
> > This should be first and foremost and then do what the Holy Spirit lays on our hearts to do to help others.

Just don't have the attitude, "Don't pray when you can worry." [7]

QUESTIONS ON CONCERN

1.   Is worry a problem with you? Why? Over what issues?

2.   How do you spiritually apply these verses to your everyday life?

3.   How do you see concern different from worry?

4.   Why is this type of concern okay to have for one another?

5.   What would you do?

6.   What has been your involvement in friends' concerns and problems?

7.   How can we learn to have concerns but not to worry?

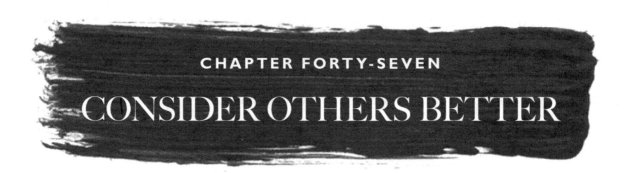

CHAPTER FORTY-SEVEN

CONSIDER OTHERS BETTER

PHILIPPIANS 2:3, *DO NOTHING OUT OF SELFISH AMBITION OR VAIN CONCEIT, BUT IN HUMILITY CONSIDER OTHERS BETTER THAN YOURSELVES.* [1]

To get an idea of what Paul is saying let's look at the whole paragraph. Paul starts off in **VERSE 1** by saying *IF YOU HAVE ANY ENCOURAGEMENT FROM BEING UNITED WITH CHRIST, IF ANY COMFORT FROM HIS LOVE, IF ANY FELLOWSHIP WITH THE SPIRIT, IF ANY TENDERNESS AND COMPASSION.* What he is saying is:

> I know you have encouragement from being united with Christ.
> I know you have comfort from His love. We are all loved by the Lord.
> I know you have fellowship with His Spirit. This brings fellowship with one another.
> I know you have tenderness and compassion. We care for each other.

Since we have all of these things, **VERSE 2** goes on to say *THEN MAKE MY JOY COMPLETE BY BEING LIKE-MINDED, HAVING THE SAME LOVE, BEING ONE IN SPIRIT AND PURPOSE.* Since we have, or in light of all of these things, we can make our joy complete by:

Being like-minded. Being selfless. Not thinking of ourselves first.

Having the same love. Total love for our Christian brothers and sisters.

Being one in spirit. We are the body of Christ, the church.

Being one in purpose. We are one. Complete unity to grow the church, and for all of us to be more Christ-like.

In **VERSE 3** he says, since we are all of these things, we are to do nothing that is:

Selfish ambition. Actions done to suit our own interests or needs. We are putting our own ambitions first in what we do. Keeping good things for ourselves and not sharing.

Or doing things for our own vain conceit. Putting our pride first.

In other words, don't do things just for yourself or just for your needs. [2]

Here are some bad examples of what can happen within a church:

I only want hymns to be sung in the church.

    I want no hymns, only choruses or new music; spiritual songs.

No drums in the church.

    We must have drums to keep it up to date.

The music is too loud. I hate loud music.

    We are to sing out to the Lord. Loud is good.

Because of the older people, it is too hot in here.

    I am too hot, turn on the air.

The pastor speaks too long; it affects my plans.

    I wish the pastor would speak longer.

This church is too formal.

    This church is too casual.

Everyone wants to change the order of the service. I like it how it is.

    We need more spontaneity in the service.

Our church needs to grow.

    I don't want new people in the church. They take my pew. [3]

This list could go on and on. These are attitudes that can destroy a church. This is why Paul says we are to *CONSIDER OTHERS BETTER THAN YOURSELVES.* What does this really mean? To regard or believe others better than ourselves is a state of mind, a new attitude. Our new way of thinking is to impact our actions. We are to see others as if they are special. **[4]**

Humility is making a right estimate of ourselves, to consider others better; we see them as better than us or of more importance. To consider others better, indicates a position of status, not a comparison of character or ability. We are not thinking of ourselves as nothing or having low self-esteem, but thinking of others having a higher position, and then we are to think of how we are to act towards them and how to treat them. If we look down on others, we will treat them differently than if we look up to them. Paul is saying we are to look up to our Christian brothers and sisters. **[5]**

Paul goes on to say in **VERSE 4,** *EACH OF YOU SHOULD LOOK NOT ONLY TO YOUR OWN INTERESTS, BUT ALSO TO THE INTEREST OF OTHERS.*

When we have the attitude of putting ourselves and our wants first, we are really saying "I am the most important." We must learn to honor and consider others better. To do this, we must get to know the needs of others, their concerns and their problems. To do this we must spend time together. **[6]**

It is evident that Jesus considered others better since he died for them. He saw others as the most important.

QUESTIONS ON CONSIDER OTHERS BETTER

1. What do you think it means to "consider others better"?

2. What comments would you add about **VERSES 1–3?**

3. What would you add to the list? Have you ever heard any of these comments in your church?

4. Is this by words or actions? Explain.

5. What keeps Christians from living like this?

6. How can you personally improve this part in your life?

CHAPTER FORTY-EIGHT

GOOD DEEDS

HEBREWS 10:24, *AND LET US CONSIDER HOW WE MAY SPUR ONE ANOTHER ON TOWARD LOVE AND GOOD DEEDS.*

GALATIANS 6:10, *THEREFORE, AS WE HAVE OPPORTUNITY, LET US DO GOOD TO ALL PEOPLE, ESPECIALLY TO THOSE WHO BELONG TO THE FAMILY OF BELIEVERS.*

We might think:

> I don't have time for doing good.
> I have my own family to take care of first.
> I am so tired at the end of the day.
> I don't even know what to do.
> That is not my gift.
> Doing good deeds is too demanding. [1]

If we look back at this list, we realize that it is nothing but excuses to keep us from doing what we are commanded to do. Doing good deeds seems to be and must be a part of our conversion. Keep this in mind through this entire study.

Paul brings up the point that as Christians, we are to prove our repentance by doing good deeds. **ACTS 25** and **26** tells the story of Paul being arrested and being brought before King Agrippa. Paul tells the King how he, as a Jew, became a Christian. He tells about the vision of Jesus and what He said to him. He tells the King in **ACTS 26:19–20,** *"SO THEN, KING AGRIPPA, I WAS NOT DISOBEDIENT TO THE VISION FROM HEAVEN. FIRST TO THOSE IN DAMASCUS, THEN TO THOSE IN JERUSALEM AND IN ALL JUDEA, AND TO THE GENTILES ALSO, I PREACHED THAT THEY SHOULD REPENT AND TURN TO GOD AND PROVE THEIR REPENTANCE BY THEIR DEEDS."* This brings up the question of how do we, who have been saved, prove our repentance by our good deeds? Aren't we saved by grace, not works? What is going on here? Paul is telling us that one brings about the other.   [2]

This follows along with what James writes in **JAMES 2:14–17,** *WHAT GOOD IS IT, MY BROTHERS, IF A MAN CLAIMS TO HAVE FAITH BUT HAS NO DEEDS? CAN SUCH FAITH SAVE HIM? SUPPOSE A BROTHER OR SISTER IS WITHOUT CLOTHES AND DAILY FOOD. IF ONE OF YOU SAYS TO HIM, "GO, I WISH YOU WELL; KEEP WARM AND WELL FED," BUT DOES NOTHING ABOUT HIS PHYSICAL NEEDS, WHAT GOOD IS IT? IN THE SAME WAY, FAITH BY ITSELF, IF IT IS NOT ACCOMPANIED BY ACTION, IS DEAD.* We should always be praying for our Christian brothers, but James is saying we need to have actions. Actions that might cost us time or money. We are to be involved with the needs of others. We cannot go around with our eyes closed to our brother's troubles and then say, "I never knew." That is just an excuse. Yes, there are times doing good deeds will take us out of our comfort zone, but our attitude needs to be, "whatever it takes Lord."   [3]

Paul points out that once we become a Christian, good deeds are expected. James says in **JAMES 2:26,** *AS THE BODY WITHOUT THE SPIRIT IS DEAD, SO FAITH WITHOUT DEEDS IS DEAD.* We cannot have faith without deeds. If we have faith and no deeds, our faith is dead. Strong words from these two Saints, but they are absolutely on the mark. Good deeds just follow becoming a Christian. It is the same as when we jump into water, we will get wet. One follows the other. James feels so strongly about this he says in **JAMES 4:17,** *ANYONE, THEN, WHO KNOWS THE GOOD HE OUGHT TO DO AND DOESN'T DO IT, SINS.* We tend to look at sin as something we have done, but in this case, James is saying we sin when we don't do something when we know we should. One is as bad as the other.

Here is a prayer from an American Anglican Sunday service:

Most merciful God, we confess that we have sinned against you in thought, word and deed, by what we have done, and by what we have left undone. We have not loved you with our whole heart: we have not loved our neighbors as ourselves.

We can sin by omission as well as commission.

There is another key reason for us to do good deeds. It shows the world how Christians are to act, it shows the world the love of Christ that is in us and thus, people should see the Lord in our lives. We are His examples here on earth. In **MATTHEW 5:14–16,** Jesus says ***"YOU ARE THE LIGHT OF THE WORLD. A CITY ON A HILL CANNOT BE HIDDEN. NEITHER DO PEOPLE LIGHT A LAMP AND PUT IT UNDER A BOWL. INSTEAD THEY PUT IT ON ITS STAND, AND IT GIVES LIGHT TO EVERYONE IN THE HOUSE. IN THE SAME WAY, LET YOUR LIGHT SHINE BEFORE MEN, THAT THEY MAY SEE YOUR GOOD DEEDS AND PRAISE YOUR FATHER IN HEAVEN."*** I can never read this verse without remembering a song that I sang as a kid: "This Little Light of Mine." The second verse says this: *Hide it under a bushel? No! I'm gonna let it shine.* Some might even remember the actions we had to go along with the song. But the key for me is I still remember the song and what it means. We as Christians are the light of the world. People need to see the light so it might attract them. Christians must do good deeds; otherwise we are hiding our light, the light of Christ. Do people praise the Father in heaven when they see the deeds we do, or is there anything to see? [4]

If others see our good deeds, they can actually see the Lord at work in our hearts and our actions that will flow from His love. No one should ever question if we are Christians. Our actions should show that we are. Doing good deeds should just flow automatically from us, and if they do not, we need to look at our lives in Christ and see what we are missing. We do not and cannot serve God in a vacuum or a bubble.

By doing good deeds and works:

It is pleasing to God.
It allows the Holy Spirit to become more a part of our lives.
It keeps us from being selfish as we give to others.
It allows the fruit of the Spirit to grow in our lives.

It is an example of Christ living in us.
It is a testimony of our faith.
It is an outward sign of our faith.
We follow His command. [5]

COLOSSIANS 3:17, *AND WHATEVER YOU DO, WHETHER IN WORD OR DEED, DO IT ALL IN THE NAME OF THE LORD JESUS, GIVING THANKS TO GOD THE FATHER THROUGH HIM.* Whatever we do, it is to honor Him. We are His ambassadors to the world.

1 PETER 2:12, *LIVE SUCH GOOD LIVES AMONG THE PAGANS THAT, THOUGH THEY ACCUSE YOU OF DOING WRONG, THEY MAY SEE YOUR GOOD DEEDS AND GLORIFY GOD ON THE DAY HE VISITS US.* Really analyze this verse. Peter is telling us that when we live our lives as Christians, we are setting such an example, that the pagans (non-Christians) will see that we are different. They will see that we are the Lord's reflection. We are His light. Some may never hear about Jesus, but they will see our lives and see Him through the way we live. They will not only see a difference in how we live day to day but also see the deeds we do. Our actions are our testimony. [6]

Jesus says in **REVELATIONS 2:23B,** *"I WILL REPAY EACH OF YOU ACCORDING TO YOUR DEEDS."* We are also told in **MATTHEW 16:27,** *"FOR THE SON OF MAN IS GOING TO COME IN HIS FATHER'S GLORY WITH HIS ANGELS, AND THEN HE WILL REWARD EACH PERSON ACCORDING TO WHAT HE HAS DONE."* Since we are to be rewarded for our deeds, we should not show up empty handed. It is not that we do good deeds for the reward, we should be doing good deeds because of our love for the Lord. But as we follow the commands of the Lord, we are laying up treasures in heaven. Paul tells Timothy in **1 TIMOTHY 6:18,** *COMMAND THEM TO DO GOOD, TO BE RICH IN GOOD DEEDS, AND TO BE GENEROUS AND WILLING TO SHARE.* To be rich in something means we have a lot of it, whatever it is. In this case Paul is saying he wants fellow Christians to be rich in, to have a lot of, good deeds. Thus, by being rich in good deeds we are to share these good deeds with everyone. Not keep them to ourselves.

Isn't it really about doing something for someone that they do not expect but appreciate? It is showing our Christian brothers the love we have in our hearts as we do good deeds. It makes us feel like we helped someone in need by just showing our Christian love. It is not that we need credit for it. Sometimes we do good deeds, and no one sees or notices it at the time.

Some of our best good deeds occur when no one knows who did the good deed. Getting credit should not even come to our minds as we follow the Holy Spirit's leading. The Holy Spirit puts the desire in our hearts to do good deeds. On more than one occasion I have had someone plow out my driveway after a major snowfall and I am not sure which neighbor did the good deed. The person who did it was not looking for credit, but just wanted to be helpful. Good deeds like this are always appreciated. [7]

How do we get ready to do good deeds? **2 TIMOTHY 3:16–17, *ALL SCRIPTURE IS GOD-BREATHED AND IS USEFUL FOR TEACHING, REBUKING, CORRECTING AND TRAINING IN RIGHTEOUSNESS, SO THAT THE MAN OF GOD MAY BE THOROUGHLY EQUIPPED FOR EVERY GOOD WORK.*** For us to do good deeds and lead a Christian life, we need to know the Bible and the teaching that is in it. We need to be prepared to be corrected as we go through life and as we are trained in righteousness. This can come from reading and studying the scriptures; by attending Sunday School classes, small groups, men's or women's groups; listening to radio or TV; and from the teaching of our local pastor. We can also watch others as they set examples on doing good deeds. We should pray daily for opportunities for doing good deeds. We must devote ourselves to doing what is good. **TITUS 3:8, *THIS IS A TRUSTWORTHY SAYING. AND I WANT YOU TO STRESS THESE THINGS, SO THAT THOSE WHO HAVE TRUSTED IN GOD MAY BE CAREFUL TO DEVOTE THEMSELVES TO DOING WHAT IS GOOD. THESE THINGS ARE EXCELLENT AND PROFITABLE FOR EVERYONE.***

GALATIANS 6:10 says we are to do good deeds to our fellow Christians. Just what are good deeds? Good deeds can be many things:

Cleaning up after a church dinner.
Doing maintenance for someone who is unable to do it himself.
Opening the door for someone.
Visiting a sick friend.
Shopping for someone who is unable to get out of the house.
Buying lunch for a needy person.
Taking food to the home bound.
Shoveling the driveway for an older person.
Raking the leaves for a neighbor.
Carrying something heavy for someone.
Making something for someone.

Helping someone financially when there is a need.
Telling someone we appreciate what they do for others. **[8]**

This list is unending, just as it should be. I was recently in a grocery store and wheeled my cart out to empty my groceries into the car. When finished, there was no cart parking places anywhere near, so I started to take it back up to the front door. On my way, I saw other carts just left in parking spaces. I picked them up as well. On my way back to the car a man who was watching me said, "That was really nice." Personally, I did not think anything of it, good deeds just come out from me most of the time. It was nice to hear though. We must never, ever stop doing good deeds. Age or health should not stop us. **GALATIANS 6:9A, *LET US NOT BECOME WEARY IN DOING GOOD*.** Actually, as we grow in our Christian walk, we should be more prolific in doing good deeds. We may retire from our jobs, but we cannot retire from doing good for others.

We are told in **EPHESIANS 2:10, *FOR WE ARE GOD'S WORKMANSHIP, CREATED IN CHRIST JESUS TO DO GOOD WORKS, WHICH GOD PREPARED IN ADVANCE FOR US TO DO*.** WOW! Think about this for a moment. God, the Master Creator, made us to do good deeds. He even created the opportunity for us to do them. We cannot let Him down. We must keep our eyes open. We must ask the Holy Spirit to help us. Help to put the desire for good deeds in our hearts and help us to see when they need to be done. **[9]**

Don't we all want people to do good deeds for us? They feel the same way. When I started work on this chapter, I started going out of my way to do good deeds for others. It is unbelievable how the spirit to do more good deeds has grown in me. Plus, I see it as contagious. When I have helped someone in a public place, I see others doing the same. The benefit for me is immeasurable. It makes me feel so good just to do something for someone. Be the catalyst for others. Today we say, "pass it forward." Look for ways to do good deeds.

For a Christian it is more "just do it" or "try it, you'll like it." Good deeds are to flow from us. They must be as much a part of us as breathing. A natural reflex. **[10]**

QUESTIONS ON GOOD DEEDS

1. What other excuses have you or others used?

2. How would doing good deeds prove our repentance?

3. Did you see this area of good deeds change in your life after your conversion?

4. What are your thoughts on **MATTHEW 5:14–16?** Do you feel like a light? How bright a light are you?

5. What else would you add to this list of reasons for good deeds?

6. What are your thoughts on **1 PETER 2:12?**

7. Have you done a good deed anonymously? How did it feel?

8. What would you add to this list?

9. Discuss this verse. How would this impact our efforts? Up the ante?

10. What is your attitude about good deeds after the lesson?

CHAPTER FORTY-NINE
BE KIND

EPHESIANS 4:32A, *BE KIND AND COMPASSIONATE TO ONE ANOTHER.*

Webster tells us kind or kindness means: *a gentle or considerate manner or conduct towards others. To be considerate, taking care not to inconvenience or hurt others.* [1]

The way the word is interpreted in **EPHESIANS 4:32,** it means to *keep on proving yourselves to be kind to one another.* Paul is not expecting us to be kind one moment and not the next. Our kindness is to be never ending, not just once in a while or when we feel like it. Or not just to people we like; it is to be to all people, particularly to our Christian brothers.

There are many verses to examine on kindness, but the key one is **GALATIANS 5:22.** This verse starts the list of the fruit of the Spirit. *BUT THE FRUIT OF THE SPIRIT IS LOVE, JOY, PEACE, PATIENCE, KINDNESS, GOODNESS, FAITHFULNESS.* Why is this verse so key when it comes to kindness? When we become Christians, the Holy Spirit enters into us and when He enters us, He brings to us the fruit of the Spirit. This fruit does not make us full of love, joy, peace, patience, kindness, goodness or faithfulness immediately from that salvation day. All of these plus others must be developed. Some of the fruit of the Spirit grows faster than others, but they all must be watered so they will grow within us. Like any growing fruit, it does not happen overnight. Just because we became Christians, we cannot expect ourselves to be the kindest people on the earth immediately.

This fruit is like a muscle, by exercising our kindness it will grow. Once it is developed, it becomes a part of who we are as Christians. [2]

In **GALATIANS 5:22A,** love is the first fruit that is mentioned. Without love, none of the other areas will develop. **1 CORINTHIANS 13:4A** says *LOVE IS PATIENT, LOVE IS KIND.* If we don't have love in our hearts, the love that comes from the Holy Spirit, it is hard to be kind to others. We should not "pick and choose" which fruit of the Spirit we want in our lives. We are to develop all the varieties of the fruit so we can be more Christ-like. The Holy Spirit working in us makes this possible. **ROMANS 13:14,** *RATHER, CLOTHE YOURSELVES WITH THE LORD JESUS CHRIST, AND DO NOT THINK ABOUT HOW TO GRATIFY THE DESIRES OF THE SINFUL NATURE.* Every day when we get up in the morning, we are to put on Jesus Christ, which enables us to look out for the needs of others and then to do generous acts of kindness. We are to do this so we are not doing things to gratify our sinful nature; things that appeal to our sinful nature. This is not inborn in us; the Holy Spirit works to develop the fruit. The Holy Spirit is in direct conflict with our flesh, our sinful nature. This battle will keep going on until we are taken home to be with the Lord. We are to live by the Spirit. Living by the Spirit is far different than living for the flesh, living for ourselves, being self-centered. [3]

COLOSSIANS 3:12 directs us to clothe ourselves with kindness. Every time I read in the Bible to clothe myself with some virtue, I envision getting up in the morning and putting it on. To put on the clothing of kindness, I am ready to walk out the door and to show kindness to all. I am to actively look for ways to be kind. It is to be ingrained in me, a part of who I am. This way people can see the Lord in my life. A smile on my face helps as well.

GALATIANS 5:17 speaks to the ongoing battle. *FOR THE SINFUL NATURE DESIRES WHAT IS CONTRARY TO THE SPIRIT, AND THE SPIRIT WHAT IS CONTRARY TO THE SINFUL NATURE. THEY ARE IN CONFLICT WITH EACH OTHER, SO THAT YOU DO NOT DO WHAT YOU WANT.* At times we do not do what we want to do, or what we know we are supposed to do. This is what Paul is writing about. We may want to be a kind, considerate Christian, but we have a hard time doing this on a consistent basis. Paul tells us how to defeat the flesh. **GALATIANS 5:16,** *SO I SAY, LIVE BY THE SPIRIT, AND YOU WILL NOT GRATIFY THE DESIRES OF THE SINFUL NATURE.*

It is not natural for us to be concerned for others and to want to be kind to them. Most of the time our only concern is "what is in it for me?" To do acts of kindness in hope of receiving something in return is not kindness at all. That is bribery.

Kindness directs me to do generous acts to others expecting nothing in return. We cannot have the attitude "but they were not kind to me first" or "they were unkind to me, why should I be kind to them?" We are to repay unkindness with kindness. **2 TIMOTHY 2:24,** *AND THE LORD'S SERVANT MUST NOT QUARREL; INSTEAD, HE MUST BE KIND TO EVERYONE, ABLE TO TEACH, NOT RESENTFUL.* We are to be Christ-like and reflect His kindness to all.

We cannot expect all acts of kindness to be appreciated or noticed. **2 CHRONICLES 22–24** gives us an example of how an act of kindness can be totally ignored. It begins in **2 CHRONICLES 22:10,** *WHEN ATHALIAH THE MOTHER OF AHAZIAH* (the king) *SAW THAT HER SON WAS DEAD, SHE PROCEEDED TO DESTROY THE WHOLE ROYAL FAMILY OF THE HOUSE OF JUDAH.* But Jehosheba, wife of Jehoiada, took Joash, the king's son, and hid him away from the dead king's mother. He was brought forth, after six years in hiding, and made king. Many years later, Jehoiada's son was killed by King Joash. **2 CHRONICLES 24:22A,** *KING JOASH DID NOT REMEMBER THE KINDNESS ZECHARIAH'S FATHER JEHOIADA HAD SHOWN HIM BUT KILLED HIS SON.* Jehoiada had raised Joash as his son. Joash and Zechariah were raised as brothers and the future king had been shown great kindness. The lesson here, when we give an act of kindness, expect nothing in return. [4]

We do see acts of kindness in the Bible:

Paul speaks to this in **ACTS 28:1–2** when he and all the rest of the ship's passengers and crew came on shore after a shipwreck. *ONCE SAFELY ON SHORE, WE FOUND OUT THAT THE ISLAND WAS CALLED MALTA. THE ISLANDERS SHOWED US UNUSUAL KINDNESS. THEY BUILT A FIRE AND WELCOMED US ALL BECAUSE IT WAS RAINING AND COLD.* This is not Christians showing kindness but people that were simply showing humanitarian aid to total strangers. We see this even today.

Another thing that comes to mind is the parable of the Good Samaritan. In this case this is a person taking care of an enemy and being kind to him; someone hated by all Samaritans, a Jew. (See **LUKE 10:25–37.**)

Jesus gives us many examples:

> Talking to the woman at the well
> Making wine out of water so the host is not embarrassed
> Bringing back Lazarus from the dead to help his sisters in their grief
> Speaking to the man on the cross and reassuring him of his future
> Feeding the five thousand
> Dying for all mankind

God is also an example of kindness to us:

ROMANS 11:22, *CONSIDER THEREFORE THE KINDNESS AND STERNNESS OF GOD: STERNNESS TO THOSE WHO FELL, BUT KINDNESS TO YOU, PROVIDED THAT YOU CONTINUE IN HIS KINDNESS. OTHERWISE, YOU ALSO WILL BE CUT OFF.* This kindness shown to us is the grace that Jesus brings to us through his death.   [5]

We do not have kindness as a prominent trait when we start our life. When we observe little children, particularly an only child, they think the world revolves around them. They see mom and dad as someone to do their bidding. If they don't get their way, they throw tantrums so they *will* get what they want. Their life is about selfishness, not kindness. We have all seen children like this, usually in the checkout line. If children are around other children that want to play with *their* toys, what do we hear? "It's mine, you can't have it." "Give it back, I had it first." Children want all their toys to be under their control, so we must teach our children kindness. Kindness can and must be taught. Children and adults must learn to give up some things no matter what the cost. First it starts with sharing of what they have, and then it goes into giving their toys away so others can enjoy them. Try giving away your children's toys even years after they do not play with them. Some children and some people never learn how to be kind, how to share. They are selfish all their lives, not caring about others. An example comes from Marie-Antoinette when she was quoted as saying about the poor having no food, "let them eat cake." Kindness is to be taught and then it must be exercised.   [6]

Being kind does not happen immediately after we become a Christian, it is to be a learning, growing fruit within us. Paul recognizes this and says in **TITUS 2:3–5** to teach the older women to train the younger women to be kind. Did we have anyone train us in kindness when we were younger? Most of us were taught as children to be kind by our parents or a teacher, but not so much after we became young men and women. But we could see the older Christians living their lives as they treated each other with kindness and respect. Their actions were teaching us how to act, how to be kind, how to love our fellow Christians, even the unlovable. As we matured, we were to take our training and turn it into our own decision to be kind. [7]

Kindness can be taught, and it can be developed. If it can be taught, then we can learn how to be kind. Look for examples in other Christians, but most of all look to our Lord, for His life was full of kindness.

God showed his kindness when He sent His Son to save us. **EPHESIANS 2:6–7,** *AND GOD RAISED US UP WITH CHRIST AND SEATED US WITH HIM IN THE HEAVENLY REALMS IN CHRIST JESUS, IN ORDER THAT IN COMING AGES HE MIGHT SHOW THE INCOMPARABLE RICHES OF HIS GRACE, EXPRESSED IN HIS KINDNESS TO US IN CHRIST JESUS.* How far do we need to go to show kindness? God allowed His Son to be crucified to show His kindness to mankind. We are to be God-like, Christ-like, and show kindness to all. [8], [9], [10]

QUESTIONS ON BE KIND

1. If you were to be kind to someone, what might it entail?

2. Have you always been a kind and considerate person to others? All the time?

3. What is your understanding of being clothed with Jesus?

4. Have you ever been kind to someone and then they took advantage of you?

5. What do you see as the kindness of God and of Jesus?

6. Why does it go against our human nature to be kind?

7. Why do we have to be trained to be kind to others?

8. Who do you know that you would consider a kind person? What makes you think that?

9. Isn't kindness a sign of weakness?

10. What changes do you need to make to be kind to your Christian brothers?

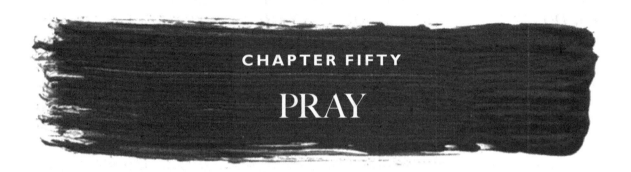

CHAPTER FIFTY

PRAY

JAMES 5:16, *THEREFORE CONFESS YOUR SINS TO EACH OTHER AND PRAY FOR EACH OTHER SO THAT YOU MAY BE HEALED. THE PRAYER OF A RIGHTEOUS MAN IS POWERFUL AND EFFECTIVE.*

Why do we need to pray for our fellow Christians? The answers are in the preceding verses, **VERSES 13–15.** Here are the reasons.

> If we are in trouble. **VERSE 13**
> If we are sick. **VERSES 14–15**
> If we have sinned. **VERSE 15**

These are the same reasons we want someone to pray for us today. If we are in trouble, whether it's financial, our home life, work, relationships or for any other reason, we covet the prayers of our fellow Christians. If we or other family members are sick, we let people know that prayer is needed. The church I attend has a weekly updated prayer list. These are needs someone in the church is asking for their Christian brothers to pray for them. This list is sent out every Monday or Tuesday via e-mail. If someone needs urgent prayer and it is a new issue, then a memo goes out to all the same way. **[1]**

One reason to pray for others is someday we personally might need prayer over a problem area ourselves. [2]

There is another reason to pray. Prayer keeps us from being anxious. **PHILIPPIANS 4:6, *DO NOT BE ANXIOUS ABOUT ANYTHING, BUT IN EVERYTHING, BY PRAYER AND PETITION, WITH THANKSGIVING, PRESENT YOUR REQUESTS TO GOD.*** But what is really key is what the next verse tells us. **VERSE 7, *AND THE PEACE OF GOD, WHICH TRANSCENDS ALL UNDERSTANDING, WILL GUARD YOUR HEARTS AND YOUR MINDS IN CHRIST JESUS.*** Prayer should be keeping us from being anxious. The definition for anxious is *troubled and uneasy in mind, causing worry*. This is reason enough for us to pray. When we pray, we are giving God our troubles and those of others. Notice the verse says ***BUT IN EVERYTHING*** bring it to God. Nothing is too small, and nothing is too big. Once this is done, God gives us peace. He gives it, but sometimes we do not accept it. We keep brooding over the issue. We give it to Him, then we take it back. We must learn to trust in the Lord for He is good. [3]

Paul, in his letters, gives us many lessons on who and what we should pray for concerning each other.

EPHESIANS 6:19–20, Paul gives the reason he requested prayer. ***PRAY ALSO FOR ME, THAT WHENEVER I OPEN MY MOUTH, WORDS MAY BE GIVEN ME SO THAT I WILL FEARLESSLY MAKE KNOWN THE MYSTERY OF THE GOSPEL, FOR WHICH I AM AN AMBASSADOR IN CHAINS. PRAY THAT I MAY DECLARE IT FEARLESSLY, AS I SHOULD.*** Wouldn't it be wonderful if someone was praying this prayer for each of us? Do not think this is just a pray for pastors and Christian workers; this prayer should be for all Christians. I was with a person who was a regional director for a major company. We had become friends over the years. While riding in a car together, he said that he could see something different in me that he wanted to know about. He said he was considering attending church with his family and wanted to know what the Christian experience was all about. Looking back at my answer, I feel like I stuttered and stammered and did a very poor job of telling him about my salvation and what it meant to me as I lived my daily life. I would give anything to get another chance at that answer. So, to me this prayer that Paul is talking about hits home. [4]

COLOSSIANS 4:2–4, *DEVOTE YOURSELVES TO PRAYER, BEING WATCHFUL AND THANKFUL. AND PRAY FOR US, TOO, THAT GOD MAY OPEN A DOOR FOR OUR MESSAGE, SO THAT WE MAY PROCLAIM THE MYSTERY OF CHRIST, FOR WHICH I AM IN CHAINS. PRAY THAT I MAY PROCLAIM IT CLEARLY, AS I SHOULD.* Paul wants open doors just like we should want in our daily lives.

EPHESIANS 3:16–19, *I PRAY THAT OUT OF HIS GLORIOUS RICHES HE MAY STRENGTHEN YOU WITH POWER THROUGH HIS SPIRIT IN YOUR INNER BEING, SO THAT CHRIST MAY DWELL IN YOUR HEARTS THROUGH FAITH. AND I PRAY THAT YOU, BEING ROOTED AND ESTABLISHED IN LOVE, MAY HAVE POWER, TOGETHER WITH ALL THE SAINTS, TO GRASP HOW WIDE AND LONG AND HIGH AND DEEP IS THE LOVE OF CHRIST, AND TO KNOW THIS LOVE THAT SURPASSES KNOWLEDGE—THAT YOU MAY BE FILLED TO THE MEASURE OF ALL THE FULLNESS OF GOD.* What a prayer he prayed for the Ephesians! He prayed they would be strengthened in the Spirit and that they would have the knowledge of the depth of love the Lord has for them. This prayer can be our prayer for our Christian brothers.

PHILIPPIANS 1:10, he prays that their love may abound and that they would *BE ABLE TO DISCERN WHAT IS BEST AND MAY BE PURE AND BLAMELESS UNTIL THE DAY OF CHRIST.* He also prays they may be filled with righteousness. Again, these are prayers we should be making for our fellow Christians.

2 CORINTHIANS 13:9, Paul prays for their perfection; to be more Christ-like.

2 THESSALONIANS 1:11–12A, Paul prays continually *THAT OUR GOD MAY COUNT YOU WORTHY OF HIS CALLING,* and goes on to pray that *HE MAY FULFILL EVERY GOOD PURPOSE.* He continues to pray *THAT THE NAME OF OUR LORD JESUS MAY BE GLORIFIED IN YOU, AND YOU IN HIM.*

In review, look at the directions Paul has given to us of areas that we should be praying for ourselves and for our fellow Christians. We also need to understand how to apply these verses to our daily living.

EPHESIANS 6:19–20

A. That we should be given words so we can make known the Gospel so people will understand.

To many people the concept of Christianity is foreign to them, so they do not understand the true meaning of salvation and grace. Pray that the Holy Spirit will speak through us.

B. We should be fearless in our testimony.

Do not be fearful, because the Lord is with us.

COLOSSIANS 4:2–4

A. We are to be devoted to prayer.

This means we are to be in constant contact with the Lord, not just a set aside time for prayer. **[5]**

B. We are to be thankful.

Always give thanks to the Lord, for He is good.

C. We are to be watchful, aware of the prayer needs that are around us.

Do not be oblivious to others and their needs and only pray for our self.

D. We are to pray that we and others will proclaim the Gospel.

We need to keep our missionaries in our prayers as well as other Christian workers.

EPHESIANS 3:16–19

A. Pray that we will be strengthened by the power of the Holy Spirit.

Without the power of the Holy Spirit we can do nothing.

B. Pray that Christ will dwell in our hearts.

This should be a daily prayer. If we continually have the Lord in our hearts, our lives will be changed.

C. Pray we become rooted and established in Christ's love.

This can only come through prayer and Bible study.

D. Pray we may grasp how huge Christ's love is for us.

    We are truly loved in a way that can only come through the Lord.   **[6]**

E. Pray we are filled with the fullness of God.

    We should be seen as Christ-like.

PHILIPPIANS 1:9–11

A. Pray that our love may abound.

    We must show the love of the Lord in our daily living.

B. Pray that we gain more and more knowledge and discernment.

    Pray that we will know how to live our lives in such a way that it will be pleasing to the Lord.

C. Pray we use this discernment to be pure and blameless upon the Lord's return.

    We must understand how to live and how to be pure in the Lord's sight.

D. Pray that we will be filled with righteousness.

    Again, this points out we are to be like our Savior.

2 CORINTHIANS 13:9

We are to pray that we become more and more Christ-like as we go through life.

2 THESSALONIANS 1:11–12

A. We are to pray that we are worthy to be called Christians.

    When we are called Christians, we take the name of the Lord with us. It is like our earthly father saying, "make us proud of our name."   **[7]**

B. Pray that we may fulfill, to the best of our ability, what the Lord has asked of us.

    We are to pray that we do not fail at what the Lord has directed us to do here on earth.

C. Pray our lives will glorify the Lord.

    We have been given gifts to be used to glorify the Lord. We must use them in our daily lives.

Jesus gives examples of how we are to pray in **LUKE 22:40.** When the Lord left the upper room, He took the disciples to the Mount of Olives. ***ON REACHING THE PLACE, HE SAID TO THEM, "PRAY THAT YOU WILL NOT FALL INTO TEMPTATION."*** This can be our daily prayer, for ourselves and for others. Pray that as we come into tempting times, and times of trials that we would remain strong in the Lord. We, on our own, are not strong enough to resist evil.

JOHN 17:15, Jesus prays this prayer to His Father, ***"MY PRAYER IS NOT THAT YOU TAKE THEM OUT OF THE WORLD BUT THAT YOU PROTECT THEM FROM THE EVIL ONE."*** My father-in-law, a devout Christian, prayed similar prayers many times. He wanted protection from the evil one for his children. We all should be praying a prayer like this to our Father, that He would protect us from the evil one.

We are not only to pray for our Christian brothers and our families, but for those in leadership. **1 TIMOTHY 2:1–2A,** *I URGE, THEN, FIRST OF ALL, THAT REQUESTS, PRAYERS, INTERCESSION AND THANKSGIVING BE MADE FOR EVERYONE—FOR KINGS AND ALL THOSE IN AUTHORITY, THAT WE MAY LIVE PEACEFUL AND QUIET LIVES IN ALL GODLINESS AND HOLINESS.* If we find this hard to do today when we don't even like our President, think how hard of a request that Paul was laying on Timothy? At that time Nero was persecuting Christians even to the point of death. But this is the point, if we pray for our leaders, we are praying that they will know the leading of the Lord as they direct the nation. We are praying that more and more nations will allow the Word of the Lord to be brought to their people. If all this takes place it will allow all Christians to live a peaceful and quiet life. If we want a loving spirit in our hearts, learn to pray for people we dislike. As we pray, the Holy Spirit will soften our hearts. This is not the only Scripture that gives us directions to pray for those who can and do harm us. In **MATTHEW 5:44** Jesus says ***"BUT I TELL YOU: LOVE YOUR ENEMIES AND PRAY FOR THOSE WHO PERSECUTE YOU."*** Jesus also says in **LUKE 6:28, "BLESS THOSE WHO CURSE YOU, PRAY FOR THOSE WHO MISTREAT YOU."** This can be anyone in our lives. If it is a boss, a fellow worker, a relative or anyone who does not like us, we are to pray for them. Why? If we turn over to the Lord those who are causing us problems, He takes the situation out of our hands. [8]

We do have some caveats to answered prayers. Here are three guidelines:

1 PETER 3:7, we, as men, are told to treat our wives with respect and consideration, *SO THAT NOTHING WILL HINDER YOUR PRAYERS.*

1 TIMOTHY 2:8, Paul gives this direction, *I WANT MEN EVERYWHERE TO LIFT UP HOLY HANDS IN PRAYER, WITHOUT ANGER OR DISPUTING.*

MARK 11:25, Jesus says, *"AND WHEN YOU STAND PRAYING, IF YOU HOLD ANYTHING AGAINST ANYONE, FORGIVE HIM, SO THAT YOUR FATHER IN HEAVEN MAY FORGIVE YOU YOUR SINS."*

These verses tell us we must be holy and right with God when we come to the Lord in prayer. We must be right in our marriages and we must be forgiving to our brothers, not have anything against them. Why? If we are not forgiving, our prayers will go nowhere, they will be hindered. [9]

It is key to our prayers to pray in the Spirit. What does this mean? We should be praying and letting the Holy Spirit give us direction and guidance. The Holy Spirit knows the will of the Lord, who to pray for, how to pray, what to pray, when to pray and when we need to pray more or when to quit praying. If we don't know what to pray, the Spirit will intervene. I personally know this feeling. My youngest son was in the hospital and they could not find a diagnosis for days. He was in a poor state and I did not know what to pray and really could not focus on prayer. I knew my friends were praying but we are also told in **ROMANS 8:26–27,** *IN THE SAME WAY, THE SPIRIT HELPS US IN OUR WEAKNESS. WE DO NOT KNOW WHAT WE OUGHT TO PRAY FOR, BUT THE SPIRIT HIMSELF INTERCEDES FOR US WITH GROANS THAT WORDS CANNOT EXPRESS. AND HE WHO SEARCHES OUR HEARTS KNOWS THE MIND OF THE SPIRIT, BECAUSE THE SPIRIT INTERCEDES FOR THE SAINTS IN ACCORDANCE WITH GOD'S WILL.* We must ask the Holy Spirit to help and guide us in our prayers. [10]

When should we pray?

ACTS 1:14. The apostles were constantly in prayer.
ROMANS 12:12. We are urged to be faithful in prayer.
EPHESIANS 6:18–19. Pray on all occasions, always.
COLOSSIANS 4:2. We are told to devote ourselves to prayer.
1 THESSALONIANS 5:17. We are to pray continually.

The key seems to be our prayers are not to be hit and miss, or just if we really want something or when we are in trouble. If we, as parents, have a child that never communicates with us, never visits, never gives us love in return for our love, how willing would we be to give them something if they asked for it and it was in our power to give? This is the same as our heavenly Father. **[11]**

Prayers do not need to be long. The Lord's Prayer takes less than thirty seconds to repeat. Prayers can be long. Jesus prayed all night prior to the selection of His apostles in **LUKE 6:12.** We do not need to pray with a bunch of thees and thous. We are just communicating with our Father. Speak your mind. The Father just wants to hear from us. What is going on in our lives? Our concerns, our requests, our thanks, our troubles and when we are asking forgiveness or for direction. **[12]**

If prayer is not an emphasis is our churches, it needs to be. **[13]**

Every church needs prayer warriors, people that can be counted on to pray for the needs of the body. Someone who says, "I will pray for that need" and we know they really will. Never, ever promise to pray for someone and then not do it. We need to keep our promises, others are counting on us. **[14]**

QUESTIONS ON PRAY

1. When should we ask for prayer? Do you have a similar prayer request system in your church? If not, are you the person to start the system?

2. Do you agree?

3. Are you able to turn things over to the Lord and leave them there?

4. Has this ever happened to you?

5. What does it mean to be devoted to prayer? Are you?

6. How would you explain God's love to someone?

7. Do you agree?

8. Can you pray for the ones mentioned in these verses?

9. Do you agree?

10. Explain praying in the Spirit. To some this means praying in tongues. Do you agree?

11. Have you ever thought about prayers this way?

12. Are we to pray about everything in our lives? Should we pick and choose?

13. Is prayer an emphasis in your church? If not, why not?

14. Who can you count on to be a prayer warrior?

ABOUT THE AUTHOR

David has been married over 55 years and has three adult children: daughter Wendy (Grant), son Todd, and son Trent (Sabrina). He also has two grandchildren, Cade and Brenna, and a brother, Dennis. David and Naomi now spend half a year in Florida and the other half in Ohio. Personally, he is grateful to his parents, Bill and Wanita, for their great Christian up-bringing.

As an adult Sunday school teacher for over 50 years, David has prepared over 2,400 lessons, teaching primarily a verse to verse study on many books of the Bible.

While preparing these lessons, David felt the urging and direction from the Holy Spirit to put together a series on the subject of the "One Anothers." Thus, this book was created on the study of Biblical commands; on how and why we as Christians are to treat our fellow Christians.

David's desire was to make the book teacher-friendly whether teaching in Sunday school or leading a small group. This book can and has been used to teach junior high students through adult seniors, as well as a personal study. To make it teacher-friendly, all scriptures used are in bold print, saving time to look up every verse. Questions at the end of each chapter should help stimulate conversation.

Enjoy the study but remember as a teacher we are to practice what we teach.

Printed in the United States
by Baker & Taylor Publisher Services